D0093756

SLEEPING
with CATS

SLEEPING
with CATS

A MEMOIR

MARGE PIERCY

wm

William Morrow

An Imprint of HarperCollins*Publishers*

FIRST EDITION

Designed by Michelle McMillian

Printed on acid-free paper

Library of Congress Cataloging-in-Publication Data

Piercy, Marge.
Sleeping with cats : a memoir / Marge Piercy.—1st ed.
p. cm.
ISBN 0-06-621115-8
1. Piercy, Marge. 2. Authors, American—20th century—Biography. 3. Women cat owners—United States—Biography. 4. Cats—Anecdotes. I. Title.
PS3566.I4 Z477 2002
813'.54—dc21   2001016845
[B]

02 03 04 05 06 QW 10 9 8 7 6 5 4 3 2 1

FOR ALL THOSE I HAVE LOVED,
TWO- AND FOUR-FOOTED

CONTENTS

POEMS

ATTEMPT AT AUTOBIOGRAPHY

A tango among the potsherds
in bare feet, soon bloody.

Ah, bitch memory, you tangle
me in your barbed hair.

How can I tell enchantment
from fact, lies from promises?

You sing to me in my own voice
but on key with harmonics

that make my bones quiver.
The familiarity of your face makes

me trust where I should close
my eyes till I see sparks.

You persuade me of scenes I cannot
have witnessed, you sing ballads

of deeds only daydreamed. I am
your fool, your lover, your liar.

SLEEPING
with CATS

A FAMILY OF SEVEN

Do I have faith in my memory? Who doesn't? How can I not trust memory. It is as if I were to develop a mistrust for my right hand or my left foot. Yet I am quite aware that my memory is far from perfect. I frequently forget events and people that my husband, Ira Wood, remembers, and similarly, I remember incidents that have slipped away from him. I rarely remember things incorrectly; mostly I remember clearly or I forget completely.

I have distinct memories of events that happened before I was born or for which I was not present. This comes from having heard the stories told vividly by my mother or my grandmother when I was little and imagining those scenes and the people in them so clearly and intensely that I experience them as my own. I have precise memories of the voice and face of my mother's father, who died ten years before I was born. Stories about him that I heard as a child were so real to me that I created him as a living personage.

I have trouble remembering periods of intense pain. The summer my second marriage was disintegrating around me was a time I so hated every moment that it has almost vanished into the limbo of repressed pain. Sometimes a sound or a smell or a voice will break that seal of willful forgetfulness and out will slither those poisonous days and nights.

Once that has happened with events, I will not again forget. They are filed in a different part of my memory and can be summoned, or will drift up unbidden to torment me. But they are no longer vanquished, vanished.

I am convinced that all those people I write about would remember events and patterns of events quite differently than I do. After all, memory changes. Our pasts constantly change. When a friend betrays us or turns against us, the past is rewritten to prefigure that betrayal, that loss of intimacy and faith. When a love affair ends, we read the causes backward into the quarrels, even the minor disagreements. Those months of the inexplicable allergic sniffles of a friend suddenly become clues once we learn of their cocaine addiction. Someone we had scarcely known becomes an important figure in our lives, and in retrospect, every small meeting or passage together is invested with significance. Remembering is like one of those old-fashioned black-and-white-tile floors: wherever I stand or sit, the tiles converge upon me. So our pasts always seem to lead us directly to our present choices. We turn and make a pattern of the chaos of our lives so that we belong exactly where we are. Everything is a prefiguring of our current loves and antipathies, work and faith. We compose a future that leads from where we believe we are at the moment. When the present changes, past and future change significantly with it.

This is, after all, my perspective on my life, not anyone else's. It is neither true nor false in a large sense, because my truth of events is not the same as that of the others who lived them with me. To create a faithful autobiography would require as many years in the telling as the living of it, with transcriptions of every casual meandering conversation about what kind of soup to have for lunch, the weather, a movie seen last week. It would be filled with dirty bathrooms and clean laundry, bills paid and unpaid, overdue library books, hems to mend. We spend more time doing dishes than we do making love, but which figures prominently in the story of our lives? We choose, therefore, only certain events, certain people, certain points of crisis and joy. It is an extremely stylized map, with most of the byways omitted, even the most interesting and lovely and dangerous byways, because we are always hastening to arrive where we now think it is important and inevitable that we live.

I try to make myself look good, but I am aware that sometimes my honesty and my attachment to what happened prevent me from presenting myself as the blameless heroine. I usually try to do the best I can from day to day, but my best is often flawed and skewed, and sometimes I try to inflict harm. I aim to be good, but sometimes I am best at being at least mildly wicked. I frequently misjudge situations and people and blunder in where I should avoid. I talk myself into relationships that are good for no one, and certainly not for me. Or if good for me, bad for the other person. As I look at my life, I like the work I have done, but I often dislike how I have behaved with other people. I have intended to be a better friend and lover than I have turned out to be.

I think for the most part as time has gone on, I have become a better person in my most intimate relationships and in my relationships with the natural world and with my cats. I do not think I am any more effective politically than I was thirty years ago—probably less so. I assume leadership more warily. I am a better writer, but I stand behind the earlier novels and poetry. My life has been full of blunders, misprisions, accidents, losses, so no wonder I forget. If I did not forget much, how could I possibly continue? At the end, I will forget everything.

Why a memoir now? Well, I am about to turn sixty-five. In common with a lot of baby boomers—the generation after mine but the one I often identify with—I am still surprised that I have aged. I got to have two adolescences, one at the normal time, and a second one in Students for a Democratic Society during the 1960s. I was so used to thinking of myself as young that I still have to correct my inner vision to what I really am chronologically and in my body. It seems like a time to reflect, reexamine, make amends and corrections—a sort of High Holidays of the soul in which I judge what I've done and left undone. I have been a busy actor in my time. People who call me prolific often imagine I do little but write, but I have had my fingers in a great many boiling pots.

In every community there is a cat lady. In the Cape Cod village where I live, there are people who have never read a word I have written and may not be aware I have written at all, but they know that if they have a cat problem, I am the person to call. They also call me when a cat has been killed or died, for they know I won't mock their grief. This story is about the central relationships in my life and how I survived the bad ones and was strengthened by the good ones. It is primarily about me, but my life has a spine of cats, and it is also about them.

I have been many people in my life. We all change as we take new lovers and partners, as we take on new tasks, new jobs, new interests. Yet there have been constants: my need to write, my drive to write what was meaningful to me and I hope to other people, my desire to love and be loved, my valuing of freedom as close to an absolute, and of course my companions, the cats whose love was there when others failed me or I failed them.

I've lived with cats throughout my life, and I have more cats as time diminishes. My cats are among my friends, different in kind but not in importance from my human friends. Your relationship with a kitten has a maternal component, but once the cat has reached what she considers maturity, long before you think she is adult, she begins to contest your will with her own considerable intent. The bond becomes more nearly a relationship in which each makes accommodations to the other, attempts to learn and to teach, strives to understand and be understood and also to dominate, to rule. The love of a cat is unconditional but always subject to negotiation. You are never entirely in charge.

I was married twice before, but I have been with Ira Wood longer than the first two marriages put together—and far more intimately. Ira is younger than me—a tradition in my mother's family. My mother was older than my father, and her oldest sister had about the same age gap— fourteen years—with her younger husband as I have with Ira. He is four inches taller than me and much stronger. He is solidly built and has a great need for physical exercise. His hair is brown and densely curly. When I met him in 1976, he wore it in a huge Afro, which is its natural condition if left to grow out. Nowadays he keeps it fairly short. He has changeable green eyes and a ruddy complexion. He has always been a very good looking man, but it was his character I fell in love with. He has a great capacity for love, a giving nature in close relationships, a delicious sense of humor and strong sensuality combined with a bright inquiring mind. Although we both have quick tempers and too much impatience, we are well suited. We feel we are each other's *bashert,* each other's true intended. When we were first involved and again when we decided to marry, many people disapproved or were shocked by the age discrepancy and told me obliquely or with great and unappreciated directness that I was going to get dumped, that a woman cannot marry a man so much younger. I lost friends by my choice, but I gained my best friend.

This memoir focuses on my emotional life, not on my literary or political adventures, or most of my friendships. When I was fifteen, my life changed radically and permanently. In that year, I lost one of my best friends to a heroin overdose; my gentle intelligent cat was poisoned by neighbors because an Afro-American family was moving into our house; and my grandmother Hannah, to whom I was very close and who was my religious mentor, died of stomach cancer. My family moved to a larger house where I had a room of my own with a door that shut, and I began to write. I withdrew from the street gang I had belonged to and withdrew from my early sexual adventures. In my life, what comes before that point almost belongs to someone else, although there are many continuities. What came afterward is me. I changed, I learned, I developed, I grew, but after those events, I became a poet and a fiction writer and the person I still am. It has, nonetheless, been a long, rough journey from central city Detroit to the edge of this freshwater marsh in Massachusetts.

Ira and I and our five cats—Dinah, Oboe, Max, Malkah and the kitten Efi—live on four acres on Cape Cod, miles out to sea. Why do I live in a village? I was born in the smoking amphetamine heart of Detroit and lived in many cities—Chicago, San Francisco, Brooklyn, Paris, Boston, Manhattan. I've traveled a lot, and being a poet means doing gigs all over. I find I can write here with fewer interruptions and fewer temptations to fuss about my "career" than was possible in New York. We are two hours from Boston and drive back and forth frequently to see friends, do readings or hear them, use libraries, buy wine, shop, attend concerts or plays.

We refuse to let ourselves blink at the commute, because we can enjoy city pleasures and country quiet and beauty.

Two of our cats are elderly. As I write this, Dinah is seventeen and a half and her son Oboe is sixteen and some months. Dinah is the smallest cat, and the feistiest. Korats are gray, cobby cats with deep green eyes and a silken silvery gray coat. Her earlier dulcet voice has changed, peremptory, almost fierce with a sharp husky insistence that pierces walls. She cries her desires like a hawk. She has always been able to throw the much bigger male cats across the room when she is annoyed, and she takes no guff. She gets stepped on all too frequently because she lies down in the center of the hall or doorway and will not move. She is six pounds of intense willpower, healthy for her age and sometimes playful. She is obsessively jealous of Ira. Her son Oboe, however, is allowed any attention. With all the other cats, she counts the strokes they get.

I sometimes call my husband Woody, his nickname, and sometimes Ira and sometimes Wood. He calls me Marge or Piercy about equally, as well as other names I will not mention. He has multiple names for the cats. Dinah is Dweeze or Dweezelle. Sometimes Munchkin or Moochie. He is a giver of nicknames.

Dinah fell in love with Ira when she was ten weeks old, and he remains her passion. It is morning. Ira gets up first and makes cappuccino downstairs. When I am home alone or he is ill and I make the coffee, it takes me an hour. Until I have coffee, I can't do anything, including make coffee, so it is a farce. Afterward ground coffee and water and milk are spilled all over the kitchen. I do 90 percent of the cooking, but not in the morning. Me in the kitchen when I am half asleep is an accident in the making. I do not rise with full coordination. I rise bleary and shambling, Frankenstein's monster imperfectly fitted together.

When Ira goes downstairs, Dinah must go with him talking in her high raspy voice, oversee his making coffee, and then she must jump up on the high ledge in the bathroom to observe his first piss. What this means to her we have no idea, but she is insistent on her privileges. If something is missing from the order of the morning, she plants herself in the middle of the kitchen floor and tells us loudly that we are out of line and must shape up. We have our cappuccino in bed and Dinah lies on Ira's chest, purring. Ira often says he has never been loved as completely as she loves him, which I presume includes me. Oboe, her son, curls in my lap, purring just as loudly. Efi, the young Siamese, climbs the padded raggedy cat tree in the corner and waits. While I am making the bed, Ira will play with her. If he doesn't, she wails her disappointment.

Routines, habits, rituals bind life together for most people, but no one can understand the pleasure or the comfort of them, looking on from outside. Such routines appear silly or time wasting. Yet like the cats, I am pleased by some appearance of the ordinary in a life that is overly hectic. I wake alone in motel rooms too often not to appreciate the accustomed round of the morning. We have created these habits, all of us together, so they are shaped to our contours.

Dinah's son Oboe, born in my bed, is a natural mediator. He has fought when necessary, but he has never been injured in a catfight and mostly he prefers to make friends with other cats. His major mode of fighting, when forced to it, consists of blowing his fur out so that he looks twice his normal size and making horrendous huge terrifying noises. I doubt if he has ever bitten another cat, and he has certainly never been bitten. He is a lover, gentle with us and his own cats, ruling more by persuasion than force. He has a heart-shaped face, soulful and intense, his green eyes large and luminous.

Two years ago, he was given a death sentence by our veterinarian, and he may well die while I am engaged in this book. I had Ira dig a grave last fall, in case Oboe should die when the ground is frozen; I try to avoid walking near that area. He is stoical about his illness and deeply embarrassed when kidney disease keeps him from reaching his box in time. Nonetheless, he is where he wants to be, with the people and cats he loves, among whom he is the universal favorite. Whatever he does has prestige. Efi, the baby Siamese, throws her arms around him and goes to sleep hugging him. Sometimes she washes him so vigorously, he is wet afterward.

Ira and I have been together part-time since 1976, and full-time and monogamously since 1980. We share the garden, Leapfrog Press—our small publishing company—writing, the love of wine and food, the Cape, politics—but the core of our relationship has always been communication and sex, the exchange of words and the joining of our bodies. Since he was four months old, Oboe has wanted to be with us whenever we make love. I have tried to understand what it means to him, who was altered young. Is it the scents, the hormones released, the animality or sensuality of our naked torsos and limbs entangled? Whatever it is, he stays clear of the action until it is safe, purring loudly, sometimes leaping over us, back and forth. When we are at rest, he crawls between us, blissful. It feels at once somewhat perverse and very natural to have him there. If we shut the door and close him out, he sets up a heartrending wail, not conducive to intimacy. It's much better to let him in.

Dinah hated nursing her kittens and had little milk, so I bottle-fed them. Oboe had two mothers, and his relationship with both of us is tender, passionate and erotic. Dinah gave birth to her lifelong companion, her lover, her best friend, her playmate. They curl up together, one ball of silver-gray fur with four sharp ears protruding. Of all the cats, Oboe is closest to me. When I meditate, he sits with me and makes no demands. He is wise in the ways of the house and does not freak as the younger cats do when the carry-on bag comes out. It is only when the big suitcase is taken from the closet that he goes into a sullen depression, head wrapped in his tail, a comma of grief, knowing this means a considerable absence. His name comes from his voice, which even as a kitten was loud, plaintive and carrying, a true wind instrument.

Max and Malkah are much younger orange tabbies, litter mates acquired from a shelter when they were runty palm-sized kittens with three kinds of parasites, respiratory infections, more fleas than fur, and a hunger so vast they seemed all swollen stomach. Now they are magnificent.

The Korats, mother and son, did not go out freely until they were eight and nine respectively. They are such gentle friendly cats, I was afraid they would cozy up to an oil truck or a Doberman. Our four acres are in a cul-de-sac at the end of a road surrounded by marsh. The Korats prefer the brick patio by the screened gazebo. On hot days, they ask to go into the gazebo, where it is shady and bugless and there is a view of the slope and into the treetops. Often Ira or I take the laptop out to work there. The gazebo is a lovely thing, octagonal with a pointy shingled roof and an octagonal table within. We look into the cutting garden with its lilies, dahlias, blue lupine and coneflowers with their blown back petals around the bronze center, single old-fashioned hollyhocks and chrysanthemums—full of bloom from June through October. The far end I fill with sunflowers—maroon, golden, bronze, yellow. I recite Blake's poem "O sunflower, weary of time" to them as I plant.

Our gardens are not the neat suburban type but combine vegetables grown in the intensive French method—close together in rich organic soil we have created—with flowers, mostly perennials, rosebushes, peach, pear and sour cherry trees, red and black currants, goose-, blue- and raspberries, grapevines, flowering bushes and trees. It is thickly planted. A neighbor once called it The Jungle. I was picking daylilies this July when I disturbed the sleep of a possum. Ira once tripped over a pumpkin-sized snapping turtle snoozing near a leak in the irrigation system. Gardening gives me peace, working with my hands in the dirt. I planted these trees and bushes on an eroding sandy hillside: we made this lush place with our own hands, learning gardening from books and trial and error, creating a living art for ourselves.

Below the gazebo is the Ram Garden, planted with potatoes or pole beans, named for a bas-relief of a ram that hangs on the shed wall. Margaret Atwood told me years ago I should grow scarlet runner beans to attract hummingbirds. I love to see them darting like jeweled helicopters, and the hawkmoths that stand in the air with blurred wings drinking from the flowers.

Come with me into the weathered gray cedar-shingled house. The front door leads into the dining room with windows on three sides, always bird activity at the feeders, a room stuck out into the garden. Right now in late September, you see eight ironstone platters of tomatoes: yellow, red, orange, pink, purple, striped. Fat ones big as babies' heads, luscious pink breasts, oblong, some cat-faced, plum tomatoes, cherry tomatoes. Behind the tomatoes are mounds of big red Cinderella

Marge Piercy with Burmese cat Jim Beam, Wellfleet, 1987. Photograph by Ira Wood

pumpkins, Rouge Vif d'Estampes you see in the fall in Paris for sale in florist shops as well as in markets, for their beauty. A basket of maroon cabbages. Buff butternut squash, striped squash, orange and green winter squashes crowd every available surface. Does anyone live here or is this an indoor farmers' market? Tomatoes are our joy and currency. I give my agent one present a year: every August we express her a box of our tomatoes, which she claims are better than any she can buy in New York. We send out tomatoes to small-press pals, we barter them for lobster, clams, oysters and fish with a shellfish farmer and a lobsterman. We give tomatoes plus other vegetables to friends with a theater background who let us stay with them in Manhattan.

I began to can after my mother died, three kinds of sauce (simple, Italian, and hot) and whole plum tomatoes. She canned constantly through the warm months into fall, putting up far more than I do. Ball jars of peaches gleamed like amber in the sunlight streaming through the kitchen window. Jars of pickled young green beans with one clove of garlic, elegant fingers. Sour cherries. Half pears. Elderberry jelly. We used to go to the farmers' market for her to buy bushels of fruit, while I admired the live chickens and mounds of rutabagas and sugar beets. Canning is a way of embodying the best of my mother in myself, to hold on to her, for I lost her younger than most of my friends lose their parents—she gave birth to me around forty-four. She had no birth certificate, so her age was approximate. We were close until puberty, and then came a long rocky contentious period; then the last ten years of her life, we were close again. I still mourn her. In some ways, she was my muse. By teaching me close observation, developing my memory and playing word games with me, she made me a poet.

In the same way, when I light Shabbat candles and say the blessings, I am embodying my grandmother Hannah, who gave me my religious education and taught me storytelling by her rich example. Both those women live in me and my work, at the same time that I never cease to miss them in the flesh. Sometimes when I am preparing holiday food, I see myself as a version of the Pet Milk cans of my childhood, the can with the cow inside the can with the cow, ad infinitum. I am a woman with my mother inside, inside her my grandmother, her mother, reaching beyond memory, all of us making the same ritual gesture. It comforts me. I have lost so many people that I need ways to remember and cherish my dead.

Or you might look at all those tomatoes and squash and simply say, I was the child of penury and now I revel in abundance, too many tomatoes, too many clothes in the closet, too much in the freezer, a calendar too full and a life too busy. Ira jokes that when he dies, his tombstone will read HE STILL HAD STUFF TO DO. We always do. I love silence but I fear emptiness.

We are a tight-knit family of two humans and five cats who live far out to sea on the land we have made fertile among our gardens and our woods. This is our chosen home. It has taken me a long time to arrive here and dig in. These are my wanderings in search of a place where I could write and be myself and have what I consider necessary and what is not perhaps necessary but makes life good enough to endure the hard times. A place and time to write is a necessity, and love is a luxury, but I have spent a great many years searching for both. I am a stray cat who has finally found a good home.

SEPTEMBER AFTERNOON AT FOUR O'CLOCK

Full in the hand, heavy
with ripeness, perfume spreading
its fan: moments now resemble
sweet russet pears glowing

on the bough, peaches warm
from the afternoon sun, amber
and juicy, flesh that can
make you drunk.

There is a turn in things
that makes the heart catch.
We are ripening, all the hard
green grasping, the stony will
swelling into sweetness, the acid
and sugar in balance, the sun
stored as energy that is pleasure
and pleasure that is energy.

Whatever happens, whatever,
we say, and hold hard and let
go and go on. In the perfect
moment the future coils,
a tree inside a pit. Take,
eat, we are each other's
perfection, the wine of our
mouths is sweet and heavy.
Soon enough comes the vinegar.
The fruit is ripe for the taking
and we take. There is
no other wisdom.

TWO

IN THE BEGINNING

The cats of my childhood came out of the alley. Alleys ran up the center of our blocks, as they often do in the Midwest, so that to a child, each house faced two ways. For me, the most important direction was the alley. I was an alley child, as my cats were alley cats.

Some of my earliest memories are artificial, based on photos in the family album, myself eight months old on a blanket at the beach near Traverse City, Michigan, near the tip of the little finger of Michigan's palm. I have rich and splendid memories of things that happened in 1912 and 1926, from seeing in my imagination scenes described with such color and emotion by my mother Bert, my grandmother Hannah and my aunt Ruth. Therefore as I begin to unpack this load of rags and riches, caveat emptor. I come from a long line of storytelling women. I have a vivid childhood memory of standing in the back alley with my brother Grant and looking up at tall buildings—in an alley lined with garages in a neighborhood where the tallest building was two stories. It is very early childhood and I am so small, all buildings are tall to me.

I remember peeing in my bed and how good it felt while it was warm under me and how nasty it felt when it grew cold. I remember the sense that the sounds my parents made were powerful and made things happen and if I made sounds, things I wanted would happen, though crying sometimes worked. The words that were only shaped noise to me felt dense as objects. I remember the sense of my parents locked in war and myself caught in the middle, torn, tormented, guilty. They were always at war, and I was one of their battlegrounds. My father had desperately wanted a son, and although he occasionally tried to turn me into one, I was never satisfactory. He related more fully to my half brother, Grant, son of my mother's previous marriage, but Grant was already a teenager and usually in trouble. In the culture of our neighborhood, that was acceptable for a male child, although my parents balked at his sexual involvements.

The hospital I was born in, at the corner of Grand River and Livernois, had failed and become a bank in the middle of a row of used-car dealers by the time I was old enough to look at it. All that stays with me from the first tiny apartment upstairs in a two-story wooden house divided into four furnished apartments: I am lying on my back and I hear pigeons cooing. I clap my hands and my mother leans over me with her flower face. All through my life if I stop and listen to pigeons, I enjoy a sense of well-being. It soothes me, which carries over to the sound of mourning doves I hear often in these woods, especially in the spring. I slept in my parents' room, as I was to do until my brother left home. Grant was thirteen years older.

We lived at first in a Jewish neighborhood, familiar to me all through my childhood because when my grandmother came to live with us each summer, my mother and I would take the streetcar there to buy kosher meat, gefilte fish, *rugolach,* bagels and bialys, smoked fish and other treats—when there was enough money. When there wasn't, Grandma had to live on canned fish or vegetable soups, for she was Orthodox. Shortly after my parents moved to Detroit from Cleveland, where they met, my father was laid off for two years. My parents doubled up with another couple, Lucy and Lon, up from Appalachia. What little we had, we shared.

When I was three, my father was rehired and we moved into a house my parents bought, where we would live until I was fifteen. It was a tiny house with asbestos siding that had been foreclosed on by the bank. My parents would be paying it off for the next ten years. It was in a working-class neighborhood largely Irish, Polish Catholic, and Afro-American. My parents had a bad Depression and it was not over, although my father was back at work. My mother was a housewife. I will not say she did not work, because she worked incessantly. My mother had been taken out of school in the middle of the tenth grade and sent to work as a chambermaid. My father had finished high school and gone to a technical night school, which had given him some sort of credential as an engineer, although he did not have a college diploma. He worked for Westinghouse installing and repairing

Bert Bunin at seventeen years of age in Pittsburgh.

heavy machinery. He worked for them at least fifty years, never promoted until the end when he was the last person left in the Detroit office; then they gave him an honorary title: supervisor—of himself.

Lucy and Lon moved out as tenant farmers to a small holding near the River Rouge Ford Plant. Every Sunday we drove to see them. I could see and smell the red smoke across the marshes. My mother would bring cakes or home-canned goods to Lucy and Lon. In exchange, they would kill a chicken for us to take home. I remember Lucy swinging the chicken and then chopping the head off, and how much blood gushed out. Through much of my early childhood, until World War II brought prosperity to Detroit, that was the only meat we could afford. I remember plucking the chickens and scorching the stumps of the feathers. Perhaps that made it easier to pluck out the quill ends. Out of the mysterious opened belly of the chicken came eggs, some with shells and some without, down to the tiniest little yellow and red worlds. My mother made a wonderful soup with the unborn eggs. Then she usually made the chicken as a pot roast with vegetables such as carrots, potatoes, celery: a dish I still make, with many variations. My mother was not a good cook, but she had her successes—most of which I have learned by trial and error to duplicate.

Even after my father went back to work, times were hard and there was little surplus. Sometimes it was difficult to make the house payments, and my mother would take me with her when she went to the bank to stave them off. My mother's only tool in the battle with bureaucracy and men with power was flirtation. She was an accomplished and persuasive flirt, a tiny woman with an extravagant hourglass figure, intense dark brown eyes and short curly black hair. She had a way of walking, a way of moving, a way of sitting that drew men's eyes to her. She moved like the dancer two of her sisters had been. Half the men we dealt with were convinced she was crazy about them, but she mostly felt contempt. They were marks. She had a job to do and she did it. She was obsessed with my father, not with any of these men about whom she had a rich vocabulary of Yiddish insults which she muttered to me after each encounter.

I shared my parents' bedroom until my brother was forced by my parents to marry his girlfriend Isabelle. Our parents came home unexpectedly and caught Grant and Isabelle having sex on the couch while they were baby-sitting me. The marriage did not last, but I inherited my brother's room—not really a room but a hallway. This was the space my grandmother shared with me every summer. Isabelle, Grant's first wife, was a redhead with creamy skin. I remember he played the guitar then. I adored him. He was warm and emotional where my father was cold and withdrawn and judgmental. I adored my father too when I was little, but I think by the time I was seven, I had learned I could not please him. My brother would get bored if I asked too much of him, but while he was paying attention, he was affectionate and funny and endearing. He looked like me. Everyone we touched looked like us, nieces, nephews, cousins. We all have dark hair and dark dark brown Oriental eyes, a stocky build.

It's hard to excavate my childhood. On one hand, I have vivid sensual and emotional memories. I know I was fearful of death. Perhaps it was my favorite aunt on my father's side dying young from complications after an auto accident on an icy mountain road near Monday's Corners—my uncle Zimmy, a coal miner, driving and presumably drunk, after a dance. Perhaps it was the death of the first cat I remember, Whiskers. For whatever reason, I was terrified that my mother would suddenly die, or that my grandmother, when she slept with me, would stop breathing. Perhaps it was my mother's melodramatic streak, for she would assume a pose and say, "You'll be sorry you did that when I'm dead!" "When I'm dead and gone, you'll remember how wicked you were to me!" "When you've put me in my grave, you'll understand what it is to be a motherless child, alone in the mean world without anybody to take care of you!"

My room was painted "robin's egg blue"—a name that impressed me because I did know what color the eggs of the neighborhood robins were, as sometimes cowbirds would push them from the nests and I would find them broken on the ground.

Until age nine or ten, I found this tiny house and yard rich and wonderful. I was fascinated by the mirror that hung near the front door, which I have to this day, one of the few relics of my childhood. It has an owl's head on top, the ornate frame made of once-gilded plaster. On a shelf stood a strange teapot from my great-grandmother back in Lithuania, the pattern long faded into the grayish curve of the sides. When my father broke it in a temper tantrum years later, I was furious, for I had always presumed it would be mine someday. I found the space under the front porch mysterious, sandy and hung with spiderwebs. I loved the front porch, screened in by my father, with its creaky glider I could lie on and stare up at the boards of the dark green ceiling. That was one piece of furniture my cat was allowed on, so we curled up there together.

We always had a car. My father's manhood meshed strongly with automobiles, and even if we were eating only oatmeal or beans and potatoes, the car always had gas. After the war, he bought a new car every two years. There was no money to go to the dentist when mother or I had a toothache. I went to school in hand-me-downs, sometimes with Aunt

Robert Douglas Piercy at thirty in Ebensburg, Pennsylvania.

Ruth's initials shaming me on my blouses; but a new car was as important to him as the fact that we owned our tiny ramshackle house. To him it meant that we were middle class. We weren't, but never mind. There was a lawn out front the size of a nine-by-twelve rug, but it had grass growing on it, and that too was a badge of his station in life. These things were very important to my parents. To my father being able to regard himself as middle class was necessary because he had been raised with those pretensions—for his family had to differentiate themselves from the coal miners around them—and to my mother, it was important because she had not been so raised. Her childhood and adolescence had been spent in vicious poverty, too many children and too little of everything else.

I remember once sitting in Austin, Texas, with the fine poet, my friend Audre Lorde (who wrote a remarkable memoir, *Zami*). We were in a Holiday Inn that had at the top one of those restaurants that revolved—a fad of the time. We were looking down into the neighborhood of working-class or poor families, and Audre remarked that living in places where people had little houses and little yards was better than living in the downtown areas of cities. I agreed, thinking of my Detroit neighborhood. At the end of every block loomed dilapidated apartment houses where some of my friends lived, or housing projects, but most of the neighborhood was composed of what were called bungalows, tiny houses, or two- and four-family frame houses. Detroit has a wet climate and the sand must be fertile, as it is here on the Cape, for if a house burns down, within a couple of months, a jungle of greenery grows in its place. Nature is avid to take back any available space. When I was a child, the streets of Detroit were lined with huge elms and an occasional oak. It gave me a vision of an alternate city of green over the grim and hostile streets. If my father cherished the minute front lawn, my mother grew vegetables, herbs and flowers in the only slightly bigger backyard. She used every inch she could pry from his vision of green lawns.

Early on after we moved into that tiny house, my uncle Danny lived with us. Maybe he had got into trouble in Cleveland; maybe he was just out of work. He and my brother were only two years apart. My grandmother Hannah had eleven children before she finally left off childbearing, at fifty-three. Danny was the last child and the only one she had the leisure to spoil. He was an anarchist and believed in the power and virtue of the working class; he loved jazz and had a huge collection of records. He was the coolest of my uncles. Danny and my brother Grant gambled together, ran after women, borrowed money. When they had any money, they lost it immediately or spent it on loud clothes and louder women. I loved but never wanted to emulate them. But I thought them both the handsomest men alive.

The first cat I remember was Whiskers, a gray tabby. My mother named all the cats. Danny brought home two bunnies he had won in a card game. They lived down in the basement until they chewed the insulation off the washing machine. Whiskers would wait on the ledge by the furnace and then pounce on one of the rabbits and ride him. Sometimes he would chase them, and sometimes one or both of them would chase him. I also remember the little raisiny turds they dropped all over the basement. Like most little kids, I was fascinated by shit.

The rabbits were shipped off to Lucy and Lon, where, for all I know, we might have eaten them. I was far more involved with Whiskers. The cats of my childhood were not long-lived. They were all males, never altered, never taken to the vet and usually put out at night. They got in fights, they were hit by cars, they fought with the huge rats that inhabited the alleys. Boys shot them with BB guns. My mother was wonderful at nursing hurt animals, but it would never have occurred to her to try to prevent those injuries.

I am enormously fond of the writings of M. F. K. Fisher and was flattered and honored that she liked my novel *Gone to Soldiers*. However, when I read her memoir of her cat who was finally torn apart by other male cats when he could no longer defend himself, I could not help wondering what was with all those women of the older generations who insisted on leaving male cats intact until they were killed. It reminds me of guys who identify with the size and power of their dogs. When I was faced with that situation for the first time, with Jim Beam, Ira and I were sentimental and waited too long to have him altered—a lapse we were to regret the rest of his life. To this day, I will find some object in the house that stinks of male cat piss, and remember Jim Beam, who expressed himself on it. But somehow to that earlier generation, the sexual adventures of a male cat were more important than his health, well-being, or even his life.

I grew up much closer to my mother's family than to my father's. For one thing, my mother and I were Jewish, and my father was not. There was a lot of intermarrying in the extended Bunnin family, and while my grandmother, who gave me my religious education, did not like that, she couldn't do much about it. My father's family was casually and relentlessly anti-Semitic, so neither my mother nor I was ever easy with them. We were always waiting for the next little insult. We were always being observed to see if we would do something Jewish like crucify somebody in the backyard. If my mother or I ever laughed, or raised our voices, or used our hands in talking, there was a look that would pass between them that would silence us, as if we had been pushed under a glass bell. They never missed an opportunity to serve ham to us. My mother would eat it politely, although of course she never cooked it, but I would not. My grandmother had trained me too well. I remember no animals in the Ebensburg narrow brick house where my father grew up and his two maiden sisters lived. I do remember that my great-aunt Jane who was Scottish had two Scotty dogs and a husband fifteen years younger. She went about the extended family visiting, for it was understood she would leave her fortune to the relatives who pleased her best. She was always on the move with her doting husband, from best bedroom to best bedroom. She made clear what she liked to eat and to drink, so was served roast lamb, roast beef and Scotch whisky or dark ale. I liked the Scotty dogs, who ran exuberantly through the houses of relatives who detested animals. It wasn't until she died at ninety that the family learned there was no money at all. The two of them had been living on the relatives, enjoying life together. A consummate con woman. I admired her. So did my mother.

The most shameful thing I ever did in Ebensburg was when I was eight, when I fell in love with a wooden doorstop in the shape of a swan. I had seen swans at the Detroit zoo. I thought it beautiful. I wanted it. Finally I asked my aunt Grace for it. She refused, in some annoyance. I still

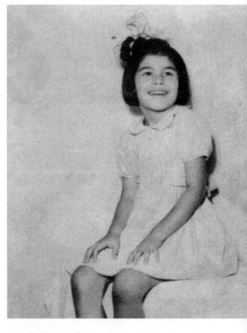

Marge Piercy at age five, Detroit, Michigan.

wanted it, so I stole it and hid it in our suitcase. I was, of course, discovered. My mother was furious. I was a born criminal, obviously, and I had shamed her before the goyim. I still wanted it, but now I knew I would never have it. How passionately I was in love with that white swan doorstop. Yet I was deeply ashamed, because I had shamed my mother.

Bert Bernice Bunnin Piercy was a small intense woman whose coloring I have: black hair, dark eyes, pale slightly pinkish skin. As I age, I look more and more like her. She had tremendous energy and a wild dramatic imagination. She was a wonderful mother to a young child. Somewhere in the books she consumed constantly she had learned that mothers should play word games with their children to develop their verbal skills. When she was giving me my bath, she would choose three words and I would have to make up a story using them. She would constantly test my powers of observation. We would play mental hide-and-seek. We would imagine ourselves walking down a familiar street and I would have to list every building and describe it. Wonderful games: I had all her attention then.

She loved toys, something she'd never enjoyed. I had a small mostly secondhand wardrobe of shabby ill-fitting clothes, but many toys acquired at yard sales. Our tiny yard had swings, a teeter-totter and lawn furniture. Sometimes the aunts gave me dolls, sometimes a book. Grandma could not give me anything that cost money, but she could take scraps of worn-out clothing and tablecloths and turn them into clothes for my dolls. My dolls were clothed in dresses Mother or I had worn in their previous guise. They were the envy of girls who had more and fancier dolls.

I had a dollhouse, two stories, very simple and covered with some indelible scribbles from the child who had owned it before: but I adored it. I was given for my birthday wooden stick figures of a mother, father and baby from the dime store, but I had quite enough of the nuclear family. Instead, I had an army of little china animals my brother's first wife, Isabelle, had given me in an Easter basket, not understanding we did not celebrate Easter. I cherished the animals, who lived out their elaborate and ongoing adventures in that dollhouse. I learned to keep the stick family sitting here and there, so that when my mother would inquire what was going on, I could break from the real action and point to them. She thought it weird that I would invest my imagination in animals, but I vastly preferred them. The leader was Captain Kitty, a small gray and white china cat I still keep on my vanity table, with her boyfriend, Terry the Spaniel. In addition, there were two other dogs, Dorothy and Bruce; a rooster, a chicken and two bunnies. All had names, personalities and ever more extensive histories. I made furniture out of dominoes at first but gradually acquired little pieces from the dime store. My first novels were composed in my head about the adventures of Captain Kitty. I do not remember the name of a single doll I had, but I remember the names of all the china animals that inhabited my dollhouse.

My childhood was a mix of abundance and penury. Once we lived on oatmeal for three weeks; to go to the doctor for my anemia was too expensive; yet I had a box full of toys and my father had an elaborate electric train set, erected every winter in the basement. It was bought used, but he was always adding to it. He loved playing railroad engineer.

For a time, my brother worked on the real railroad and was in the Brotherhood. My childhood was in the era of the romance of trains, their plaintive hooting, their promise of other places, the excitement of big formal bustling stations. My mother's relatives arrived on trains and my brother departed for the marines and came back on furlough. Four blocks away three busy sets of railroad tracks ran. In my older childhood, I hung around those tracks. I imagined leaving on a train, hopping on like a hobo and traveling, traveling. It was not until my last year of high school that I learned this was the Detroit Terminal Railroad that ran no place but around Detroit.

My father making the switchman emerge from his little house and wave his lantern, creating bridges out of odd parts left over from his work, turning the transformer high to race fast and crash on the curves, that was my father boyish and grinning. When I could play with him, we got on well. Playing cards was another time he was jolly with me, for I could remember the cards and the rules of the games they regularly played with friends: hearts, Michigan, rummy, canasta, pinochle, poker. It was a skill he could appreciate, and I had a great need to please.

My father seemed tall to me in my childhood. Certainly he loomed over my mother, who was four ten. He was probably five eight or nine. He had gray eyes. I remember his hair as silver although I know it was brown in my childhood, but, unlike my mother's, it turned early. He wore gold-rimmed glasses and smoked incessantly. The scratch of a match and his smoker's cough were the first sounds I heard in the mornings. He had a favorite chair where he sat wreathed in smoke, reading the newspaper slowly. Sometimes he smoked a pipe and always he smoked cigarettes. Except for poker, he did not gamble much, but he liked to drink and held his liquor well. He preferred beer or rye whiskey, sometimes bourbon. My mother liked only wine, which she made of whatever she could find to ferment: sour cherries, elderberries, Concord grapes.

Mother had a great capacity for joy, stunted by her life. She had enjoyed school, but was taken out halfway through the tenth grade to go to work. The histories of my mother's two earlier marriages do not belong to this memoir, but I knew what a hard time she had throughout her life, and I could see how little she was getting in the present. She could enjoy fully and passionately the flowers of her plot, playing with the cats or me, getting dressed up when they went out, traveling, staying in hotels or tourist cabins or cottages we rented for a week, seeing her family, learning all the secrets of the neighbors and telling them to me. I was the repository of her past, the previous husbands and boyfriends never to be alluded to in my father's presence, the complicated tales of her family, the local scandals, complaints about my father. She poured her emotions, her fantasies, her resentments into me. An intensely nosy child, I was always asking *why,* far more often than was pleasant to anyone around me, but I was at least a good listener. I was an obnoxiously curious child, always into everything, always poking and prying and asking impertinent questions. I loved to sneak into the room and listen to neighbors telling her their troubles. I still am that child. I eavesdrop on the conversations of strangers in restaurants, in airports and supermarkets. I drive my husband crazy with questions sometimes; but I am still a good listener and I still keep secrets.

The most mature person I knew was Grandma, Bubbeh, Hannah Levy Adler Bunnin. Actually Adler should come last. After my grandfather's murder, his head bashed in by thugs hired by the owners of the bakeries where he was organizing a union, a few years later she married again: the owner of a shoe store. He lost the shoe store in the Depression and died soon afterward. Grandma did not talk about Adler. He had been a compromise and a disappointment. She talked only of her first husband, my grandfather. He was the love of her life and caused her the greatest pain, for he was not faithful. He was a radical and irreligious, a deracinated Jew from St. Petersburg; she was the daughter of a shtetl rabbi from Lithuania. Like my parents', it was a marriage of passion between ill-matched lovers.

My grandmother had a cat named Blackie, who has appeared in my poems and in *Gone to Soldiers.* He was a gentleman, in disposition much like my Oboe, well mannered, affectionate, clean with a shiny black coat unmarred by a fleck of white. I admired him greatly. Seders were special at my grandmother's, and Blackie always attended. My grandmother insisted he prayed, and she confided that when no one else was there, he ate with a knife and fork. I believed. It was no more wonderful than the stories she told of the golem, dybbuks, rabbis who could fly. My grandmother took me to shul, where I was perfectly happy behind the *mehitzah* with the old ladies who smelled of lavender and sweat and camphor, who fussed over me, who spoke little Hebrew but a great deal of Yiddish. I felt intensely cherished with my grandmother and her friends. In Grandma's apartment, I learned to drink hot tea from a glass with a sugar cube clenched in my teeth, and there too I heard all the neighborhood gossip as well as fifty-year-old scandals and escapes. Some of the most intense pleasures of my childhood were listening to adults tell stories. I pieced a world together from these rich fragments.

We went regularly to Cleveland, where several of the Bunnins lived: Grandma, Aunt Ruth, one of my mother's brothers, Frank, and his wife, Mickey, and Danny, his wife and then ex-wife and their two daughters. Uncle Frank and Aunt Mickey were interesting to me because they were childless and happy. They both worked and had a pleasant apartment and money enough to go off on trips for pleasure. My mother spoke of them with pity, as she did any childless couple, but I thought their life looked pretty good. Cleveland was a place I always felt welcome. Indeed, when I was twelve, I went to stay with Aunt Ruth—my mother's youngest sister, also childless and a working woman—for a couple of weeks by myself, taking the Greyhound bus. Ruth was intermediate in age between my mother and myself. Sometimes she seemed almost a girlfriend. Sometimes she betrayed me and sided with my mother. We looked alike, as everyone in the Bunnin family did. They were a volatile lot, given to late phone calls to my mother full of trouble and excitement, given to unfortunate romances and hasty marriages, given to lofty plans, financial disasters, failed ventures. I admired Ruth. She worked, she wore slacks long before they were common. She was the only athlete in the family, putting her overabundance of energy into sports. A line of trophies stood in her living room. I don't remember going with her to the bowling lanes, before she married and took up golf, but I remember being her caddie on the links. The game itself bored me, but my aunt never did. She was merry, lively, shrewd. She laughed easily and read mysteries. She had been told many times if she had a degree, she would have moved up in the navy. She had a civilian job and did extremely well at it. Whatever she did, she performed well. I strove to emulate that trait. She seemed far more focused to me than most of the rest of the Bunnins, and I already admired focus by late childhood.

She had RH-negative blood, as I do. Wanting children, she suffered a string of miscarriages. The negative factor was little understood then. Most members of that generation of Bunnins were childless by choice. Growing up with so many babies in such poverty turned off the desire to procreate. Danny had children—two families' worth. My mother had my brother and me. That was it, except for my mother's oldest sister, Rose (the stage name she took; her name was Rivka), who adopted a son.

They got married, they got divorced, they had affairs, they had adventures. Except for my uncle Harry, an unsuccessful magician who married a rich widow with four daughters, none of them owned much. Frank and Mickey were comfortable, but mostly when the Bunnins did well and were beginning to be solidly middle class, like Ruth, something came up. Her husband was abusive, and she left him for another man, left the middle class, left everything except Grandma, who was living with her by then—except for summers with us. The Bunnins talked a lot, about everything. They were full of laughter, of anger, they were sexy, they were smart, and they were usually in some kind of trouble. My mother would have a sudden premonition that something was wrong. Late phone calls. Whispers. Don't tell your father, she would say to me, but Ruth is leaving Barney. Danny has run away from Lil. They gossiped about one another, they fought and made up, they told stories and they exaggerated and they swore unapologetically. How could I resist them? Why should I want to? They had wit and politics. When they were in a room, the air vibrated with loud laughter and put-downs and jokes. They had strong opinions about books and music and popular culture. Three of the uncles had been in vaudeville, and my mother's two oldest sisters had been dancers in the Ziegfeld Follies, George White's Scandals, even the movies. They ranged politically from Roosevelt Democrats to the anarchism of Danny and general left sympathies. Conversation never lagged. They told dirty jokes and acted out scenes from their lives, to wild laughter.

My father's side consisted of an extended family of many Welsh coal miners he barely acknowledged as kin, many of whom I liked. My favorite relatives on that side were my aunt Margaret, a schoolteacher whom the rest of the family felt had married beneath her to a coal miner, my uncle Zimmy. Zimmy hunted, legally and illegally, to supplement the bad meat from the company store with venison, supplying the entire family on occasion. He drank, and he smashed up their car one night after a dance at Monday's Corners. Margaret died slowly, over a year. At her funeral, he keened for her. The immediate Piercy family was shocked at the open display of grief, but they went on eating his venison.

Going to Pennsylvania a few times a year was a mixed experience. I loved the mountains, the switchbacks in the roads, the rocks cleaved open for highways or railroads, multicolored, stained with water, stained with iron, bearded by shining ice in the winter. I loved the reservoir cut into rock on the end of town, I loved the way the streets dipped down from High Street, the main route then where my aunts lived in a narrow three-story redbrick house on an ample lot. On High Street, I was walking on the backbone of a great animal, whose ribs were the streets curving down. Ebensburg felt superior because it was the county seat and served the surrounding coal towns but was not one—like my aunts and the uncle who lived there, who felt superior to the miners. I was uncomfortable, but the area drew me. All night long, I could hear trucks laboring up the mountain into town. After I saw *Fantasia* (the only Walt Disney movie I saw, as my mother considered it culture; otherwise we boycotted because my mother called him a fascist and a union breaker), I imagined the trucks as dinosaurs bellowing and groaning as they struggled upward.

I loved going to Horseshoe Curve and watching the long freights strain up and go brakes squealing down. We lived near the railroad tracks in Detroit, but there, trains never went fast. We waved to the brakemen and they threw us fat pieces of chalk perfect for scrawling obscenities on sidewalks and walls. Here the trains seemed more dramatic. The drab company towns with the made-up names—Revloc,

Colver—fascinated me: a string of identical little wooden houses, almost shacks, riding the razorback of a mountain and straggling down the steep sides, no color because unpainted or stained with coal dust. Ebensburg was a place my mother and I felt on display, judged, but mountains filled me with sharp ecstasy. I suppose they fed the great hunger for beauty that gnawed at me as a child. As I got older and was still coerced into going, I brought girlfriends with me, to serve as a buffer.

My brother's first marriage ended in divorce and he joined the marines. On his last furlough, he married Florence, a woman from a working-class family, an office worker, self-supporting but living at home. After Grant was sent overseas, my niece Suzanne was born. I took being an aunt seriously, pondering presents for my niece, much later trying to interest her in college. During the war, my father worked lots of overtime. Detroit was overcrowded and buzzing. He was chosen air-raid warden of our block and went about making sure people observed the blackout regulations. He was always chosen as a leader by other men, for he got on well with them and he was bright, capable and full of jokes. He had the capacity I still lack of remembering jokes he had heard and delivering them well. He was a shop steward in his union. We followed the war closely. Mother told me about what was happening to Jews in Europe—it is foolish to imagine people did not know. It was all over the Yiddish papers, and my grandmother talked about it constantly, worrying about her family back in Lithuania. It was terrifying to me. I was intensely patriotic and did wonders on the scrap-metal drives, the paper drives. I was a hero of trash. Mother half expected the Nazis to arrive any moment and kept saying, "Don't tell anybody you're Jewish," as if everybody couldn't tell anyhow.

The first cat who was vitally important to me was named by my mother Buttons, a tuxedo cat with great yellow eyes, long-legged and slender. I think he arrived around the time my career as a tomboy ended with the German measles followed by rheumatic fever. I came close to dying. My grandmother came and prayed over me. I remember waking to the smell of burnt herbs. She changed my Hebrew name from Miriam to Marah—bitter—so the angel of death, *Malach ha-moves,* would pass over me. I remember the sense of burning, burning, and days going by blurred. Afterward, I was not as afraid of death as I had been. It was more mundane to me. Been there, done that, perhaps I felt, because I had been pronounced as dying by the doctor who finally came to the house for five minutes. We never had much to do with doctors. My mother, like Bubbeh, believed in herbs and poultices, tisanes, hot and cold baths—to which Grandma added amulets and lots of praying.

I was turned from a sturdy child to a pale blue neurasthenic and anemic creature who fainted easily and was often ill with minor complaints like tonsillitis and sinusitis and chronic sore throats—no doubt exacerbated by my father's nonstop smoking. Until that point I had little interest in school beyond the trouble I caused with my big mouth, and I was pleasing to my mother and close to her. I was born the wrong sex to please my father, but I was acceptable until disease turned me into an unattractive and sickly thing. I began to read a great deal, although my eyes had been weakened by German measles. Soon I was put into glasses, which annoyed my parents. An unattractive girl child was a liability. Now I was too weird to make friends easily, and after I began to do well in school, I was double-promoted and younger than anyone in my class.

For the next years till I went to summer school and graduated in order to cut one more semester off my prison sentence, I hated school. I liked some teachers, I liked some classes, but the entire experience of going to a ghetto grade school with its emphasis on discipline and ignoring what violence could not be contained, with the bored teachers and the even more bored students putting in their time, with the stench of urine and the yellowing dirty halls and busted lockers, old books, old desks, and the contempt of the teachers for us and themselves—for decades afterward, when I dreamt of imprisonment, it was always my grade school I saw. I lived in a state of high tension and fear, never knowing when just being who I was would get me into trouble. I was in fight after fight. I was poor at defending myself at first, because I tended to faint. But I learned to fight. I had to. When I had protectors, they were Black. Most of the time I had to depend on my ability to duck, to punch, to survive. But I was small, slight, and while I was fast, I had little physical strength.

Eventually I learned to carry a knife and to act fierce. The combination was a bluff that usually worked.

The tough kids, the riffraff of the neighborhood, the kids from poor or broken families, the foster children taken in for money from the state, these were my friends. Some streets, some families, were much more middle class; the girls from those families were my tormentors. They dressed prettily and the teachers preferred them to all the lumpen rest of us. I would be the storyteller; they would be the princesses in school plays. After my illness, I did better than I was supposed to in school, so I was seated with them. Of course I wanted them to like me and was easily fooled, but they were unremittingly nasty as only self-righteously vicious little girls can be. I was their preferred victim until I escaped into high school and never spoke to them again.

I can still close my eyes and taste that prevailing fear, mixed with boredom, mixed with disgust and shame. Years later, when I was under surveillance by the FBI and the Red Squad in New York, I knew that same underlying ground of fear and tension, and sometimes it made me feel like a child again. When I think of certain years of my childhood, I seldom call up innocence or joy or a sense of safety: it is that whining rumble of fear like the sound of traffic as you lie awake in a high-rise that I remember.

I had for the next few years two comforts, two pleasures: escape into reading and other worlds, other times, other bodies; and my cat Buttons. He was very much mine and gave me the only strong affection I experienced besides my grandmother's. My grandmother did not mind that my eyes had become weak and myopic and I must wear glasses. My grandmother thought I was beautiful. My grandmother thought I was brilliant. Whatever was wrong with me, Grandmother could produce someone she had known who had had the same complaint and had done something wonderful. However, Grandma was only around in the summer, and Buttons was with me almost all of the time—when he was not wandering or in fights or lying injured someplace. I cannot count all the times I searched for him and found him with his leg swollen up by an abscess, or all the times he came limping home. I spent hours combing the alleys for him, and sometimes I found him and sometimes he dragged back on his own. One of the great frustrations of my childhood was that I was not permitted to sleep with him. He was not allowed on my bed, although when I was alone with him in the house, we both understood that rule was in abeyance. I was an emotional child with few outlets for my affection, inclined to be weepy and self-involved. I did not grow out of the copious tears until I was twenty-one or so. I became less engrossed with myself as I became more interested in the external world and more able to explore it.

Buttons was reasonably friendly with other cats and sometimes brought them home, including, once, a young female kitten I was permitted to keep for a short while but who then disappeared. My mother gave me a fanciful story, but I imagine they dumped her someplace enough blocks away so she could not come back. My mother did not hold with female cats, whom she considered immoral. It was from my mother I learned that you can teach a cat that it is permitted and in fact encouraged to hunt rodents, but that birds are forbidden, because my mother fed the birds in our tiny yard—fed them stale bread, leftover cereal, spaghetti, as well as growing sunflowers for them. She kept a compost pile, managing to grow great vegetables in a plot the size of your average dining room table and she understood that birds ate insects. None of our cats ever took a bird more than once.

My father liked Buttons and sometimes gave him a small saucer of beer. I can't imagine this was good for the cat, but he liked it. He would weave around chair legs and then go to sleep and snore. My father was kind to animals. I wrote silly stories about Buttons, his exploits, his heroism, modeled on the dog and horse stories I consumed. I was extremely fond of animal stories: first of all, unlike stories about humans, females were as powerful as males. Lassie might be as heroic as Lad. Second, animals were not anti-Semitic, and I was beaten up regularly at school. *Anti-Semitism* was a word I learned very early.

My parents were ill suited. Mother had been married to the father of my brother Grant when she met Robert Douglas Piercy, a bachelor. Mother was seven years older than my father—we think. The three oldest girls in her family did not have birth certificates. My mother talked to ha Shem (God) all the time, personally, vehemently. My father considered all religion superstition, although he would attend the Presbyterian Church in Ebensburg when he was there and make us accompany him and his sisters. He did not believe in a deity, but he strongly believed in societal roles and how things were supposed to be. He considered the world mechanical and predetermined by the nature of its laws. Society was a machine. The universe was a bigger machine. Both required that everything stay in its proper place. His views were grim and rather puritanical.

He was a Roosevelt Democrat who later became a Nixon Republican. My mother was always at least liberal and usually radical. She had strong class politics, and in spite of her helplessness and dependence on my father, there was a streak of feminism in her. For instance, she admired women who kept their own names. She was keenly aware of the disadvantages of gender as it is constructed in this society, but also fatalistic. If I did not stay within the strict gender roles with which she was familiar, I would be punished, I would be killed. My father really considered women inferior in all respects. Unlike my father, who read only the paper and an occasional story in the *Saturday Evening Post,* Mother devoured books. With little education, she had no framework in which to retain what she read and little sense of how to read critically. All statements had the same validity to her, and she was often impressed by writers who struck me as charlatans. She was hungry for knowledge, but little in her environment encouraged her intellectual curiosity or fed it—except for the random books she carried home from Gabriel Richard public library. Sometimes we took the Livernois bus there. Sometimes my father would give us a ride. Mother never learned to drive. Every week we went to the library, that repository of dreams, ambitions, alternate lives, shimmering possibilities, hard and false information, history, belief, story. Every week I brought home receptacles containing hints that my life might be different, wider than my mother's.

What she wanted for me was a clean pink-collar job. To her, the ultimate in refinement and ambition was to work in an office, and the top of the pile of women was the boss's secretary. College was unreal. Her only images came from musicals, to which she was addicted. No one in our family had experienced higher education. When I enrolled in college prep in high school, instead of the commercial course, I did so without her knowledge or blessing. When she realized halfway through my freshman year what I had done, she was furious. I soothed her by taking typing courses. I am to this day a rapid typist, more than a hundred words a minute. My father's only reaction was that he wasn't going to pay for college: indeed, he didn't.

My mother was sensual, highly sexual. My father had been passionate in the early days of the relationship, but once he had reduced her to housewife, he had contempt for her and indeed for all women. He gradually lost sexual and romantic interest, which made her bitterly unhappy. My childhood was lived in the trenches of their war. My mother liked food flavored with onions and herbs. My father liked things simple—the stuff he was used to eating in diners and restaurants as a bachelor. "I'm a meat and potatoes man." My father's pleasures were playing poker or other card games, drinking beer or whiskey, tinkering with his car, going fishing, fiddling around in the basement with power tools he relished. My mother loved music, romantic movies, books, gardening, gossiping and managing the affairs of the neighbors. She had liked to dance, to get dressed up and go out. He was dogmatically realistic; she was mystical and overdramatic. She raised flowers—chrysanthemums, irises, old-fashioned roses, black-eyed Susans—and vegetables and herbs; he wanted only grass. The small front and back yards were war zones. He would run the lawnmower through her flower beds. She would dig up his sod and plant beans.

The backyard, when they were not fighting about it, was heaven to me. From the time I was little, I loved to lie in the grass, looking into the spears of the iris bed where huge spiders lived, looking at the tiny cities of broken bricks with which my mother tried to defend her beds from his mower. I saw them as pueblos, whose pictures I had studied in the encyclopedia my mother bought at a yard sale. I caught caterpillars and attempted to raise butterflies in jars. My mother had read a book about organic gardening, so she had a compost pile about two feet by three feet in which she put everything that could decay and then used the soil to raise vegetables. It was right beside the lilac bush I loved. From the time I was six, the little space between the lilac bush and the alley fence was my own garden, where I could plant whatever I could, always mint and nasturtiums. In school in spring they sold seeds through special catalogs, and I would order the seeds my mother wanted and also some I could choose. The smell of lilacs recalls to me the best aspects of my mother. I still love seed catalogs, and every year, I order far too many packets of seeds, for the joy of them. Hollyhocks grew along the alley fence, outside, and my friends and I played with them, making hollyhock ladies dance on buckets of water, making heads from buds and impaling them on the open blossoms that became skirts. One girlfriend who lived kitty-corner across the alley was the daughter of a cop. I especially liked her because when we played dress-up, she wanted to be the rescued princess and I could do the rescuing. She was obsessed with what went on at burlesque shows, which her father regularly attended and her mother reviled. They were confused in her mind with whorehouses. We could locate those houses in the neighborhood, beside the streetwalkers we also knew. As I grew older, some of my friends joined their ranks.

Mother was a storyteller, as Grandma was, but even when they told the same stories, the emphasis, the characters, sometimes even the outcomes were different. I have often said that I learned about viewpoint long before I wrote my first novel from listening to the different ways my mother and my grandmother saw the same people, the same events. If it was a family tale, then Aunt Ruth would also have a version. Mother's stories were more dramatic and sensational; Grandma's were moralistic or spiritual. Her best stories came from the rich pack of folklore of the women of the shtetl, a world of brutal violence and powerful magic. The story of the golem that I used in *He, She and It,* I first heard from my grandmother. Ruth's versions of family stories emphasized the facts, what really happened, how she figured it out. They were little detective stories. Mother had tales about everyone in the neighborhood, for if they had secrets, she would know them sooner or later. Women came into her kitchen to consult her, to drink her coffee and eat her apple cake, to weep and sometimes giggle like me and my friends, and tell stories that made the hair stand up on my arms, when I could manage to keep quiet and overhear. Sometimes she read their palms. All this coming and going was in my father's absence and never could be mentioned when he could hear it. He had forbidden her to read palms; it was one of our many secrets. *Don't tell your father* was a refrain of my childhood, along with the threat *I'll tell your father if you do that.* One of our weapons against his domination and his temper was to withhold information—little excursions we might have taken downtown, a dress she bought on sale and hid away, the visits of neighbors, the stories she told me of her previous boyfriends and husbands, the secrets of the neighborhood added to ours.

Violence was a daily part of the neighborhood—not the violence of today, drive-by shootings. Hardly anyone had a gun, but many of us had knives or razors. Violence was in the family, between the races, among neighbors. The man next door used to come home on payday tanked to the gills and throw his entire family out of the house, one at a time. He would work his way through them, starting with the youngest, swat them around, rough them up and then hurl them out the grade door so they slammed one at a time against our house so it shook. The youngest son was my on-and-off-again boyfriend, and it made me feel bad to hear him pleading and then crying. We would lie in bed waiting till it was over to sleep, but of course, we never said anything. The father was the breadwinner: a Lithuanian immigrant, he worked as a bus driver. He had the right to beat his wife and his sons. We knew it was coming when we would hear his voice, never otherwise raised, lamenting his brood of bloodsuckers. Then we knew the beatings were about to start. That did not surprise me, since I was frequently beaten.

It was not that my parents were cruel. My father never hit my mother, although he terrorized her with his temper, as she in turn went into blind crazy rages. Once when they were fighting about whether to go to Ebensburg for Thanksgiving, she pulled the tablecloth fully laden with supper off the table, flinging it at the window. My father did hit me, quite often.

If he got angry enough, he kicked me, hard. The worst thing was being beaten with a wooden yardstick that leaned against the wall behind two doors that always stood open, where the mangle and the vacuum cleaner were kept. That continued until I took the yardstick and broke it into many pieces.

My father was impatient, and working with him had a dangerous side. He might let go of the ladder when I was climbing, he might drop a hammer on my foot, he might let a table I was helping him move pin me to the wall. It was a tamped-down hostility suddenly leaping out of control: a desire to be free of my mother and of me. A desire to be alone again. On the afternoon of my mother's memorial, many years later in Florida, we returned through the sweltering humidity to their empty house. My father seemed oddly jolly.

"I want to get a burger and a beer. I always wanted to try Harpoon Louie's."

That was the local TGI Friday's imitation. "You want to go out now?" Woody asked.

"Why not?" My father chuckled. "Now that I'm baching it again."

That desire to get rid of the burden of the two of us may have been behind his terrifying impatience. I have a crushed misshapen finger, the index finger of my left hand, because I was too slow getting into the car to go to Sears, and he slammed the door on my hand. He might have been a fine uncle, full of jokes and singing off-key and playing cards with enthusiasm and skill, letting his nephews and nieces have a sip of his beer, but he should never have been a father. I understand. I would not be an adequate mother. Having to put up with us was more than he could easily endure.

But he was an honorable man with a strong sense of duty, so he stayed, where another man would simply have taken off. If he had left, we would really have been reduced to poverty. Mother had no ability to earn a living. Not only did he stay, but he also paid monthly for my grandmother's keep, a woman who meant nothing to him, however important she was to me. That was a lot of money going out every month from what was never an ample salary, but I didn't hear him complain.

One charming thing he did was recite poetry that he had learned in school. This love of poetry was something my parents gave me. In the Ebensburg school system, every child learned certain poems by heart. "On the day we French stormed Ratisbon / a mile or so away / on a little mound Napoleon stood. . . ." "The boy stood on the burning deck." He liked to recite in a loud sonorous voice. I loved those times. It would happen in the evenings, over coffee and cake at the kitchen table. I would ask for the poems I particularly liked. My mother would reel off "The Owl and the Pussycat." The owl and the pussycat were happy, for once.

My parents were simply obsessed with each other and after my early childhood, in which I pleased my mother, found me more of a nuisance than an asset. I began doing very well in school after my illnesses, but neither of them was interested in grades. My brother had done poorly in school but had been their idea of a proper boy. I seemed incapable of learning when I carried home my dim accomplishments—all A's, my spelling bee victories—how little such things were valued by my parents. They would much rather have had a healthy flirtatious little girl, a sort of minor-league Shirley Temple. When we were given intelligence tests, I was made to take mine over again. The score was inconceivable. It was embarrassing for my mother and annoying to the school. The principal did not know what to do with me. Since I read way above my grade level, I was sent out of class to tutor the kids who could not read. I rather liked that, and I liked them. Usually they were from Afro-American families just up from the South to work in the nearby factories. They liked getting out of the classroom and so did I. We were misfits together.

I confided my ambitions only to Buttons, who listened approvingly. Like many cats, he loved to be talked to. I had dressed Whiskers in doll clothes, but I never did that to Buttons. He was my coconspirator. I did not know much about college, but I knew it was where you learned the things you needed in order to understand the world, I knew it was the way out of the neighborhood I wanted to escape. By the time I was twelve, I knew. I listened to my aunt Ruth saying that with a college diploma, she could have been a professional, she could have achieved a high civil service rating. Staying was death. It was drinking too much or doing drugs. Staying was going on the streets as some of my girlfriends soon did, running numbers like the guys, working at dead-end jobs, having babies too young and too many. It meant violence or tedium, dying fast or slow. It meant reform school and then prison. That was all I could see before me if I did not get out.

Buttons had an unusual habit: when I went out into the alley to scavenge or make my way through the neighborhood, often he would walk at my side. He trotted along beside me, giving an occasional chirp or meow of comment. If we met a dog, he climbed something. If I ran into a friend, he dropped back. Those were our secret walks.

Buttons disappeared when I was twelve. We never found his body, although I spent endless afternoons and weekends looking for him, always hoping to find him still alive. There are so many ways a cat living half on the streets and in the alleys could have died. I mourned him violently.

Shortly thereafter, I found a way to have a sense of community, of belonging—by joining a street gang.

THE NEW ERA C. 1946

It was right after the war of my childhood
World War II, and the parks were wide open.
The lights were all turned on, house
lights, street lights, neon like green
and purple blood pumping the city's heart.
I had grown up in brown out, black out,
my father the air raid warden going
house to house to check that no pencil
of light stabbed out between blackout curtains.
Now it was summer and Detroit was celebrating.

Fireworks burst open their incandescent petals
flaring in arcs down into my wide eyes.
A band was playing "Stars and Stripes Forever."
Then the lights came on brighter and starker
than day and sprayers began to mist the field.
It was the new miracle DDT in which we danced,
its faint perfumy smell like privet along the sidewalks.
It was comfort in mist, for there would be no more
mosquitoes ever, and now we would always be safe.

Out in Nevada soldiers were bathing in fallout.
People downwind of the tests were drinking
heavy water out of their faucets. Cancer
was the rising sign in the neon painted night.
Little birds fell out of the trees but no one
noticed. We had so many birds then.
In Europe American cigarettes were money.
Here all the kids smoked on street corners.
I used to light kitchen matches with my thumbnail.

My parents threw out their depression ware
and bought Melmac plastic dishes.
They believed in plastic and the promise
that when they got old, they would go
to Florida and live like the middle class.
My brother settled in California with a new
wife and his old discontent. New car,
new refrigerator, Mom and Dad have new hats.
Crouch and cover. Ashes, ashes, all fall down.

THREE

A LIFE IN WORDTIGHT COMPARTMENTS

You must not imagine the gang I joined at age twelve was like the gangs of today. We were not part of a drug distribution system, for that was in underworld hands. Heroin and marijuana and uppers existed in school and in the neighborhood, but we were more interested in alcohol and tobacco. We had no guns. When turf fights existed, they were sporadic and a matter of fists, baseball bats, Sam Browne belts, occasional knives and razors; since no income was involved, they were not pursued long or vigorously. Nobody much wanted our turf, from the gasworks to the railroad tracks. I was stronger by then, no longer fainting. I learned to pick easy locks and I could run like hell. I had quick hands. I was gifted at shoplifting and never caught. My gifts were appreciated in the gang, who forgave me for doing well in school—something I never gave up. I would not allow my grades to falter no matter what I did in the hours afterward, because of my dream of somehow escaping to that place called "college."

We specialized in petty theft—stuff found in unlocked garages and cars, what we could get by shoplifting, opening basements, stealing bikes and running mild scams. We played "scavenger hunt," working up the side of a block, asking for a buffalo nickel. Almost every house would give us one. With a couple of dollars, we felt rich. A package of cigarettes was a quarter. We were just street kids working the blocks we could reach on foot. We climbed on the roof of the White Castle, a local fast-food chain, and blocked the chimney or threw garbage down it. We stole hubcaps and, a couple of times, shirts left out on a line. We got older brothers to buy beer, which we'd drink till somebody puked. We all needed money for cigarettes. I smoked Lucky Strikes. Mostly we stole stuff we could use, but if we found something like a good saw or electric drill, we could sell it to an older kid who acted as agent for a fence. He would give us a dollar for something his boss could sell. We knew about marijuana and heroin, but none of us touched it—yet. We did get our hands on white lightning from a local still in a garage. It was cheap, strong and merciless and burned the lining off my throat. I did not enjoy it but drank it out of pride, not to seem afraid.

Another skill I acquired around this time was lying. When I was younger, I was truthful with my mother. She could empty me out like a pocket and I would tell her everything. She would have been a terrific interrogator, as she could play either soft cop or tough cop. Her skills at reading body language were intense. As I entered puberty, she began frantically to police me. She went through my things, she violated my privacy daily. After all, my room was hardly private. It held her sewing machine; it was the route to the attic and storage. I returned her hostility and became master of the quick and easy lie. She never knew where I had been, although she imagined she did. I created lies within lies, tangles of obfuscation in which all of the invention I would later put into my novels was developed and perfected in keeping my mother at bay. I still have an overdeveloped and paranoid sense of privacy. I become hostile if someone, even Ira, picks up objects on my desk or dresser and appears to be looking through them. I am nosy about other people, but I hate being questioned myself.

As I said, my mother was forty-four when she had me, so when I began to menstruate, she must have been well into menopause. Certainly her response to my first period was close to anger. She went down to the corner drugstore, returned with a box of menstrual pads and a sanitary belt. "Go in the bathroom, shut the door and put it on," she yelled.

Obviously I had done something wrong. I managed as best I could. I had no idea how to attach the pad to the belt, so I hung a string of safety pins from the belt down to the end of the pad and put the belt around my waist. This was extremely uncomfortable and prone to stick out in back or front in a embarrassing way. A year later, my aunt Ruth saw me putting on a menstrual pad and showed me how to loop it through the sharp end of the belt and wear the belt and pad properly.

When I had my period, Mother would not let me near wine she was making or dough that was rising, and I had to take my pads out to the alley and burn them. At first I had to ask for each pad, as if I might use too many. I took to stealing them by the box from the drugstore and then I did not have to ask. I was an accomplished shoplifter from twelve on through college. It was how I got the things I did not have the money to pay for. I stole my first brassiere. I needed a bra from the time I was twelve, but my mother would not let me wear one, saying I wasn't old enough. I began walking all hunched over. I stole one and hid it, so when I went out, I could slip into a bathroom and put it on. Finally in high school, she bought me a couple of bras. At the same time, she presented me with my first girdle. Since I weighed ninety pounds, this was superfluous by any rational standard, but not by the mores of the 1950s. If you might jiggle, you needed a girdle. I hated it. It was a white rubber contraption with garters hanging down. I could see only one advantage in growing up: being able, I imagined, to control my own destiny and make my own choices.

Another cat walked into the backyard, a long-haired tabby someone had taken the trouble to have altered. I was picking lilacs from the bush by the tiny compost pile. A strange tabby stood at the alley gate and stared at me expectantly. He did not meow, he did not do anything except look straight at me. I walked slowly to the gate, expecting him to run away. Instead he held his ground. I opened the gate and he stepped intelligently out of the way, then strolled onto the cement walkway that led from the alley gate to the grade door of the house. He walked to the door and I followed. He waited to be let in. "Mother!" I called. He was gravely polite with her, allowing both of us to pet him. He was very hungry but ate carefully, without getting food on the floor.

My mother named him Fluffy. He was an exceptionally mild and sweet-tempered cat, although he would sit on the fence and tease the dog next door, who could not reach him. I would wait till my parents went to sleep and then sneak down to the basement (where he unlike Buttons was permitted to sleep) and carry him up to my bed. I don't think I slept much those years, as I had to sneak him out in the morning. Like Malkah he enormously appreciated having a home and was demonstrative with all of us. He wanted to be a lap cat. He quietly and inexorably worked on my parents with his charm and his patience and his persistence until he was allowed to sleep inside, until he was taken on vacation with us, until he had at least some of the privileges he strongly desired. He had little interest in the life of the alley and would eat almost anything presented to him, including cantaloupe and tomato sauce. He would try anything you offered him, out of politeness if not hunger.

The neighborhood in Detroit was Black and white by blocks, like a crazy checkerboard. I had always gotten along with the Black kids in my grade school; in fact some of them protected me from the white kids. Being one of the only Jews in the neighborhood, I was not white and I was not Black, but something in between. Jews were not whites and were kept out of most neighborhoods in Detroit by covenants, as were the Blacks. My first boyfriend in grade school (I had a couple earlier) was Black, but that earned me a beating and got him into trouble too. He took his mother's brooch to give me. That didn't help either of us. But his sister Josephine looked out for me. She knew I had really cared for Joey. I was casually prejudiced but at the same time recognized I had more in common with the two brightest Black girls in my class, who had also been double-promoted with me and who were hard and fast, than I did with any of the doll-like white girls the teachers liked. My white friends were all kids up from Appalachia or tough girls placed in foster families.

Cats were my usual pets, but I had others: turtles bought from the dime store that promptly died; tadpoles or frogs from science class in school that I would keep in the house for a week or so and then get my parents to picnic someplace where I could free them; a garter snake a boy named Floyd gave me. I thought it much better than presents other boyfriends gave me, silly jewelry from the dime store or half a bag of candy. I named it Slinky and got books from the library about how to care for it. My mother disliked that snake intensely. Her neighborhood ladies did not want to come into the house. One day I came home from school to find that Slinky had disappeared. I tore the house apart looking for him. I was consumed with guilt, imagining him dying of starvation or thirst in some ventilation duct. It was not until ten years later, my mother told me she had taken him out to a vacant lot and let him go—which was probably the kindest thing to do, but I wasted a lot of time and guilt looking for him. I brought home all the amphibians because I had a crush on my general science teacher, Mrs. Williams. I loved her cool rationality combined with enthusiasm for her subject. I thought I might be a scientist, if I were not to be a successful thief.

One tremendous pleasure of my childhood from the time I was perhaps four years old into adolescence was travel. I mentioned the regular trips to Cleveland and Ebensburg. My father was sent by Westinghouse all over the state to repair machinery—in steel mills, paper mills, foundries. In summer, Mother and I accompanied him. Sometimes in the spring or fall, I would skip school and we would go. I remember my mother and me hanging around parks in Port Huron, in Lansing, in Kalamazoo. I was particularly fond of the Winona Hotel in Bay City, which was fronted by a big old-fashioned verandah with vines where I could often find Isabella woolly bear caterpillars. I thought of them as the pussycats of the caterpillar family. Also in the dining room they had a relish tray that went around before the meal was served. I was impressed by that—as I was by anything that gave me a choice. Radishes, cottage cheese, scallions, olives—that was luxury. Travel seemed to me a wonderful freedom from daily life, and I think it was so to my mother, as she was often playful. We would find something free or cheap to occupy our stolen time, perhaps a small ratty zoo, a museum of coins or local history, a park, a fountain, a river. This was her escape from housework.

In the summers, my father would have two separate one-week vacations, and we would rent a summer cottage. They were rather primitive but on a lake or river. Fluffy alone of our cats was a good traveler. He would get into the car willingly and sit in the backseat with me. He liked those cottages. My father fished and brought home sunfish or perch. My mother would fry them, and Fluffy would have his share. What a stupid name for an amiable, intelligent creature, one of the world's gentlest.

One place we returned for several years was a cottage colony on a river in the thumb area of Michigan, near Bay City. Fluffy liked to sit on the pier and dabble his foot in the running water of the river. My mother insisted he was trying to fish, but I thought in the heat he simply liked the sensation of cool water. Always there was some kind of water, always a rowboat, always a few battered pots and frying pans. Often it was damp. I loved those vacations, especially when we brought along Fluffy. More than once, I took him out in a boat with me. I liked to row; he liked to be rowed. He found it all amusing. A benign overseer, he was interested in everything we did. The magic for me lay in these little cottages being somebody else's. There might be odd or interesting books. The furniture was different. The beds were uncomfortable, but no worse than mine at home. Even looking in closets and cabinets was fascinating. I walked a great deal from the ages of ten to fifteen, walked miles, exploring I called it. When we rented a cottage up at Crystal Lake, I worked picking cherries. It was child labor but who cared. My mother made exquisite pies from them. She was not much of a cook, but she was a terrific baker. Apple pie, peach pie, plum, chocolate, lemon. Hermits, Toll House, raisin molasses, sugar, oatmeal cookies.

My parents were different on the road. My mother played games with me, my father and mother and I sang, all sorts of old songs including many popular when they were first together: "Did You Ever See a Dream Walking?," "Tea for Two," and barbershop favorites of my father, like "Shine on Harvest Moon." They were jolly, they behaved affectionately toward each other. It was a briefly happy family, unless one of us wanted to make a stop the others refused. That was usually my mother, and she would sulk. My mother was a champion sulker. Ira, who only met her once, remembers her sulking, sitting in a restaurant—the wrong restaurant because we could not get into the one she wanted—refusing to speak a word, balling up bread from the basket in the middle of the table and throwing the tightly wadded-up balls of bread in all directions, pouting.

From the time I could sit up and make out the lines on maps, I became the navigator. My mother hated maps and could not even fold them. The maze of lines confused her. I always filled in, rushing to prove competent where my mother would not or could not. It kept the peace, and my father's temper was always looming over us. I usually had a reasonable idea what would please them in the way of routes and activities. So after World War II, when we were able to take a journey westward to Yellowstone, I picked out where we went and what we did. I tend to do the same thing today when Ira and I are traveling. Old habits hang in there. I'm good at itineraries and at finding offbeat but fascinating places. My ambition after that trip was to be a park ranger.

I had a couple of girlfriends up from Appalachia who lived in a swaybacked house by the railroad tracks. We spent a lot of time in the fields by the tracks, finding baby rabbits, chasing pheasants, poking in the water holes for what we might find. It was a patch of industrial wilderness between the streets of little houses and the factories. By my later childhood, it filled up with new houses we played in as they were being built. Then they were finished, rows of identical two-bedroom houses speedily sold to veterans and their new families. We called that row Babyland. Soon we were baby-sitting there. I discovered sex with these girlfriends. It was more a game than anything else, but a pleasurable one. The first time I had an orgasm—I was eleven—I was astonished and also I had a feeling of recognition. Of course, that's it. As if that was what I had been expecting or looking for. We touched each other, first one being the "man" and then the other. Usually there was role-playing— kidnapping, Robin Hood, plots taken from movies or books with sexy scenes, the bodice rippers we weren't supposed to read. In the next few years, until I was fifteen, I had sex with twenty-odd girls, usually as the seducer. Some of my girlfriends used the sex to manipulate me into doing what they wanted, such as lifting things for them—lipsticks, bottles of Evening in Paris, a dime-store perfume.

I spent a great deal of time up in the unheated attic of our house, where I had some old furniture and a bookcase with tilting glass doors. At some garage sale, my mother had picked up a collection of books, the Harvard Five Foot Bookshelf. Each volume was a collection from a different culture: not only Greek and Roman myths, but also myths from India, from Native Americans, from the Norse, from *The Arabian Nights* (bowdlerized of course). I read and reread those stories and they helped form my imagination. Once the attic had been my playroom, where I kept the dolls various aunts gave me and the wonderful doll clothes my grandmother made. Now it was my retreat, where in spite of the cold, Fluffy would join me, sitting on my lap in a child-sized rocking chair painted dark green with scrolls on the back that was rapidly growing too small for me. But I was a small person.

My parents bought a cottage of their own, an hour out of Detroit. It was a tiny lot on a weedy little lake called Pardee. I thought this a made-up peculiar-sounding name, but nobody could tell me what it was named for. The cottage was run-down, had a leaking roof and no inside plumbing, only a pump in the yard. It was not winterized. There were holes in the walls. In short it was a complete mess and very cheap. My father began rebuilding it and continued to do so until they sold it thirty years later. It was an ongoing fix-it project never intended to be completed, a toy for him. He did all the work himself, and sometimes he was successful and sometimes it was a disaster. The first plumbing job he did exploded shit and hot water simultaneously.

At first, I loved going out there. Fluffy often accompanied us. Purple martins occupied a white birdhouse, a miniature colonial up on a high pole on the lot next door (the lots were extremely narrow and the houses almost touched), and used to dive-bomb him, so he preferred the screened-in porch to the actual outside. I sometimes slept on that porch and sometimes in a tiny room whose partitions did not go all the way up to the ceiling. The cottage was heated by an old potbellied wood-burning stove, which I loved to feed. My father's first project was to add a bathroom on the back, put in a water heater, and then bring running water into the kitchen. I think there was almost no fix-it job beyond him. He enjoyed mastering plumbing and carpentry and tiling. In my adult life, I have often expected more from the men I've been with than comes easily to them in the way of the ability to repair and fix up, because of my father.

Our back fence at the cottage gave onto the land of an immigrant everybody called The Russian, who grew black walnuts. A canal he had dug to give himself more privacy—perhaps I should call it a moat—separated our land (and that of ten other people) from his. Frogs twanged from the canal and snapping turtles raised their snouts like U-boat periscopes. He lived in a year-round house he had built of logs. My father never had anything to do with him, but my mother, who knew a few Russian phrases, charmed him. He was always inviting us to come over to collect walnuts. The pulp stained our hands, and I went to school with brown palms. Mother flirted with him, as she did with most men. It was her standard tool for getting what she hoped for, second nature. She had a well-honed contempt for women who couldn't or wouldn't flirt—like my aunt Ruth and like me. Her flirting embarrassed me until I would turn my back and pretend I could not hear her. I was an awkward mopey creature still painfully skinny but with visible breasts, a source of terrible embarrassment to me, with whacked-off black hair and a permanent slump, wearing too-big plastic glasses and clothes that never quite fit, since few of them had been bought for me. My aunt Ruth was one source of my clothes. We were close to the same size, but my breasts were already bigger, so nothing buttoned completely.

When I was twelve, I began reading my way through the mysteries in the Gabriel Richard branch library because Aunt Ruth read them, and what she did was glamorous. For the next year and a half I must have read 90 percent of the mysteries in that library. Then, abruptly, I stopped. I was bored. The last ones I really loved were Dorothy Sayers's. Rereading them in adulthood, I still liked them, although the class attitudes made me gag. I began reading biographies. Perhaps I was looking for role models, for lives to try on mentally. When I turned fourteen, I began to read real novels—Dickens, Hemingway, the Brontë sisters, as well as a lot of 1930s through 1950s fiction.

Strange the things I remember vividly. A tree stood to one side of the sand road at the cottage. We called it fish head tree because local fishermen, if they had caught a particularly big pike or bass, would nail its head to the tree. We used that tree as home base in hide-and-seek and other games. Yet when it came back to me in dreams, it was sinister and dangerous—a portent of death.

Bert Bunin Piercy in 1945, Detroit, Michigan.

We had not had Fluffy for more than two years when I found a kitten. I was always cutting through the alleys of my neighborhood and I always had my eye out for anything salvageable, little treasures like interesting bottles or a stool somebody might have thrown away. This time it was a tiny abandoned kitten thrown out in a box. I thought her adorable and I brought her home. It was late spring and my mother was in a good mood, I have no idea why. She also thought the little tricolored kitten was cute and said that if Fluffy accepted her, we might keep her, at least for a while. I don't know why I thought it was a female, for she was quite young and I did not know how to sex a kitten. This was Friday after school and the next morning, we drove out to the cottage.

I had not named her yet, as mother for the first time had given me permission to name a pet myself. Since I had disliked Fluffy's name, I took very seriously my right to name my new kitten. Fluffy accepted her and proceeded to wash her. He was, as I have said, an exceptionally friendly and adaptable cat. He even played with her. She tried to suckle him, which he discouraged. I had never had a kitten before, and everything about her enchanted me. In the car, she was a little frightened but crawled into my blouse and hid there, little nameless ball of white, orange and tan fluff purring loudly, pleased to be fed and warm and held. I made lists and lists of possible names. Perhaps she was my first poem.

I was intensely proud of her, and I wanted to engage my friends out at the cottage in the naming. After we had lunch, I started up the dirt road, carrying the kitten in my jacket to a cottage that belonged to another family from our neighborhood. While visiting them we had first learned of the run-down house for sale cheap on the same road. I had left the lower houses behind and was climbing a hill through the woods to their house when a large hunting dog came leaping out of the bushes. I held the kitten to me but the dog knocked me down, biting my arm and ripped the kitten from me. In front of me as I beat ineffectively at the dog, kicking and screaming, it tore the kitten into pieces of gore. I chased the dog through the woods, screaming, still somehow thinking I could recover my kitten. I was hysterical. I was brought home in shock. For years, I had nightmares. I went over those few seconds again and again, trying to think what I could have done. It was my fault for taking the kitten to my friend's house. My parents were embarrassed that I made such a fuss. Nothing was done to the dog.

I never liked the cottage so well after that. What I did like was walking. At that time the area had thick forest and trails through it. On the other side of the small lake, deer came down to drink in the morning. I made friends with a man who lived down the road. His name was Tom and I thought him an old man, although probably he was no older than I am now. He was Native American, a Wyandot, married to a white woman who worked in an office in a nearby town. My mother said his wife did not love him any longer, wanted to be rid of him. He had worked in construction, but his heart was bad. Now he did odd jobs— build a shed, repair a roof, put up a fence. Around the clump of cottages on the lake forest stretched, crossed only by trails. In the other direction, there was an old gravel pit near a smaller lake where I often saw massasauga rattlers sunning themselves. I had no fear of snakes and left them alone, simply admiring them. I never bothered them and they never bothered me, although a couple of times, I inadvertently came within inches of their dusty sleekness. Past that were meadows I was fond of and past that were farms and apple orchards.

Tom showed me the old trails through the woods. To this day I dream of those woods, because I had never to that time tasted freedom such as I knew there. I walked and wandered in the city, but always it was somebody's turf and I had to be careful. I had to watch out for boys, for men, for trains, for trucks, for the cops. In the woods, I feared nothing, if I avoided hunting season. I rarely saw another person. I saw deer, raccoons and foxes, toads, weasels, box turtles. The woods were mine. I tried to persuade friends to accompany me, and sometimes they would, but they saw little point to my wanderings. My girlfriends out there were boy crazy, movie star crazy. I kept a scrapbook of movie star photos, but I never looked at them when I wasn't with my girlfriends. With an apple and a piece of cheese or bread in my pocket, I would go out as soon as I had finished my daily chores and walk six miles, eight miles, ten miles, returning only for supper. Walking alone was a fierce high joy. I didn't have to explain or justify myself. I was accustomed enough to navigating the streets of my neighborhood alone after dark; the country roads and wood trails felt safe. Once when I heard men's voices, I simply hid in the bushes. I could move far more quietly than they could. They passed by and I continued. Being wary of men when I was alone was second nature to me. If guys in cars or trucks stopped on the roads, I just gave them some story and moved on quickly. Mostly nobody ever bothered me around the cottage, except for a local boy who got me down on the floor once, when I came over to see his sister, but I punched him and got away. I didn't take it seriously. To me, that was just how it was. If you didn't want some bozo pulling your panties down, you had to fight him. I was never afraid to hit, and I had certainly taken enough punches by early adolescence to know I could stand being hurt, if needed. I combined that with screaming my head off. I had boyfriends, and I let them rub against me or touched them through their clothes—what "good" girls did—but I was too terrified of pregnancy to exercise my strong curiosity about sex with males. By eighth grade, several friends had gotten caught, as we said, and had to leave school. That looked like the end of their lives. Often they were sent away from their families or just disappeared. Some went into prostitution.

I felt Tom had given me the gift of the woods. He was the one who finally told me that the name of the lake, Pardee, was an amalgam of the names of the two men who had sold off the land on one side for cottages, bringing the sand road in. He had stories too, like my mother and my grandmother. Who had ever heard of a man with stories? Except for my brother.

When Grant came home from the marines and the war in the Pacific, he talked compulsively about it in a graphic and realistic way that stayed with me for years and years until I wrote about it in the Murray sections of *Gone to Soldiers*. He told me what war had been like, poured it out. He talked of the landings where men on either side of him had their heads blown off, where the ocean was red and sticky. He spoke of shooting wounded Japanese soldiers. He spoke of the smell of the trenches on Okinawa, the smell of rotting meat that was human and the smell of shit. He told about how his sergeant had persecuted him for being Jewish and how he finally punched him and was thrown into the stockade. Visiting us, he was on some antimalarial drug that made him high. But a couple of years later, when I recalled those stories, he was already telling tales of a glorious, heroic war. I did not believe the later stories, as the earlier ones had burnt themselves into my brain.

My father rarely talked about his childhood or his adolescence. In fact, he rarely talked about his life at all. I would ask him questions and he would answer one or two and then he would get annoyed. He had an intense dislike for the emotional, the irrational, the personal. So I was astonished and moved when Tom told me wonderful stories, stories of his people, stories of the history of the area—where his family had lived for a thousand years or more—stories of the towns, stories of animals. I formed a strong sympathy for Native Americans I have never lost. I had been reading adventure stories about the settling of Ohio and Kentucky, written I think by somebody named Altshuller, in which renegades were villains. But I thought if the Indians were right and defending their land, Altshuller was wrong, and if you were not an Indian, the only right thing to do would have been to be a renegade and join up with them. I even learned to count in Wyandot from one to ten, long since forgotten. Tom died of a heart attack a couple of years later. He was up repairing a roof. It was not clear if the heart attack or the fall killed him.

When I found a new trail, when I found a new road, I had to know where it went, and since I was twelve, thirteen, then fourteen years old, I did not drive. Occasionally I hitched a ride on the running board of a farm truck, just for the fun of it. Some roads were called corduroy roads. They were made by laying logs down and putting sand or gravel over them, so driving on them was a bump-and-bump, tooth-rattling, bone-shaking experience. I was chased by a bull. I watched deer from hiding. I found an old icehouse long abandoned and climbed up a rotting staircase to the loft. I bought cider gushing as it came from the press. I picked apples from roadside trees. That time, my mother sent me back with a bag and eventually I filled enough to stock our cellar for the winter. I love the smell of apples. I gathered hickory nuts; my mother gave bags of them to friends. I took my role as scavenger seriously. Once I brought home Osage oranges, but they turned out to be inedible. I picked raspberries, blueberries, elderberries, from which Mother made pies, jellies and wine. Wherever I went, I kept an eye out for windfalls.

In summer, my father would fish the lake for largemouth bass, for sunfish and perch (pretty high-colored fish that flashed as they were landed to die gasping) and bearded slimy catfish. Catfish were not kosher but my mother cooked them, because my father caught them and liked to eat them. I liked the largemouth bass the best, not only because they tasted good but also because catching them was a bit of a battle. I fished with my father, more to try to please him than because I liked it. I did enjoy casting with the spinning reel, watching the lure arc and dance away. I did not enjoy the mosquitoes or cleaning the fish. I was always cutting my fingers on the fins or slicing open the gallbladder.

In winter he went ice fishing with local guys who had little shacks they lugged out on the lake. They would bring a stove and set that up too on cinder blocks or bricks. Then they would saw a hole in the ice and sit there hour after hour. I liked being way out on the lake which was pretending to be a snowy field, while hiding a mysterious dark world under us, the fish circling, the water weeds growing, the water lilies asleep in the muck down deep under our feet. But I found the actual process of ice fishing boring, and my presence inhibited the guys. I was happy to stay inside the cottage with Fluffy and the potbellied stove, but the disadvantage was that soon my mother would set me some task I found meaningless, the housework that was never even half done, and soon we would be fighting. Better to get away and walk, beating a path through the snow in the winter woods, no matter how cold I got—and sometimes I came near frostbite. I loved the stillness. I got drunk on silence. There was not much silence in my life.

One May, I had my first mystical experience lying on a hillside in a clearing that had probably once been a farm. I experienced total oneness with everything as I rose above my body and then sank back into it. It was ecstatic as nothing I had ever felt before. I swore I would never catch a fish or harm an ant again. The resolution did not last the week, but the feeling of kinship with all living has not left me. I have never since been able to see myself as outside or above nature. That kind of experience of unity has been accessible to me during some periods of my life, particularly since I moved to the Cape. I value such moments but not in the way that some people do; I have never organized my life around them.

I still dream of those woods. Often I am searching for the way in. Sometimes they are compounded with the woods around where I live, whose sand roads and old trails I have walked since I moved here. Once with Ira, I went back to Lake Pardee. Suburban sprawl stretches out from Detroit to encompass that weedy little lake. There is no mystery, no wildlife, no forest. It was insanely depressing. There was no way I could show him what I had experienced, for not a trace of it survived.

My life was intensely compartmentalized. There was school, where I was a brain but not really white and badly dressed compared to other white girls. I hung out sometimes with boys in my neighborhood and then in the gang, and that was weird to the other girls. They all wanted to have a boyfriend, but they didn't play with boys. Sometimes I still did. I always had boyfriends, although I did not care much for them. They teased too much and always wanted to be poking at me or telling stupid dirty jokes. I had an on-and-off flirtation with the youngest of the family next door. Sometimes we fought. Sometimes he teased me and sometimes I teased him. His feelings were easily hurt. Sometimes he wanted to live in our house. He had a need to try to exert power over me by tying me up. I did not quite trust him and never let him render me helpless. I desperately wanted a best girlfriend, but until I joined the gang, I never got on that well with other girls, not the ones I wanted to, but in the gang, the girls respected me. I followed the same rules they did.

There was the life with the gang and the friends I had made there, feverish connections, passionate, sometimes tormented. With one of my gang girlfriends, I began baby-sitting. We sat for people who worked late—restaurant workers, nurses. I would come home by myself at one or two in the morning, running through the streets. As long as I was baby-sitting and made money, my parents never questioned me. From twelve on, I was always doing something for money, odd jobs until I was sixteen and could get a regular job. Often when we were baby-sitting, we had brief furtive sex.

My mother was always telling me how easy I had it and how little I knew about life, but I knew a great deal more about the neighborhood than she did. I knew some of the prostitutes and what their lives were like; I knew the numbers runners; I knew the gang structure, far less visible in those days of no colors, no guns and minimum graffiti. You could easily make a mistake about turf and pay for it. I knew where the nearest still was, and I had sampled the stuff cooked there, driving up in a car full of gang kids. I knew about hot rods and playing chicken and how dope was hidden in cars. I had seen people cut with knives and razors, beaten to raw meat, but I had never seen anyone shot. I saw how badly girls who were raped were treated by everyone, how they were punished and classified as whores afterward. I fought off three rape attempts, never mentioning them to my parents, for they would have blamed me. The first was the boy at the cottage. One was a guy in the gang, not my boyfriend, whom I had persuaded I would not do it. I bit and kicked the other guy in the balls and ran like hell, yelling that I would tell my boyfriend. The third was a guy who had come to use my girlfriend Kim, but she was with another customer. I was sitting outside in the hall waiting, because we were going to a Humphrey Bogart movie afterward. We shared a crush on him. The guy decided I would do and didn't want to take a refusal. He was much bigger than me, but I made such a ruckus, he let go. I knew how to call up a violence in myself that could cause males much bigger than me to back off. It was not only that I would readily punch and kick, but I could seem fierce.

At the same time, all my dreams came from books, and I was full of fantasies and invented tales of escape and high adventure, nothing like the ordinary grimy terrifying daily life of the streets I knew too well. I was a Jew, and thus an outsider. My mother was always saying, *Don't tell anyone*. She was terrified that the Nazis would appear and carry us away to a concentration camp. My grandmother was proud of being a Jew. She practiced her religion openly and wore her identity in the world. When my grandma learned that everyone, everyone she had known in Lithuania was dead, she grieved and mourned. I promised her I would always be a Jew, like her.

Kim was already on the streets as a prostitute at fourteen. We read Edgar Allan Poe together. We would lie on her bed reading aloud until we were ready to scream, an excuse to hold each other. Our touching was not only sex but had an element of tenderness, of caring. By fifteen, she already had a drug habit, acquired from her pimp. Reading was as important to her as it was to me, as much an escape. We handed books back and forth and shared our favorite parts out loud. We both got into Walt Whitman when I was fifteen. I dared to love her, because I could share my dreams with her—her and my cat. I was important to her because I was not in the life or on drugs, and still was her good friend.

My parents finally paid off the tiny house. It was the 1950s, my father felt prosperous. We even bought a television set on which my mother and I watched McCarthy and Kefauver hearings and my father watched sports and cowboy shows. They wanted a house in a less grungy neighborhood. The only people who would consider buying our house were Blacks, and my parents sold the house to a Black doctor. As my parents did not go through a bank but collected the monthly small payments themselves, I saw over the years how he improved the house. I was impressed that he was a professional man and had enough money so that when he moved in, he remade the house almost completely and enlarged it. It became something far more spacious and comfortable.

In retaliation, our Lithuanian neighbors—actually my boyfriend—fed Fluffy rat poison on a piece of hamburger. Fluffy died for an entire day. He shook with pain and moaned and writhed as I held him, squatting or lying on the worn linoleum of the kitchen floor. I have never forgotten or forgiven. I have never poisoned anything in my life, not a mouse, not a beetle. Years later, when I was active in civil rights, I knew where my militancy about race had started, with that sweet affectionate creature dying in acute agony in my arms, hour after hour, because we had sold our house to an Afro-American doctor. I wanted to kill the boy who gave him the poison, but mostly I understood hatred as I never had. I thought race hatred the worst crime imaginable. I was fifteen.

That year I lost my girlfriend Kim to a heroin overdose, but I did not cry over her any harder than over my cat. I understood why she had let her pimp get her hooked: it numbed her. I was never judgmental about sex, for she had to make money. Everybody did. That was just a way unappealing to me. I missed her, and her open and affectionate acceptance of me. Both deaths marked and changed me for the rest of my life, as did the third: my grandmother—my source of Jewish ritual and story, the one person in the family I was quite sure loved me—died of stomach cancer. My fifteenth year was cut in two and so was my life. That was the year of loss and death when everything changed.

CRESCENT MOON LIKE A CANOE

This month you carried me late and heavy
in your belly and finally near Tuesday
midnight you gave me light and life, the season
Kore returns to Demeter, and you suffer
and I cannot save you though I burn with dreams.

Memories the color of old blood,
scraps of velvet gowns, lace, chiffon veils,

your sister's stage costumes (Ziegfeld
didn't stint) we fingered together, you
padding in sneakers and wash-worn housedresses.

You grew celery by tucking sliced off
bottoms in the soil. You kept a compost
pile in 1940. Your tomatoes glowed
like traffic signals in the table-sized yard.
Don't kill spiders, you warned.

In an asbestos box in Detroit where sputtering
factories yellow the air, where sheets
on the line turn ashen, you nurtured
a backyard jungle. Every hungry cat
wanted to enter and every child.

You who had not been allowed to finish
tenth grade but sent to be a frightened
chambermaid, carried home every week
armloads of books from the library
rummaging them late at night, insomniac,

riffling the books like boxes of chocolates
searching for the candied cherries, the nuts,
hunting for the secrets, the formulae,
the knowledge those others learned
that made them shine and never ache.

You were taught to feel stupid; you
were made to feel dirty; you were
forced to feel helpless, you were trained
to feel lost, uprooted, terrified.
You could not love yourself or me.

Dreamer of fables that hid their own
endings, kitchen witch, reader of palms,
you gave me gifts and took them back
but the real ones boil in the blood
and swell in the breasts, furtive, strong.

You gave me hands that can pick up
a wild bird so that the bird relaxes,
turns, and stares. I have handled
fifty stunned and injured birds and killed
only two through clumsiness, with your touch.

You taught me to see the scale on the bird
leg, the old woman's scalp pink as a rose
under the fluff, the golden flecks in the iris
of your eye, the silver underside of leaves
blown back. I am your poet, mother.

You did not want the daughter you got.
You wanted a girl to flirt as you did
and marry as you had and chew the same
sour coughed up cud, yet you wanted too
to birth a witch, a revenger, a sword

of hearts who would do all the things
you feared. Don't do it, they'll kill
you, you're bad, you said, slapping me down
hard but always you whispered, I could have!
Only rebellion flashes like lightning.

I wanted to take you with me, you don't
remember. We fought like snakes, biting
hard at each other's spine to snap free.

You burned my paper armor, rifled my diaries,
snuffed my panties looking for smudge of sex,

So I took off and never came back. You can't
imagine how I still long to save you,
to carry you off, who can't trust me
to make coffee, but your life and mine pass
in different centuries, under altered suns.

I see your blood soaking into the linoleum,
I see you twisted, a mop some giant hand
is wringing out. Pain in the careless joke
and shouted insult and knotted fist. Pain like knives
and forks set out on the domestic table.

You look to men for salvation and every year
finds you more helpless. Do I battle
for other women, myself included,
because I cannot give you anything
you want? I cannot midwife you free.

In my childhood bed we float, your sweet
husky voice singing about the crescent
moon, with two horns sharp and bright we would
climb into like a boat and row away
and see, you sang, where the pretty moon goes.

In the land where the moon hides, mothers
and daughters hold each other tenderly.
There is no male law at five o'clock.
Our sameness and our difference do not clash
metal on metal but we celebrate and learn.

My muse, your voice on the phone wavers with tears.
The life you gave me burns its acetylene
of buried anger, unused talents, rotted wishes,
the compost of discontent, flaring into words
strong for other women under your waning moon.

FOUR

BRUTUS THE GREAT

At fifteen, abruptly, one section of my life closed with a great thud that reverberated through me with our move, the death of my grandmother, the murder of my cat and the drug-overdose death of my friend Kim, the withdrawal from the old neighborhood. I felt isolated. The neighborhood into which we carried our battered old furniture was solid working-class, almost middle-class, with neat lawns and single-family homes. There were no gangs, no street-corner boys, no action in the alleys or the hallways of decrepit apartments: only houses side by side, and trees. Zoning was loose in those days, and my mother got away with running a rooming house. She could not put a sign outside but placed ads in the papers.

I left street life. I swore off sex. Now I had a real room of my own, upstairs away from my parents with a door that shut. I shared the upstairs with roomers, usually hapless hopeless traveling salesmen who were separated, divorced or whom no one had the bad sense to marry. They filled their rooms with girlie magazines, how-to-succeed books, paperback detective stories, an occasional photo of family or some pretty girl you knew was not theirs. I collected their discarded pink and white and blue forms, requisitions, sales reports, and began writing poems and stories on the back of them. My mother knew everything about them within two weeks of their arrival, their adventures and traumas and problems. One drank, and she worried he would set fire to his room. One had come home early to find his wife in bed with his brother-in-law. Another had lost his plumbing business to his own ineptitude and now was on the road, trying to sell space heaters. Another had gambled his life away on the horses. I had little to do with them. The exception was the sole time my mother took in a couple.

The woman, only two years older than me, was pregnant. I spent a lot of time with Lureen because she seemed lost and in a way she reminded me of Kim. There was something wistful and victimized about both of them, and I was a sucker for a hard-luck case. Like Afro-American friends I had back in the old neighborhood, she played the numbers according to dreams and a dream book she had, or from some incident of the day, a license plate she saw at an intersection, a telephone number that stuck in her head from a radio jingle. She was convinced she would hit and their money problems would be over. Her husband worked at a dry-cleaning plant, long hours, low pay.

Six months into a difficult pregnancy, one Sunday Lureen came home from some beery picnic with friends and miscarried, almost in my arms. She had really wanted children but had no prenatal care. We simply didn't go to doctors. The hospital had been a threat in my childhood: if you don't stop getting sick, I'm going to send you to the hospital, my mother would say. My teeth were rotting in my mouth, mostly from poor diet, so I chewed aspirin to control the pain. We never went to the dentist; it did not occur to me as an option. My mother had gone once when I was eleven and had all her teeth pulled. She returned disheveled and bleeding, in great pain. With poor people, they just pulled your teeth. When I finally was forced to go to a dentist after I went to work for the telephone company, he pulled three of my teeth. I was sixteen.

Lureen was devastated. She had carried twins, perfectly formed by then, two little boys. The first fiction I ever wrote was an attempt to re-create her sorrow in a short story. I had not been in my own room for more than a month when I began to write both poetry and fiction. My first poems were about death, of course. I was death obsessed. My room was upstairs at the front of the house. My parents had a bedroom down-stairs by the bathroom that I too used. This was a house three times as big as our old one, with a spacious living room, a big dining room, a kitchen with a breakfast nook, three bedrooms plus my little room, two baths (one used only by the roomers) and a big back porch. In the rear stood a two-car garage and a sour cherry tree I loved. In spring I would lie under it, staring at the miracle of blossoms thrusting out of wood. The two-story house was made of yellow brick. All through my childhood brick had represented something fine and stable, for that was what the houses were built with far out from the center city where we lived. We would drive out there around Christmastime to look at all the lights on the houses. I took the bus in that direction—to go to the all-white high school, to go to Rouge Park, several miles distant, where there was a pub-lic swimming pool, although I never really learned to swim.

The house was a complete mess, and we had spent two months before we moved in stripping and painting and carting out the filth and the trash of thirty years of the previous owner. My parents got the house at a good price because it had stood vacant for a few years. The only way we could afford it, however, was to take in roomers, which covered the mortgage payments. In front against the cement porch we never used, two tall Norwegian spruces loomed. Their gloom suited me: I thought them dark and romantic. My room stood across a hall from those of the roomers, in a gable overlooking the street. It was tiny and unheated. The roof sloped on both sides, but my father, a good carpenter, took an old dresser and a discarded bookcase and built them into the walls, into the wasted space under the eaves. I had a daybed and a small desk, a radio and a turntable that played through it—both of which I purchased from jobs I did after school. I wrote for a neighborhood newspaper, paid by the inch of copy. When I was sixteen, I began working downtown for Sam's cut-rate department store. I worked in better dresses, $4.98 and up, where the older "girls" treated me as a pet. They reminded me a little of my aunt Ruth, for they could make a living, operate in the business world, dress well, tease one another about men without seeming to take them too seriously. My senior year, I went to work part-time for the telephone company, as a long-distance operator—a job I continued to do during certain vacations all through college. Christmas meant little to me, so I didn't mind working it.

I painted the walls pale green. They were imitation rough plaster. In the wall opposite the daybed I slept on was a bas-relief of a sailing ship. The two casement windows were narrow and opened onto the street. I thought casement windows romantic. I adored my room. When I was home, that was where I preferred to be. Fortunately, high school gave homework. No matter how quickly I actually did it, homework provided me with a defense for my retreat.

I appreciated what my father had done for my room, and I tried, briefly, to please him, as I had tried when I was younger, with even less success. I was skinny, dark, opinionated and with strange habits. While I had a tortured love-hate relationship with my mother, my relationship with my father was distant and wounded. I had the impression he disliked me. I could never quite give up trying to communicate with my mother. She should, I felt, have been able to understand if only she would try. I was always explaining things I had learned to her, which must have been a real pain in the ass. I lectured her about race, about mythology, about history. With my father, conversations tended to peter out quickly. We would talk about the Tigers and the weather. I could ask him about some process, how steel was made, how electricity was generated. That about finished it off, except for Brutus. Once he had sauntered into our lives, we could talk about the cat. He was a strong personality.

I put the old typewriter my aunt Ruth had given me on the little desk. I had my books, I had my writing. I had girlfriends now like other girls did, middle-class girls who seemed to me quite naive but who were special because of that. If they were naive in some respects—sexually, streetwise—they had vast arcane knowledge about clothing and makeup and body hygiene. They taught me to shave under my arms and use a deodorant. They told me that lipstick was supposed to match what you were wearing, and that you didn't mix silver-toned jewelry with gold—not that I had much to mix. What I had, boyfriends had given me, probably swiped. They cared about all sorts of things I was indifferent to but knew I was supposed to take an interest in. I began to follow certain white singers whom other girls had crushes on. Basically they tried to show me how to be a proper girl, and if I had wanted to be one, I would have learned more than I did. But I was resistant to sex roles and I wanted something larger and deeper and darker, yearnings I was skilled at keeping mostly out of view. Still, I understood their tutelage was necessary, even to get a scholarship. I was learning to pass. I am not reading this in from contemporary feminism. My writings at the time—1952, 1953—are full of these feelings. I did not feel the way a girl was supposed to. I must be something different.

I was well educated for my age in some respects: I read Freud and Marx, not books about them; I read Hemingway, Dos Passos, Dickens, the Brontës and an enormous amount of poetry. I had zero social graces and no manners, table or otherwise. My parents ate as if the food might disappear any moment, and I gobbled even faster, to get away from the table. I was ill dressed and had no idea how to use makeup. My skin was always good, for my mother trained me to eat fruit and drink water. I was still painfully thin and had little idea how to talk with middle-class boys. The things that aroused my enthusiasm—the novels, the poets, the analytical books that were tools to grasp the world—were not familiar to my peers. My dexterity with a knife and my ability to run like hell were not useful skills for impressing girls in my classes or boys I might date. Actually I hated dating. It was a minefield. I had no better idea how to behave than someone pulled from a tribal culture and dumped in a middle-class muddle. I stumbled through dates, hoping to pass for normal.

I did not play tennis, I did not swim, I did not bowl. I knew how to dance, but mostly the wild dancing of my old neighborhood rather than the social dancing of high school. I could jitterbug but couldn't fox-trot. I knew a fair amount about baseball from my father, for we had even gone to see the Tigers at Briggs Stadium. Friends dragged me to hockey games (this was the heyday of Gordie Howe), but I understood little about the rules. Basketball and football were alien to me. I did not watch TV because I would have had to stay downstairs with my parents and risk confrontation and questioning. I was enamored of foreign movies and went sometimes with Edith or with one of my other friends. Edith was the daughter of a foreman at Fords, from a Finnish-American family. I saw *Les Enfants Terribles*—Cocteau—ten times. I remember adoring *The Man in the White Suit* with Alec Guinness and *Kind Hearts and Coronets*.

I was an editor of the school paper and joined clubs, the way adolescence was supposed to be. Much of the time, I saw myself playing a role at school but occasionally I lost it and got into arguments. I was an open socialist, thrown out of social studies classes a couple of times. I was pleased not to have to defend myself physically, very pleased. I was leading a far more normal adolescent life with the sense that all of me that counted was underground. That first fall, just as the weather was turning crisp and cold, another cat came to our door.

At first I thought he looked like Fluffy, but his legs were longer, his brown tabby fur a bit darker and with clearer markings, and he had lynx-like tufts in his ears. We thought he was a mature cat. We were wrong. He was only half grown. At his full size, he weighed twenty-two pounds, and not much of that was fat. He became quite simply enormous. In that section of Detroit in all the years my parents lived there and afterward, there were a great many very big dark brown tabby cats with tufts in their ears, for he populated the neighborhood with his progeny. He maintained a large territory but seldom bore a mark of fighting. He was aloof but not hostile to other cats, and they rarely challenged his benevolent rule. He was simply the dominant animal in his domain.

I named him Noble Brutus, as I was studying Shakespeare's *Julius Caesar* at the time and I had read Caesar's *Gallic Wars* in Latin. I did not like Caesar. I thought Brutus had done a good job on him. I might call my new cat Brutus to my heart's content, but to my parents, he was Butch. He came to either name. Edith said he would probably come to any name at all and tried that out: "Come on, Felix. Come, Bugs Bunny." He sat down and stared at her. Then he turned his back and stalked away. He knew his two names.

He had an equable nature, affectionate but strong willed. He would not do what he did not want to do. He wanted to sit in our laps, but soon, he was much too big. When my father lay on the couch, he would climb on his chest, covering it completely. Otherwise he sat beside me or overflowed a hassock. Sometimes he wanted to be out at night, busy with his courting and caterwauling. Mostly he wanted to spend the night inside. In this house I had far more privacy, and the front and side doors were far from my parents' bedroom. I could easily let him in and take him upstairs. He was better than the high setting on the heating pad in that cold room. He would get under the covers and stretch out next to me. As he came into his full size, he warmed most of my torso as I curled around him. I slept with him until I went away to college.

In the old neighborhood, I knew who lived in every house, their financial situation, their family troubles, their religion, their ethnicity, their virtues and vices. In this new neighborhood, I knew none of the neighbors. Gradually, around the time I left for college, Mother began to gather a coterie of women who came in through the kitchen door to talk, to gossip, to consult. By the time Father dragged her from the neighborhood many years later, she had wide acquaintance there. During the early years in the house, however, she was busy with the roomers and with making the yard and house her own. My mother never visited neighborhood friends. She made them come to her.

When I worked at Sam's cut-rate department store, I brought a sandwich from home or bought a hot dog and ate it standing, gulped down with Vernor's ginger ale, the Detroit spicy specialty, so I could spend the bulk of my lunch hour in the downtown branch library. Edith and I bought a dress together that we thought very adult: navy taffeta that rustled invitingly and was cut out in a diamond pattern on the neck and shoulders. We imagined it daring. We passed that dress back and forth for the next three years, for parties. Finally I gave it to her, since the color suited her better and my notion of sophistication had changed by then.

I bought books: Frazer's *Golden Bough;* poetry by Whitman and Emily Dickinson, my mentors; T. S. Eliot. An anthology of postwar poets, including Randall Jarrell, Delmore Schwartz, and above all important to me, Muriel Rukeyser. But 90 percent of the money I earned, I saved for college. These are the years when up in that room, I became who I was to be, began to write both poetry and fiction. The world—the intellectual and political and literary world—was opening to me, although it was tremendously difficult for me to sort it out. I remember reading Faulkner before I had the tools to understand what he was doing, and the feeling I had that this writing was a code I must learn to break. Every six months I would try, until finally I suddenly understood, and then he was mine. I had begun reading poetry seriously and passionately with the Romantics—Byron and Shelley and Keats—and had early and never abandoned passions for Whitman and Dickinson. But I had moved on to more contemporary models by my senior year of high school.

I listened to music on the little turntable I had bought, often getting albums out of the library. I was in love with Russian composers, Shostakovich, Prokofiev, Scriabin, Rimsky-Korsakov. I also discovered blues and jazz. I was crazy about Duke Ellington. Brutus liked music, making little crooning noises along with it. He did not care for dissonant music. He particularly disliked a symphony of Shostakovich, and if I played it, would insist I open the door and let him out—which actually involved going downstairs with him and letting him outside through the front door or else opening the door to the downstairs and letting him into my parents' part of the house.

I had grown up listening to urban blues, although to me it was just music. As a young child, I had lobbied my parents for a piano—friends of my parents had one I adored. Finally my parents got a battered and stained upright with a lovely tone. I was accepted into the Detroit Conservatory of Music and was a gifted pupil, so my mother was told, but to reach the conservatory, my mother and I had to take a streetcar and two buses. She did it with me for a year—amazing. Then she found a piano teacher who was much cheaper, McGillicuddy. We hated each other. Mutual torture went on for the next four years of my childhood. My finger got crushed in the car door shortly after I started working with him, and thereafter it would unaccountably go numb, giving me an uncertain left hand. Besides, I loved to play with feeling and a lot of pedal. It's not hard to understand why I drove him mad. He loved exercises, like the *Little Pischna,* technical brilliance. It was a bad match, but he drank and came cheaply. He lived at the Y. Around age eleven, my lessons stopped. My parents sold the piano. I did not have one again until we moved to Ward Avenue. A neighbor was selling a much smaller piano, what was called in the furniture parlance then, a spinet. I was pleased, but probably did not say so. I was so guarded I wouldn't admit to liking chocolate.

I read *The New Yorker* religiously, sure I was becoming sophisticated with every page I turned. I read the listings for theaters and cabarets, as if even the mention of performances I would never see and perhaps would never want to see, could liberate me from Detroit and my parents, with whom I was at war. Although my life was far more proper after we moved, they were annoyed by what I did, read, listened to in the privacy of my room. I was developing tastes that were not theirs, and my mother resented that. She would denounce books I read. I remember her throwing a fit about Aldous Huxley's *Point Counter Point.* She dipped into it and considered it pornographic. I had forged a note in her handwriting to the local library so I could take out adult books. Since I still cut school oftener than other good students, I had become adept at creating notes from my mother. Sometimes I went to the Art Institute of Detroit, a space I had appropriated as a seventh grader, where I felt safe. Sometimes I wandered downtown. Other times I went to the main public library. High school was a time of pervasive massive boredom, boredom as thick as peanut butter, as bland as vegetable shortening. Almost all I learned was on my own, reading books nobody encouraged me to read.

I had more time to think and brood and scribble than ever before in my life or ever again. I thought about family stories and the contrast of my father's and mother's families. I thought the Piercys lacked curiosity, tolerance, sensuality, joie de vivre, warmth. I thought the Bunnins lacked the ability to choose something and stick to it. They were brilliant and flighty. They began well but did not follow through. They were warm but scattered. Love blew them before it like papers in a wind. I would not be like that. I would avoid, I told myself, the defects of both families. But I was painfully aware of my own. I felt myself to be so much less than I wanted to be that I mocked myself, huddled in my chilly room with my cat. I did not particularly like myself. I thought myself ugly, cowardly, lumpy. I saw myself as someone who imagined great deeds and did nothing but cower.

I fantasized obsessively. My daydreams, the stories I told myself, were like knitting I carried with me and took up at any odd moment, riding the bus, doing the endless housework, sitting in class, sitting at supper trying to shut out the quarreling voices of my parents. Meals were fraught. I learned to eat sparely and quickly, to shovel in some food and flee. My mother cooked chicken well as a pot roast, and the same with beef. Vegetables were possibly dangerous. She was convinced a brother of hers had ruined his stomach and died of pneumonia (how these were related I never learned) because he ate too many raw vegetables. She cooked vegetables until they were soupy. Often we ate canned vegetables. I think most people under forty today have reached maturity without the horrid experience of eating canned spinach or canned carrots. Such is true progress.

She also put sugar in or on almost everything: on lettuce, on tomatoes, on cantaloupe and grapefruit. My parents both had keen sweet tooths. Before going to bed every night, they had cake and coffee. I would fly out yammering through the roof if I did that. Most of the sweet things were cakes, pies, cupcakes, cookies my mother baked. If she was an indifferent cook, she was a fine baker. I am the opposite, but I still make an apple cake, a flat European-style coffee cake, that is an imitation of hers.

In daydreams I lived great heroic adventures and tragic romances. How could love end happily? I hardly saw anyone who seemed happy in marriage, and the last thing I wanted was to be married. That seemed to me a kind of death for a woman, in which she lost not only her will and her power but even her name. I was determined never to marry, but I wanted sexual and romantic adventures. I knew from my mother and girlfriends that women were not supposed to think that way, so I felt myself more of an outsider than ever.

Typically, I read hunched on my daybed wearing a bathrobe over my clothes for warmth, with Brutus lying beside me, often under the bathrobe to be closer, although he did not really fit. He had a soft but melodious purr that seemed to rise and fall in its harmonics. In all those years, he never scratched me, even when I occasionally had to give him medicine, always home prescribed. In later years, my parents actually began to take Brutus to the vet, a change in their lifestyle, which is probably one of the reasons he lived to be twenty-two. He was by far the longest lived of any of their cats, and he was certainly the healthiest.

Of course he also had exceptional vigor and strength. He is the only cat I ever knew who could catch squirrels when he chose. He would sometimes demand to go up in the attic and hunt them, for he was furious when they came into the house and ran back and forth over his ceilings. Outside he left them alone. He was not a great hunter, for he lacked motivation.

He was certainly a lover. He had a regular mate who bore him litters and litters of kittens, or rather bore them to the long-suffering people in the next block who owned her. She was a pretty solid gray cat, but apparently the tabby gene was dominant. He went with other cats and sometimes brought them home, but he and the gray female had an ongoing affectionate as well as sexual bond. When he was fed on the back porch in hot weather, he would often bring her along to share his food.

He did not much care for car travel. By this time I rarely went to the cottage with my parents. I felt I had outgrown it and prized the time in the house alone. He and I got on quite well. As I had when I was a child and my mother was sick, I would open something we both liked, tuna fish or sardines, and share the can with him. Once when I was little and my mother was sick, she got out of bed to find me and Buttons eating sardines from the same plate. She was scandalized. I could not understand why. I was saving dishes that I would have to wash. Anyhow, Brutus and I were quite content to loll around the house. Of course, I had to go to work.

In my last year of high school, I developed a close friendship with a young woman a year behind me. Let's call her Henrietta. We were both sixteen, but I had been double-promoted in grade school. Although they lived on a street much like ours, the atmosphere was different. Both her parents worked, and she had a closet full of feminine clothes. She played the piano seriously, also wrote poetry, not very good but I wasn't about to tell her that. It was hard enough to get her to show me her poems. She had long wavy brown hair almost to her waist. I decided to grow my hair, over my mother's protests. She thought long hair was messy, unhygienic and reeked of the old country. My grandmother had long hair till the day she died, worn in a braided bun she loosened at night. Then she would sit on the edge of the double bed we shared and let her hair down like Rapunzel. I was in love with her when she did that, but before I was sixteen, it had never occurred to me to let my own hair grow.

My grandmother had died slowly of stomach cancer. At her funeral I had revolted against Orthodox Judaism. I was freshly aware of the situation of women. I found the rabbi a joke. He knew nothing of her character, her life, her escape with her husband who had a price on his head from an unsuccessful attempt at revolution, her clandestine passage to America, her persistence through poverty, but instead turned her into a stereotypical Yiddishe mama with no personality, no past. I hated hypocrisy at sixteen and I saw it everywhere—except in myself, of course, and in Brutus. I wrote poetry of loss, of death and desolation, but I already had learned from the culture you did not write love poems to your grandma, so I invented a dead male lover. It was Hannah I was mourning in this guise. They were called the Lil poems and later I won my first Hopwood contest at college with a short manuscript containing several of them. In reaction to what I saw as hypocrisy, I flirted with Buddhism. I was fascinated by mysticism but was ignorant of Jewish mystics, was repulsed by the Christianity that had been shoved at me at school, and found Buddhism in its sanitized Americanized version clean and sweet and enlightened. I tried chanting, controlled breathing, meditation. I discovered if I let my mind go, I saw visions—often frightening but sometimes ecstatic. I wrote bad poetry about my visions in endless spiral notebooks.

This aspect of my life I shared with absolutely no one, except, of course, Brutus. Henrietta also had a cat, Pooh-bear. I had not been raised on Winnie-the-Pooh, so had no idea where this name came from. Pooh-bear was an altered female cat who never went out. She had a sandbox in the basement instead. She was clean, dainty, well fed and well groomed. When Henrietta played piano, Pooh-bear sat on top like the dog in *Peanuts,* swishing her tail. Everything in this house was different, from the Constant Comment tea I had never tasted to the pretty clothes and the porcelain cups, the middle-class amenities. It had never before occurred to me that clothes should match. My mother had no idea of that kind of taste. I had a limited number of sweaters, blouses, skirts, jeans, and I put on whatever was clean. The notion of coordinated outfits was as strange to me as it would have been to a Bushman. I had certain favorites from clothes mostly picked up at rummage and yard sales, favored because they were soft or of a color I liked. I had never put intelligence or aesthetic judgment into clothing. I understood this made me a barbarian. My friend told me how special her family was and how special she was, and I agreed. I was a little in love. Everything in her life seemed to me refined and elegant. I felt common and loud and ashamed. Yet I never wavered in my opinion I was a better writer.

I admired everything else about Henrietta. If Pooh-bear had done anything as vulgar as have fleas, they would have been trained fleas and done tricks. Henrietta had a streak of cruelty that caused her to turn on me and make fun of me from time to time, so I never could quite trust her. There was much to make fun of, my house with its roomers, my shabby clothes, my bad teeth. The odd jobs I did, which I was always running off to. Henrietta did not have to work.

Henrietta had another friend, the first out Lesbian I ever met. Kiki viewed me as a rival for Henrietta's affections. She played the piano masterfully. Henrietta once tricked me into playing Chopin while Kiki hid in the next room, so they could make fun of my playing. Kiki kept telling me I was really a Lesbian and should admit it. I had no idea what I was. My sexuality confused me. But I resented being pushed into a category I had not chosen. I knew one thing for sure: I had to escape home and my mother to have any chance of exploring my own sexuality. I was not attracted to Kiki, because I found her domineering and flamboyant. I'd had enough of that.

They laughed together at the way I dressed and spoke. My childhood had been totally different from that of middle-class girls, although I did not share my wilder adventures or my sexual exploits. The only being with whom I talked with total honesty was my cat: and the poems I hid from my mother, who went through my room frequently looking for just such signs of my inner life. Much of my energy went into protecting my thoughts, my desires, my work, my plans from her. During those years I developed a handwriting so illegible it protected me from her—and unfortunately, from everyone else who tries to read it. Sometimes I can't read it myself. It wasn't until I went away to college that I had a friend with whom I could be honest about myself. Until then, friendship was a log over a pit of alligators. I wanted to reveal myself, to blurt myself out. But I could not. Even much of what was visible was unacceptable; how revolting my inner life would have been. Like many adolescents, I thought of myself as a monster. I had other friends on the school paper. One was a Jehovah's Witness who tried to convert me. Such a marginal religion fascinated me, who had grown up only one of two Jews—the other Black—in my neighborhood. I went to services with her, and my mother accompanied me, willing to go anyplace where other women were pleasant to her. However, we were not about to get seriously involved.

Another friend, Edith, was naive but energetic. I learned a little Finnish as I hung out with her, and she was one of the only friends to whom I showed my writing. She was far less judgmental than my other friends but easily shocked. Although at times I enjoyed pushing writing or opinions at her that were bound to overwhelm her sense of how things were, mostly I respected her innocence. She and her brothers were not allowed to have pets. Her mother considered them unsanitary and a waste of food. Therefore Edith made a great fuss over Brutus. We were both bound for Ann Arbor together, but her mother did not want her to room with me, for she mistrusted me.

I had another friend from the school paper, Louise. I liked her but thought her silly, the stereotypical ditzy blonde. Her hair was almost white and her eyes a pale but startlingly clear blue. In college I would room with her by my second semester, after discovering we had elements of our past in common and that we were both more experienced and tougher than we appeared. She was to become as close to me as anyone in my life ever has been, but I would never have guessed that from the role she played in high school. Later she would be beautiful, but then she was too frantic, too nervous to be more than pretty, with tight curls around her face that did not go with her delicate features.

All through my senior year, I was counting time toward my flight. It wasn't that I became detached or uninvolved with the people around me, but that I endured the boredom of high school, the war with my parents, the sense of being invisible—all as a temporary condition soon to be erased by my departure. I was walking through the maze of what was expected of me while putting my best effort into trying to understand what I read and trying to write. My fiction suffered from being a strange uncouth hybrid of Faulknerian characters and situations, and plots from the girls' novels my friends were reading. I burned that first novel in the fireplace a few years ago, when it occurred to me I could die at any moment in a highway accident or an airplane crash, and someone else might actually read the ghastly thing. I scattered its ashes in the woods. Somebody may read my old love letters or my angry letters, bad enough, but to permit anyone to read that gangling adolescent mix of baroque storytelling and simplistic notions of dialogue and romance, was unendurable to any dignity I still possess. Still, some of the poems I wrote then do not embarrass me. I included a few in *Early Grrrl*. My poetry developed earlier and quicker than my fiction. I grappled with dialogue. I would write "I mize well do it," and only after some weeks figure out that while that was what I heard, what was meant would be written as "I might as well do it." I figured out on my own that long semitranscribed conversations about what to have for lunch were realistic but boring. Writing dialogue was not transcribing what people really said. These were important lessons.

Once in a while, I went out with a boy from school or the neighborhood, but none of them interested me. I went out with them because I was supposed to. That at least pleased my mother, although she felt I did not treat them well. Once I went out with a jazz musician, a trumpet player I met downtown. I realized very quickly I was out past my depth and retreated. I am sure if any benign older man or woman had appeared and offered to seduce me and carry me away into a better or at least more interesting world, I would have accepted in ten seconds. I would have fallen into bed or gone off with anyone who spoke kindly and patted my head. Fortunately—I suppose—no one did. In some ways I knew a great deal and in other respects I was an idiot—a fool like the one on the tarot card who walks off a precipice whistling to herself.

Brutus developed a friendship with the dog next door, two-thirds his size. They would play together—chasing each other around his yard. Then they would lie in the sun. Normally he ran dogs off if they came on his lawn or his property, but he liked that dog. After the dog died, many years later, he developed a close bond with the young woman who had owned it. He used to visit her. When my father retired and my parents moved to Florida, he—at twenty years old—decided he didn't want to go and instead adopted that woman and lived out his life with her. I have never had a cat who did not want to go off with me wherever I went, but my parents had been going down to Florida for months at a time, and he stayed with her when they were absent. He was a great survivor, Brutus was.

My relationship with him was not as intense as that with the two previous cats, because I was already partly gone—ready to get out and away. I had been applying to colleges and trying for scholarships without my parents' knowledge or cooperation. When I got a full tuition scholarship to the University of Michigan in Ann Arbor, they were not pleased and started arguing that if I insisted on college, I should live at home and go to Wayne, in Detroit. I had no intention of doing that, and I had been saving money since I was twelve.

After I left home, when I visited, Brutus never came back to my bed. He did not forgive me for going away, although he knew me and was still affectionate. I was no longer his; he was no longer mine. I had thought I would take him back after college, but it became clear he did not care to go with me. He was now my parents' cat. My father was able to give

Brutus more affection than I ever saw him lavish on any person—including his sisters and brothers, Grant, his nephews and nieces, myself and especially my mother. For many years, they were good companions. Butch followed my father into the garage when he was working on carpentry or on his car. My father talked to him. I think Brutus was his idea of how a creature should be: big, strong, manly, quiet, dignified and mostly undemanding.

The one thing Brutus did that annoyed my father was that occasionally he would piss on the television set. It was the only object in the house he sprayed, but I viewed that action as social criticism. The TV was a rival for my father's attention, so the cat marked it as his own. He intensely disliked the gunfire noises when my father was watching his favorite westerns or cop shows.

Brutus was in his way a strong personality, a match for my father in dignity and stubbornness. I did not begrudge him Brutus, but I was surprised. My father was never otherwise as likable as when he was with his own and only cat. It made me think that if I had been born a particular type of boy, a good athlete, say, or a whiz with machinery or cars, he might even have loved me.

THE GOOD OLD DAYS AT HOME SWEET HOME

On Monday my mother washed.
It was the way of the world,
all those lines of sheets flapping
in the narrow yards of the neighborhood,
the pulleys stretching out second
and third floor windows.

Down in the dank steamy basement,
wash tubs vast and grey, the wringer
sliding between the washer
and each tub. At least every

year she or I caught
a hand in it.

Tuesday my mother ironed.
One iron was the mangle.
She sat at it feeding in towels,
sheets, pillow cases.
The hand ironing began
with my father's underwear.

She ironed his shorts.
She ironed his socks.
She ironed his undershirts.
Then came the shirts,
a half hour to each, the starch
boiling on the stove.

I forgot blueing. I forgot
the props that held up the line
clattering down. I forgot
chasing the pigeons that shat
on her billowing housedresses.
I forgot clothespins in the teeth.

Tuesday my mother ironed my
father's underwear. Wednesday
she mended, darned socks on
a wooden egg. Shined shoes.
Thursday she scrubbed floors.
Put down newspapers to keep

them clean. Friday she
vacuumed, dusted, polished

scraped, waxed, pummeled.
How did you become a feminist
interviewers always ask
as if to say, when did this

rare virus attack your brain?
It could have been Sunday
when she washed the windows,
Thursday when she burned
the trash, bought groceries
hauling the heavy bags home.

It could have been any day
she did again and again what
time and dust obliterated
at once until stroke broke
her open. I think it was Tuesday
when she ironed my father's shorts.

FIVE

INTERLUDE IN THE PRESENT: THE FEBRUARY LESSON

Of the cats we have now, Max is the golden prince, a long lean red mackerel tabby with aquamarine eyes and a patrician nose. His color is changeable, golden under the sun and deep orange under artificial light. Max has perfect tabby markings like the striations on a sandbar at low tide. His mew is tiny and seems to belong to the kitten he was. He is the most outdoor of all our cats. He could not be kept in any enclosure or on a leash. He turned himself into water and slid out. A thirteen-pound cat, he can slip through cracks. He is extremely affectionate—on his terms. When we annoy him, he swats us the same way he cuffs Efi the kitten when she bothers him. He views us as helpless in the important things.

All the cats have various nicknames: Max's is Mr. Pitiful, as in the old Wilson Pickett song. His whole body inscribes an arc of sorrow or dejection. When he is hungry, his spine, his posture, his magnificent full white whiskers, his tail all speak starvation and neglect. When he comes in soaked with rain, he runs to me, cries his distress once, twice, and then throws himself down at my feet and stays there making an occasional exclamation point over himself until I get a towel and properly dry him. Every morning Max and Oboe go out with eagerness and some apprehension: is everything in place out there, have any strange cats pissed on their bushes, what scents reveal adventures during the night, passing coyotes, strange dogs, raccoons on the porch.

When I was younger, I would travel anyplace, anytime, in the same way that I would pursue casual sexual adventures. Now like the cats, I am rooted. For me the ideal vacation is not to go off to the Caribbean or London, but to stay and immerse myself in my chosen life. I remember the first extensive tour I went on in 1973, ten California schools in two weeks, two hundred dollars a reading. At that time I was living in a group marriage. My youngest partner wanted to go to graduate school. We needed money for his tuition. Two weeks in California, up and down the coast, what could be more fun? Two weeks of sleeping on couches, floors, eating fast food, being driven from Chico to Fresno to Sacramento to Irvine to San Diego by strangers, sleepless and babbling. I got home exhausted, with no lining left on my stomach. I enjoy performing, but I dislike planes and motel rooms. When I am on the road too long, I grow morose and irritable. I complain as pitifully as Max.

Many writers go on about how writing is painful, born of blood and pain, torn from the gut. But the truth is, I very much like to write. I enjoy writing poetry and I enjoy fiction. I get to exorcise my impulse to autobiography in my poems and in what were until now short memoirs. In fiction, I exercise my nosiness. I am as curious as my cats, and indeed that has led to trouble often enough and used up several of my nine lives. I am an avid listener. I am fascinated by other people's lives, the choices they make and how that works out through time, what they have done and left undone, what they tell me and what they keep secret and silent, what they lie about and what they confess, what they are proud of and what shames them, what they hope for and what they fear. The source of my fiction is the desire to understand people and their choices through time. I am a repository of many people's stories and secrets. Immersing myself in other lives satisfies me.

Malkah is the largest of our cats. The vet says she is the largest female he has ever seen, not only rotund but big boned, big framed, the size of a pregnant raccoon. She is apricot and creamy white, impeccably clean, plush. Her face is round, her eyes are moonlike, round and pale greenish yellow. Almost no one else ever sees her. Some friends maintain we have only four cats and pretend to have five. There is something of the odalisque in Malkah, a quality languid and opulent. After a period of her hiding when we first brought her home, I seduced her, gradually, painstakingly, with food, attention, soft words and patience. I have patience for little, but I had it for her. She loves Ira, but she is my cat. I wake sometimes in the night and she is pressed against my side kneading me and purring, purring, an engine of passion.

Guests seldom see Malkah, unless they sleep over, when they catch a glimpse of her stealing a peek at them or wake in the night to see two enormous round eyes watching. For the first two years, she did not go out. Then one sunny July morning, she sidled to the door, looking into my eyes, asking. She plunges out the way a swimmer will throw her body into cold ocean water: all at once, as if daring herself. Her farthest journey is into the two upper gardens. She has never walked down the drive or seen the two lower gardens. Max is adventurous and roving; Malkah is careful and tied to the house by a mental leash of no more than fifty feet. Even the way she moves is cautious. She is fast when she hunts, but generally, she looks quite hard before she leaps. In spite of her girth, she never knocks things over, because she places her big furry feet so painstakingly.

In spite of her fearfulness she is the happiest cat I have ever lived with. To eat and to have a home and feel loved is bliss. I understand this, for I am the same way. I inherited from my mother the capacity to take great joy in small things, in the taste of a salad fresh from the garden, the scent of a just plucked rose, Ira's company, a friend, the pleasure of making a favorite dish or inventing a new soup, a walk. When I am allowed to be happy, I am, like a state of rest I naturally return to—now, that is.

The youngest cat is Efi. When the vet gave Oboe only a matter of weeks, I became very depressed. Ira bought me a kitten on Valentine's Day of last year, a chocolate-point Siamese. That very first night this creature, no bigger than a lab rat and, like many Siamese kittens, rather resembling one, crawled boldly into bed and plastered herself against Ira. She is the most confident kitten we ever brought into the house. It took Dinah five months to fully accept Max and Malkah. Efi simply refused to be rejected. They would spit at her, growl, then when they went to sleep, they would wake up with her purring in their arms and think, *Oh, obviously I must like her*. Two weeks, and fierce Dinah was washing her and permitting Efi to chew on her tail. Oboe regained a strong interest in life.

Efi believes Malkah is her mother. Malkah believes Efi is her kitten. There is no physical resemblance: Malkah is enormous with medium-long orange fur and everything round, her face, her eyes, her body; Efi is long and lean like Max, muscular, lithe, with extremely short fur. Her body is ivory with chocolate markings, her ears pointy, her tail extremely long, high-set muscular legs and pure large dark blue radiant eyes. But whenever Malkah purrs, Efi comes running. The sound makes her dance with pleasure.

Malkah is a natural mouser and has set out to teach Efi. At first it was a farce. Malkah is a patient hunter. She outwaits mice and never forgets where they are in the walls or under the wallboard radiators. She would sit meditating on mousiness and willing the mouse to appear, for hours if necessary. Finally the mouse would creep out—and then Efi would get so excited, she would hurl herself at the mouse and under the radiator it would go for another two hours. Now they hunt together, with great success.

Efi grows more affectionate. She climbs in my lap often now and she comes up to me as I sit at my computer and demands to be petted. If I do not pet her, she takes my hand in her paws and pulls gently on it, to remind me of my duty. She begins to express a personality. When you acquire a kitten or the kitten acquires you, you can only guess what kind of being you have brought into your life. Some of the personality is there from the beginning, born in or burned in by genetics and the early days and weeks of life, but much of it flowers as the animal grows and matures. You have brought in a being to share your time and your space, and like a new lover, you cannot be at all sure what you have opened yourself to. Efi is still becoming who she is. She is on my computer monitor right now. We quarrel about her tail passing back and forth like an extralong windshield wiper across my screen.

She is as beautiful as a Siamese can be. Exquisite. She and Malkah wash each other with a housewifely seriousness, holding on and madly cleaning; they do this daily, as part of their bonding. Efi is constantly learning. That posture with the head tilted, sitting bolt upright like a statue of Bastet, is one of her signature poses. What does that mean, she is always asking. Malkah and Efi play structured games, reaching through the bars of the coffee-table legs to count coup on each other's paws. With Max, Efi plays rough. I imagine wrestling was invented by someone watching cats play. They throw each other, they pin each other. Efi is as athletic as Max. Their romps are like choreographed scenes from kung fu movies. They race from one end of the house to the other, they hurl themselves down the steps. They collide, they dodge, they feint. They roll over and over. They lunge at each other and tumble. They climb and pounce.

Tomorrow I will start the first seedlings downstairs in the former darkroom—a mad gardener's laboratory full of bags of starting medium, sphagnum moss, envelopes dated in black marking pen when the seeds inside are to be started, bird food in twenty-five-pound sacks. Two days ago as we drove into Boston for me to fly off to a gig in Michigan, we noticed the first red blush, almost a mist, among the swamp maples, and the chartreuse of some weeping willows. It begins to begin to imagine being spring. Spring to me is not a matter of temperature, but of what is happening with trees and bushes, birds and skunks.

I never truly experienced seasons before I moved here, just as I never noticed phases of the moon. Living out to sea on this sandbar, gardening, walking in the woods and by the marshes and along the shores have attuned me to the changes of wind and weather, of sun and moon. It has greatly enriched my poetry. Everything a poet experiences becomes part of that strange irrational cauldron of images cooking always in the back brain. If you truly look at a bird—a red-shouldered hawk, a towhee, a tufted titmouse, and you see how that bird moves and what it eats and how it flies, if you listen to it—then that bird is lodged in you. It is accessible to your imagination and will probably appear someday, an unexpected gift to a poem needing just that bird. Everything that I ingest— history, zoology, botany, anthropology, paleontology, astronomy—becomes part of that lore stored away. Spring moves in me when it is only a faint softening of the soil, a lengthening of the light and a shortening of the shadows, long before I ever noticed change when I lived in cities.

Now, four days later, it is snowing, thick white blankety stuff muffling everything. I view it with a sharp sense of betrayal and anger, although I know it is ridiculous to be surprised by snow in February in New England. Nonetheless, the cats line up and stare through the bay windows and we all are briefly melancholy together that yesterday was only a promise not to be fulfilled for weeks. Because I love spring so fiercely, love even the mud and the messiness of it, I mourn. Yes, it will come, but I have not yet learned to be patient enough, no matter how long I study to be so, no matter that every Rosh Hashona I try to throw away my impatience in *tashlich*. It is the renewal I long for, the first sharp blades of grass poking up through the mat of last year's dead straw.

Ever since we finally got cable, years after friends in the city would gush about shows invisible on the Lower Cape, I have been addicted to the Weather Channel. I certainly had little interest in weather when I was younger, but it seems to come with middle age. Besides, I have the excuse that I travel a great deal and have to keep an eye on what it will be like where I am going.

The cats too take weather personally, viewing wind as animate. Out here on our sandbar, wind is a potent player. Hurricanes are the extreme danger, but nor'easters can be rough. We lose power several times a year, usually for a few hours but sometimes longer—for days, after a hurricane or an ice storm. As I write this, a wet snow is plastering everything, shrouding the gardens and hiding the paths. Only Max is outside, picking his way along. Sometimes Malkah plays in the snow, digging at it with her huge plush paws and tossing it up, but this morning, she has not ventured out but lies with her paw across Efi as they curl spoon-fashion. They have relinquished the hope of spring.

WINTER PROMISES

Tomatoes rosy as perfect baby's buttocks,
eggplants glossy as waxed fenders,

purple neon flawless glistening
peppers, pole beans fecund and fast
growing as Jack's Viagra-sped stalk,
big as truck tire zinnias that mildew
will never wilt, roses weighing down
a bush never touched by black spot,
brave little fruit trees shouldering up
their spotless ornaments of glass fruit:

I lie on the couch under a blanket
of seed catalogs ordering far
too much. Sleet slides down
the windows, a wind edged
with ice knifes through every crack.
Lie to me, sweet garden-mongers:
I want to believe every promise,
to trust in five pound tomatoes
and dahlias brighter than the sun
that was eaten by frost last week.

SIX

MY LIFE AS A 1950s COED

Up until I left home, I was not free in any sense. My life like those of most children of that time was constrained, confined, coerced. I could only get what I wanted by lying and subterfuge. Once I left my parents' house in 1953 when I was seventeen, I was on my own. I am from this point on responsible for my own errors. I made a lot of them.

My first semester, I roomed with two girls from Grand Rapids with whom I had absolutely nothing in common. However, I began to know Louise much better than in high school, and we formed a close, intense bond. In January, I moved into her room. We were both poor, rebellious, experienced sexually and accomplished in school. We had been in gangs. We had ambitions that felt exotic and dangerous to our parents. I fictionalized this relationship in *Braided Lives.* For the next year, we shared a triple with another woman from a working-class background. She always felt we were closer to each other than to her, as indeed we were, but rooming together helped all of us survive in an environment for which we were not prepared and in which we were not fully respected.

Coeds of that era had chests of cashmere sweaters under the bed, sweater sets, proper little suits and sheath dresses, pearls and circle pins. We had a couple of skirts apiece, two pairs of jeans, some nylon or woolen sweaters and not much else in our closets. We stocked up in thrift shops and wore the same clothes, especially Louise and I—exactly the same size except for brassieres. We were small and quick and nasty. The sexual mores of the dormitory were that you could do anything with your boyfriend except "it." You did not do "it" unless you were engaged with a diamond big enough to license the act, or finally married: the days of the Mrs. degree. That was not what the three of us had in mind.

I wanted to learn everything at once, to master every discipline in the catalog. Like an addict, I craved knowledge: I had to know whatever I could cram into my brain, and I was a fast study. I probably believed that the more I knew, the less likely it was that I would be shunted back to my old neighborhood with its choices of early violent death or early brain death. I did not want to be pregnant at nineteen and never have a chance to write, explore the world, know other cultures.

Louise was attracted to Jews, which was probably one reason she befriended me. Her first boyfriend at college was Jewish and so was the man she eventually married. Louise made few friendships. She had a certain contempt for other women and was sometimes sarcastic, sometimes jealous of my other relationships. In college I found myself no less odd than I ever had been, but able to find others with writing ambitions, left politics—misfits and rebels and intellectuals. I had many close friendships and many of the intermediate level and several hundred talking acquaintances. I was the youngest chosen to give a public reading that spring with a group of poets, many of them graduate students, some Korean War vets. For a freshman, I already had high visibility. I also acquired my first male lover, a poet a year older than me, also from Detroit, from a German Jewish family I could scarcely identify as Jewish, their mores and attitudes and temperature level were so different from my own family's.

I was besotted with him, to the point of helpless adoration. He was large, he was broody, he had intense dark eyes and great sexual appetite. He had read widely, had the classical background I lacked, wrote poetry already getting some attention and was the type of sorrowing narcissist every piece of romantic crap I had ever consumed trained me to desire and immolate myself on. O Heathcliff! O James Dean! O kamikaze love.

I was obsessed. I considered it the fulfillment of my wildest fantasies that he should be attracted to me and want me. He was possessive, jealous of every friend I had. I was foolish enough to tell him about my sexual adventures. From then on he feared all contact I had with other women. It hurt so much, it had to be great love. He got his way mostly by reducing me to incoherent tears. He was jealous of my closeness with Louise, but I would not let him interfere. She was too important to me. She was the first person who had ever come to know me as I was, and with whom I could be honest. We shared not only a common background, but also ideas, politics, passions, tastes in music and literature. I trusted her absolutely.

He had been reading D. H. Lawrence, so we fought constantly about contraception, which he viewed as unnatural. He was always swearing that he would not come inside me. His family considered me unworthy of him, and he kept trying to decide if I was good enough or if they were right. He was constantly testing me, making me perform, till I began to rebel. He would demand I stop reading Dylan Thomas or Yeats; that I renounce this or that friend. I got pregnant that summer, and since I had no money and no access to an abortionist, and no intention of having a baby at eighteen and quitting college, I had to abort myself. I have written about this summer in *Braided Lives,* in all its agony. My mother and I were already fighting about her accurate suspicions that I was having sex with him, when she and I realized I was pregnant. She tried to make me marry him, but I succeeded in persuading her that I would not do so in any circumstances. I knew by then he was bad for me, that he would destroy me in the name of possession and his idea of love. I convinced my mother that if she tried to force me into marriage, as she and my father had made my brother marry Isabelle, I would walk out and she would never see me again.

She told me what to do, then turned away. She kept saying I would not have the strength to do what I must. I tried all the folklore of the time, mustard baths, harsh douches, jumping off the porch, quinine pills. Finally I succeeded by opening my womb, but I almost bled to death.

The pain of forcing it open caused me to black out. I came to on the floor with blood gushing out of me. My mother gave me ice and I went to bed; but when my father was expected, she had me get up and pretend to be normal so he would not guess. I could barely sit up, so I said I had a bad toothache. That was common enough to pass. I did not tell my lover I had aborted myself, but only that I had miscarried. I lost so much blood and was so weak, it would have been impossible to keep from him that something was wrong, and I had no intention of having sex with him. I feared he would enter me again without protection. I lost fifteen pounds and was pale blue under my mass of black hair. I must have looked peculiar. By the time I had gone through the pain of aborting myself, I was out of love with him. I had almost died, and that had permanently cured me of extreme romantic fantasies and the desire to immolate myself on any hard object.

But after that I had more respect for myself, because I knew I had the guts to do what I decided, no matter how painful and dangerous. I had been emotionally bullied and devastated during that first real affair. I would never again be so completely vulnerable and helpless in a relationship. For about a year, I could not write poetry. I had been persuaded that since I did not write in imitation of Ezra Pound, what I wrote was worthless. It was too emotional, not in syllabics, too simple, too female. I wrote only fiction for the next year, which he had not criticized because he did not take it seriously. In my junior year, I began writing poetry again and have never stopped.

The sexual part of the relationship had been easy and pleasurable once we drilled through my iron hymen, but the emotional part had been hell. I would never again accept another person's opinions as holy writ, no matter how attractive I found him or how much I liked going to bed with him. From then on, I preserved a certain independence of judgment and decision, no matter how delightful I found a man's company. This has never changed.

After that summer between my freshman and sophomore years, a smoking disaster, I did not visit my parents' home for more than four days at any time except at Christmas, when I worked for the phone company a split shift mornings and evenings every day. Since I was in the house only for a few hours in the afternoon and took no meals but lunch with them, I could stick it out for ten days, but otherwise, things would explode.

Too much about me made them furious. They were aware that I was sexually active. They mistrusted college and higher education for a woman. My father thought it unseemly I should have more education than he had enjoyed, and my mother thought I would wind up with my throat slit in a gutter. This was one of her favorite images of my probable fate, although when I thought about it, I considered it was much more likely to happen had I stayed in Detroit. Both of them vociferously considered me a bad, bad girl. I preferred to avoid all that. I tried to talk to my mother honestly. That would start out well, but she would wait until I had told her things she could use against me, then she would attack. It was emotionally devastating to both of us. It was better to keep some distance, physical and mental, for her sake and my own. I could not be truthful with her, and I was weary of lying, so it was better to write simple cheerful letters while receiving jeremiads from her. In her letters it always seemed to be raining, it had been raining for days, something ached or felt feverish and my father had recently done something ghastly. Her letters made me sad, but I learned that responding to them was inviting trouble. Any advice I gave angered her. There was always a reason nothing could be altered, nothing could be ameliorated. My insistence there were solutions, options, angered her.

My parents could not abide the choices I made. They could not understand my going to college and then to graduate school. I maintained a scholarship through college, had a better one my last year I could live on. My tuition was fully paid throughout the four years, but until my senior year, I had to work while in school. I also began winning Hopwood awards for my poetry and my fiction, which helped financially. Avery Hopwood was a popular Broadway playwright who wrote farces such as *Up in Mabel's Room*. Upon dying, he bequeathed tons of money to the U. of M. to finance prizes for the kind of literary writing he did not do.

I lived in a dormitory my first two years, as was required by the university. It cost too much and I ran up several hundred hours of lateness. We were always supposed to sign in and out and to be back by ten-thirty on weeknights and twelve-thirty on Friday and Saturday nights. I was called before the House Judiciary Committee, and had I gone on living in the dormitory, I would have spent my last two years making up tardiness, mostly from covering events for the *Michigan Daily,* the school newspaper. We were always in trouble in the dorm because of eating in our room, cooking, hiding liquor, putting up posters considered subversive or nasty—in general, being ordinary rebels.

I worked on the *Daily* my first two and a half years in college until I was a night editor, but then I quit, finding it was taking time away from the writing I really wanted to do. What I liked best about journalism was interviewing. I was good at it—something I still enjoy when I need to conduct interviews for research on a novel. I loved meeting professors who had done research on schistosomiasis in the Nile Valley or work on the vast Middle English dictionary being compiled at Michigan. Spring vacation of our sophomore year, we piled into a car with Louise's boyfriend and went to New York. I stayed the first couple of nights in the Bronx, where her boyfriend's working-class family lived, but after that, I stayed at the Y in Manhattan—I could not impose on them longer. I discovered that, having just turned eighteen, I could drink legally, and lived on hot dogs and beer. Louise's relationship with her boyfriend was coming apart, and I ended up getting drawn into their fights. He began to dislike me, partly from sympathy with my old lover, who paraded his broken heart around campus for another two years.

I remember our first glimpse after driving all night of the crown of towers in lower Manhattan from the Pulaski Skyway over the marshes of New Jersey. It was love at first sight. I wanted New York, I wanted to be a New Yorker, I wanted to eat New York like a steak, close to raw and hot enough. Everything seemed marvelous. The subways were as wonderful as the museums. From then on, if anybody from Ann Arbor was going to New York for a long weekend, I would throw everything aside and go off with them. I did not long for the Grand Canyon but for the canyons of Midtown. I found everything beautiful and sizzling.

I was not well suited to the regimentation of dormitory life for females. Between the high cost of the dormitory and my difficulties adapting to a controlled life, I had to find another option. Because of our schedules, we often missed meals and improvised supper in our rooms, where we had an illegal hot plate. To this day, there is a stain on the yellow brick wall of the dormitory we lived in, from a stick of butter put out on the window ledge that melted in a sudden thaw. I started exploring other options for housing just a little too late in my sophomore year to get into one of the co-ops run and owned by students. Louise was still my roommate and coconspirator. We moved into one, Stevens House, for the summer, but for the fall, all existing co-ops were full.

So we organized a new one and got the Interco-operative Council to buy an old run-down house, which we spent much of the summer fixing up. Called Osterweil House, it still exists. When I was doing a stint in Ann Arbor in residency for a month a few years ago, I had supper election night at Osterweil. I saw my old room there. It is rather fancier nowadays. What were doubles are now singles, and what were triples are now doubles, but in some ways, the ambiance is similar. We had a cat there we picked up pregnant. She was black and called Eartha Katt. She was a general house animal, although she belonged to some of us more than to others. Eventually we found homes for her and her kittens by prevailing upon guys who lived in apartments and were interested in various of us. I served as the personnel secretary of the ICC that year and took on the dean's office over the question of whether applicants had to identify their race. I took part in a few mild civil rights actions, protesting a degrading float one of the fraternities mounted at Homecoming; picketing a barbershop that would not cut the hair of Afro-Americans.

My life continued to be stranger and stranger to my parents. When my parents happened to meet my boyfriends, they detested them. My hair was halfway down my back, which they found uncouth. Only peasant women had long hair. Since her teens, my mother had kept hers short. One vacation, she bribed me to go to a salon and have it cut and styled, by paying for some dental work I needed. Having short hair represented being modern to her, not an immigrant like my grandmother. I let it stay short for the rest of that semester, then started growing it out again. I liked it long. I liked the weight and heft of it.

One shameful fact I shared with no one was that I intensely disliked being in my parents' house. The bathroom stank. They did not flush the toilet often, and my father missed the bowl frequently. My mother did not keep herself clean or wear deodorant. Smells I had never noticed assaulted me, and I was ashamed of my fastidiousness. My parents' home was full of tchotchkes, miniature wooden shoes from Holland, Michigan, birch bark wigwams and painted cacti, bric-a-brac my mother thought artistic and I found hideous. I had become a snob, and I judged myself harshly. The very education I had fought so hard to acquire was making me forever different from my family and my old friends from the neighborhood. I hated myself for feeling as I did, for gagging when I entered the bathroom, for my difficulty eating what they ate, for having no idea what they were talking about—the TV programs they watched constantly. I spent enormous effort keeping them from guessing my reactions, for if I had hurt my mother's feelings, I would have hated myself even more. I understood very well what was happening to me—and had no intention of altering my path. If I said to myself mea culpa, I did not hesitate to fly out the door as fast as I could.

Because I won two Hopwood awards my junior year, one in fiction and one in poetry, and because my mentor Robert Haugh had gotten me a bigger scholarship for my senior year, I did not have to work while going to classes. Now I was freer to choose what I would do. Two friends from the co-op had graduated and were returning to New York. That summer, before my senior year, we sublet an apartment on East Twelfth Street near Second Avenue. While we were apartment hunting, I stayed with a friend in Rockaway Beach. The ocean obsessed me. I quietly left her parents' home one evening and brought a blanket with me to spend the night by the ocean. I did not think of rapists or muggers or anything but the fascination of this breathing water. I was awakened in the middle of the night by that water lapping over me. Thus did I learn about tides. I got up, wet and disheveled, and marched back to the house and let myself in, as quietly as I had left. I was mortified by my own stupidity and never mentioned it.

When our other friend arrived, her family took exception to staying in what they called the ghetto, the old Jewish neighborhood they considered dangerous and demeaning. I liked that sublet, tiny as it was. I was not appalled by the roaches, as some of my best friends in grade school had lived in roach-infested housing and I was used to them. I liked the Lower East Side. On East Twelfth Street, we settled in—a kitchenette with a magnum wine bottle covered with candle wax, a living room and one bedroom. We alternated sleeping two to the double bed and the third on the couch in the living room. New York was mine, at last. I began work for a temp agency. My typing was extremely fast, so I never had trouble finding secretarial work. I had been doing it on and off for years, as well as working switchboards.

Next door was the Sons and Daughters of Israel Home for the Aged. Our small apartment faced a courtyard where eighteen cats cavorted, and I thought how much quieter the night would be if cats practiced oral sex. I was fascinated by glimpses of our neighbors, as no one seemed to bother with shades. I became a voyeur that summer and invented stories about the two young men who went about half dressed and seemed to spend hours rubbing a towel across the upper part of their backs; the guy who played the guitar with a friend who had an accordion, and another who played the mouth organ. Another man sat at a green kitchen table with his head in his hands staring at a half-empty milk bottle while his wife yelled at him by the hour. I did most of my shopping at a market on Second Avenue with barrels of pickles and olives, of oysters and clams and ropes of smoked fish. Everything fascinated me. New York was my fair.

I learned about espresso and ate my first lobster—I had never seen one. Neither fondness has deserted me. I was taken with things my roommates probably considered beneath their notice: walking endlessly, sometimes driven around by one or another temporary boyfriend, I was fascinated by the care that had been put into the physical plant of the city earlier in the century. It astonished me that people had once cared enough to make attractive bridges, that the walls and grillwork along the Hudson were so beautiful, that minor edifices in the parks were built like little castles. It seemed magical to me, rather romantic, public places important enough to have been ornamented. It never occurred to me I would live anywhere else after college.

My last year with the help of the good scholarship and the money from Hopwoods for fiction and poetry, I moved into a small apartment at the end of town, near the railroad station. It was a funny apartment, the living room and tiny kitchen up on the second floor with the bathroom, but the bedroom off the hall stairway over the garage. The bedroom was light, with windows on three sides, cold but no colder than my own room up in the gable on Ward Avenue. I was writing seriously and needed the privacy and the quiet. Not holding down a job or several meant I had time to spend on my honors thesis on James Joyce and time to write a novel and lots of poetry. I loved living alone, although I was usually involved with one guy or another. The only work I did during my senior year was a little posing for some artists in town. That paid very well then, four times as much per hour as secretarial work.

My parents never gave up issuing propaganda for returning to their house, returning to Detroit, getting a nice pink-collar job. They kept expecting me to come to my senses and behave as they expected girls to. They were utterly horrified when I went off to France with Michel, a French Jew who was studying particle physics at Michigan with Donald Glaser, who had not yet won his Nobel Prize for the bubble chamber, but soon would. I knew Glaser because he was dating a friend of mine, and it was through him I met Michel. My parents had never been out of the country except to Canada across the Detroit River, and they thought of Europe as barbaric and dangerous. To my mother, it was the place they burned Jews. Why would I voluntarily go there?

I had a fierce and fraught relationship with the university. I majored in English honors, but I had a smorgasbord of minors: zoology, anthropology,

Romance languages and philosophy. I was accepted into philosophy honors too, but then I got caught. Students were not permitted to be enrolled in two honors programs at the same time. I could not see why, but I relinquished philosophy, although I kept taking courses. I was least appreciated in my own department, because I was opinionated and my opinions were not the fashionable sort: I was not an imitation English gentleman carrying a black umbrella and trying to emulate Eliot, although I learned much prosody from his work. I hated Ezra Pound, who was at the zenith of his influence. I loved Yeats and began to study the tarot, not a popular approach to him in the English department. I still adored Whitman and Dickinson, a decidedly minority taste. When I discovered the Beats a bit later, everybody including my best friends thought I had lost my mind. Within a year of its publication, I was carrying around Ginsberg's *Howl* and trying to press it on friends.

I would have been just as much an outcast in philosophy, because I was passionate about existentialism. I was reading Sartre and de Beauvoir and Camus. I tried to look like Juliette Greco, whom I had admired in movies and magazine spreads on existentialism. I even tried to write in the nearest equivalent of a café, the Student Union, but I found it distracting. Besides, my handwriting is too bad for me to write longhand. I was, during those years, always trying to figure out who and what I was with the help of the books I read and sometimes films I saw. I was always trying on roles and characters and poses, to see if they fit. My tastes were neither fashionable nor traditional. Usually answering a question honestly about what I liked or admired was sufficient to start an argument. In spite of everything, I had a pretty good time in college. I was far freer than I had ever been and much more engaged. I had many friends, and in spite of my outsider status, I made excellent grades, Phi Beta Kappa as a junior. By my senior year, I was writing steadily and sometimes well.

I coedited the school literary magazine my last year, having served on the staff since I came to Michigan. My coeditor was Eric, a close friend who was in philosophy honors. In that era, an enormous amount of reading was required. We read several books a week, long poems, long novels, complete books of essays. I read all that and more. I wanted to consume everything. I am the only person I know besides specialists who has read *The Dunciad*. I actually liked Alexander Pope, although I knew no other student who did. There was a group of us would-be writers around *Generation,* the literary magazine. We exchanged work with one another and continued to do so for the next few years: Victor and Padma Perrera, David Newman, among them. Nadine, who was passionate about writing fiction and with whom I exchanged work for some years after Michigan, stayed with me briefly, but most of that year I lived alone and liked it.

Fighting the dean's office about race was only one activity; we were also collecting clothing, food and goods for voter registration in the South—yes, even way back then. Since the execution of the Rosenbergs in 1953, repression had been very real for people in my family and those I knew who had been active in Detroit. I remember talking with Pete Seeger in the back of a car, because he did not want to use the telephone. I organized a concert for him. The administration did not like it, but they chose not to forbid it. What we did then politically was weak, mild, ineffective, but we were not completely passive.

Until my senior year of college, I drank too much. People liked to get me drunk because words would flow out of me in intricate monologues they found amusing and original. My senior year, I intentionally stopped and have seldom been drunk since. My prevailing vices in college were falling passionately in love, imitating books I read; and talking. I had too many friends, I had too many people who told me their lives, I wasted too much time blabbing about myself. I was somebody people came to when they had to talk, when they were in trouble, when they were confused, when they felt desperate. This was one of the things about me that Louise despised. She felt it was promiscuous. It certainly did use up hours and hours. I was accessible emotionally to almost everyone. "I feel your pain." Well, I did, quite physically. Anyone could capture my attention and my empathy. I was vulnerable to anyone's needs. I dispensed advice like a soda machine. I took any man's or woman's troubles instantly to heart. I practically had a line out the door at my room in the co-op. I would feel like a dentist saying, Next. They would glower at one another sometimes, waiting for my solitary attention.

I would walk into a room and instantly feel the emotions of people there. If someone was in pain, I had to do something. Eventually I had to become harder in order to survive. I was so accessible and vulnerable that anyone could have a piece of me for the asking. I was an emotional free lunch.

That summer in New York, I had attempted to take charge of my feelings. Many men passed through my life, and I liked them. I was fond of some, very loving, but I was not besotted. That was a great improvement. I also attempted not to be quite as accessible, and my roommates disliked that change, although my relationship with both of them survived the summer. I was haunted at twenty by the sense that I was talking my life away instead of writing. I thought of myself as almost middle-aged, for I expected to die young, as my mother had always told me I would. She said it was in my palm.

I discovered during college I was attractive to men—lots of men. I was involved with men older than me and younger; with scientists, mathematicians, musicians, composers, a thief, a medical student, a lawyer. I don't know why this ability to conjure a male companion out of any party or gathering came as such a surprise, since I always had boyfriends since I was four.'But I had been told I was ugly, funny looking; and indeed, I looked nothing like blond Miss America. I did not take any of this seriously. I considered it a kind of con job, a matter of acting confident, and everyone would take you at face value as sure of yourself.

I was not what a 1950s coed was supposed to be. For one thing, I had a sexual past. I had studied Freud and decided he knew little about women's desires and responses: this at a time when the height of sophistication was to be psychoanalyzed and Freudian categories were widely applied by almost everyone with a college education. I had been having orgasms since I was eleven, so the theory of the clitoral versus the vaginal orgasm did not impress me—it was all pleasure, and the point was to enjoy myself and come however I could. I was ambitious in my work but never thought that made me less female or afflicted with penis envy, and I had no desire to be feminine and passive. Louise was in therapy and always telling me I should be too. My wardrobe was minimal, a problem

I solved my senior year by dressing in black—which did not show dirt. I could not afford a winter coat, so I wore an old leather jacket—what male hoods wore, but not young women of good family looking for Mrs. degrees. I affected a tough veneer, which wasn't all affectation. I had stopped drinking too much, but I smoked unfiltered cigarettes and lit them with kitchen matches brought to life by slicing my thumbnail across. I no longer carried a knife—college had tamed me—but I carried my temper with me and my knowledge of alleys and night.

The truth was, by my senior year I was running a little scared. Everything around me told me I was not what a woman was supposed to be, and I could not see what would become of me. Louise withdrew from me, partly because she had fallen in love with a recent ex-boyfriend of mine, and partly because she was seeking respectability and I could offer none. My friends were scattering to marriage, to graduate school, to jobs in Detroit or New York. What would become of me? I could not guess and all scenarios seemed depressing. There were no role models for a woman like me.

THE CRUNCH

Like the cat the Doberman has trapped,
like the rabbit in the fox's jaws
we feel the splintering of our bones
and wait for the moment that still may flash,
the white spaces between pains
when we can break free.

It is the moment of damage
when already the pricing mind
tries to estimate cost and odds
while the nerves lean on their sirens
but the spine sounds a quiet tone
of command toward a tunnel of moment

that drills the air toward escape
or death. I have been caught.
Biology is destiny for all alive
but at the instant of tearing
open or free, the blood shrieks and
all my mother's mothers groan.

SEVEN

ONE DOES NOT DO THAT

There are things we all do in our lives that afterward we ask ourselves again and again and again, *Why?* What was I thinking of? What did I imagine would happen? How could I do it, to him and to me? I invent, I elaborate reasons, but the fact of stupidity remains. Stupidity is a great mystery to me, how I can sometimes do something so counter to reason and evidence that it amazes me when I have a little distance from it. I had no desire to marry, and yet just before I entered graduate school, I married Michel Schiff.

I thought I was smart because I was avoiding my mother's mistake of marrying a Gentile, so I would not be living with anti-Semitism. Nonetheless, I married someone so different from me, as she had, so unable to perceive me, let alone understand me, that I was replicating the marriage of the cat and the dog, my parents' fiasco. It was a romantic vision of Europe, of the left, of France, I was responding to. It was someone who had survived the war against Jews while I was safe except for casual beatings in the school yard or the street.

Michel was a graduate student in particle physics who could quote poetry. I did not know that every French student memorizes a certain amount of Racine and Corneille, and that he didn't understand the simplest poem. Once in the second year of our marriage I spent an afternoon trying to get him to "see" Robert Frost's poem "The Road Not Taken." He could not grasp the concept of metaphor. To him it could only be literal: "two roads diverge in a yellow wood" is talking about two roads, and so what? My work could mean nothing to him, because it was nonsense. Fiction was more accessible to him but not interesting unless it dealt with something in France he was familiar with, like *Les Thibeaults,* which he had me read. Strangely enough, he loved Saint-Exupéry's *Le Petit Prince* and gave it to me as a courting present. Tame me, he wrote in French on the card, as the fox says to the little prince. Absolutely, I thought, but I was much wilder than he and much fiercer in my appetites, and it was me he aimed to tame. I was not unwilling, because I was afraid of who and what I was.

After I received my degree from Michigan, Michel and I—we had been dating for several months—went to France together and stayed mostly with his family in Paris. They lived in the tenth arrondissement, near the Gare de l'Est and the Gare du Nord. It was a stone working-class section then. When I revisited the neighborhood last year, the building I lived in still stands, although some of the others on that block have been torn down. The neighborhood has begun to gentrify: new apartment buildings, a glossy supermarket, with little businesses, factories and repair shops replaced by travel agencies and boutiques. The neighborhood has green lungs now, patches of tenements torn down and parks planted. The canal at the end of the block has been cleaned up and made into a kind of park.

His family had a flat on the third floor, as I remember, but I slept in one of the narrow old servants' rooms on the sixth or seventh floor, depending on whether you count in the French manner or the American. The toilet was down the hall, a Turkish toilet as they called them. If I could endure waiting, I would run downstairs, turning on the light and trying to descend before the stairway plunged into darkness from the automatic timer, to use the W.C. in the Schiff apartment. "Turkish" toilets are a hole in the floor with two big footprints. You aim at the hole. Most people seem to miss. The smell made my gorge rise.

I liked my father-in-law. I think I would have been happier with him than with his son, because he had more joie de vivre and more vigor. I did not please Madame. I made the mistake of addressing her as *tu,* since she was my putative mother-in-law, and I was severely corrected. I was to address her as *vous.* She would have liked, I think, to instruct me to do the same with Michel, but as we were having sex, she could not persuade me to do so. However, we had sex only occasionally in Paris. He was too inhibited by his mother's proximity. I did not take this seriously, although I should have. I was experienced in some ways and naive in others. I had not had much experience living with middle-class people, so it took me a while to decode his mother's attitude. In my family everybody yelled their criticisms and bellowed their anger. I was not clever at understanding subtle and indirect hostility. Much of it rolled off me, because I was too busy being curious about everything else and because it was all going on in French, which when I was tired became background noise.

It was a very hot summer in Paris, and many nights we could not sleep. Sometimes we went out together and wandered by the Seine, went to the flower market, went to Les Halles—still the market district then and extremely busy at four in the morning. Everything was new and exciting to me—the stalls, the onion soup, the sausages. I liked to go down to the St.-Martin canal nearby, my escape hatch from tensions in the flat. In the next block, two sets of locks began. The canal was lined with lindens, horse chestnuts, sycamores. I became friends with a large yellow cat who lived in a restaurant nearby. We would sit together overlooking the canal and watch the barges and the canal boats. I never knew his name, but I called him Jules, because I thought of him as a topaz, a jewel. Michel had various things to do with the government and the educational apparatus, to confirm his status as a graduate student in the sciences abroad and thus deferred from the draft, and to inform all the requisite departments that he was transferring from the University of Michigan physics department to that of the University of Chicago. While he was away, I would wander the neighborhood and visit with Jules. He was the only one in Paris who did not correct my French. The canal and Jules kept me sane, because there was so much that was weird to me and unintelligible— besides the strain of operating in a foreign language. My days sometimes felt a series of disguised traps. I was always doing or saying the wrong thing and being corrected: *On ne fait pas cela:* One does not do that. That is not done. That is not the way. Watching the guys raise and lower the level in the locks, the white water rushing in and out, the boats edging past each other with perhaps an inch to spare between them, that was entertainment for Jules and for me.

Paris did dazzle me. It was a pearl gray city such as I had never seen. Detroit felt used; this felt ancient and modern at once. I remember walking into the Louvre for the first time and being so fascinated that I stared at everything except where I was going and fell full length into an ancient mosaic. Michel's friends for the most part accepted me more readily than his mother did. We met with his friends rather formally. We also dined with various friends of the family—members of that close-knit circle. I met in Paris men and women who had been active in the Resistance and some who had been in the Hagannah to create a Jewish homeland. They were tough and supremely capable and I admired them. Michel's friends were active as he had been in opposing the war in Algeria. While he was still a student at Physique et Chimie in Paris, he had been arrested by the police and interrogated intensively about his role in the antiwar movement. It had been a painful and terrifying experience he had trouble talking about but which caused him nightmares all the time I was with him. I believe they tortured him, but he could not talk about it. We went to some demonstrations, but he hung back, far more afraid of the police than he had been.

My room was tiny and the walls were covered not with wallpaper but with some rushlike substance. One night I woke and a huge furry spider the size of a tarantula was walking on my arm. I shrieked, threw it off, put on my robe and rushed downstairs, letting myself into the Schiff apartment, where everyone was sleeping. I sat down in a chair in the dining room. I stayed there the rest of the night, too shaken to return to my room. I dozed off. When I woke, M. Schiff was standing over me asking me why I was there.

I could not think of the word for *spider* in French, so I said, "The beast with eight legs has walked upon me in my bed."

Soon the whole family was standing about staring at me. To this day, I cannot recall the French word for *spider,* although I must have looked it up over the years seven or eight times. Madame got up, swept them all before her, and soon we were eating breakfast and pretending nothing had happened, as in fact nothing in particular had.

For the last forty years I have had a recurring nightmare in which I am on a subway train in the bowels of the earth, twisting squealing climbing descending, squeezing through tunnels far too small for the train. It is a nightmare of claustrophobia and suffocation. It is hot and I cannot breathe. I had interpreted this dream quite Freudianly, as the birth canal. While I have been back to Paris many times in the intervening years, usually on my way someplace else or doing research (*Gone to Soldiers; City of Darkness, City of Light*), I usually take one of the newer renovated Métros, such as line 1. This time Ira and I went by Métro to my old neighborhood and to several working-class neighborhoods. Suddenly I found myself in my nightmare. These are old narrow tunnels, older trains. They do constantly twist about squealing and groaning. They climb, they crawl down, they creep about deep in the earth. I broke into a cold sweat. Suddenly my sense of being lost and out of my element that summer came back to me. My nightmare was a reliving of that summer with Michel. In Paris Michel changed. I felt caught in a situation I had backed into but which was set up as win or lose.

Certainly I had been quite competitive in my college years; how not? I competed for scholarships, I competed for better scholarships and fellowships; I competed in class, in exams, I competed in the Hopwood contests, whose prizes were prestige but also money I desperately needed. Now I competed to win Michel. It was almost instinctive. It was almost suicidal. On some level I must have known that. Yet I could not give up. I was caught in the net of his family, and my only reason for being there seemed to be to marry him.

Back at Michigan, he had courted me, quite formally. I was the prize. I was used to being pursued by young (and sometimes older) men and pretty much took it for granted. I had not thought much about going off to Europe with him. He had talked about marriage, but so had other boyfriends, and I had not seriously contemplated marrying any of them. I had gone to New York with friends, I had gone to Chicago with friends. I loved to travel, and the idea of going to France with him seemed great. I had a good fellowship waiting for me at Northwestern, so I could afford to blow my Major Hopwood award money on a trip to Europe. Staying with Michel's family simply cut costs. I had no idea how it would affect me. I thought of it almost as a student exchange, rather than a process of being integrated into his family and redone into something acceptable.

Of course having me in Paris with his family meant that Michel was looking at me far more critically than he had in Michigan. It was a question of whether I measured up to his mother's standards. It was a question of whether he would commit himself. Probably if he had remained certain he wanted to marry me, I would have gotten cold feet and we would never have married. But his very hesitation hooked me. I would never be stupid in that way again. If someone was not sure, I would get out of the way. But it seemed to be a contest, and Michel was now the prize—not me—and I must win. Certainly I cared for him, but that somehow wasn't the point. I found him very attractive. He was slender, of medium height with dark brown eyes and hair, a winning wistful smile and considerable charm and integrity. But the need to justify myself by winning got in the way of my ability to see past his charm and be clear about what marriage to him would actually entail.

His parents went off on vacation with his brother to Normandy and we had the apartment to ourselves. There was no refrigerator, but there was a maid. They lived in a very different style from anyone I had known. Meals were rather formal and very good. I ate my first artichoke there (and my second and my thirtieth) and had veal for the first time and mussels. They did not keep kosher and did not even light candles on Shabbat. Their circle was Jewish, but they seemed to have ceased practicing any of the rituals decades before. They did not observe the holidays. Michel knew far less Yiddish than I did. I had greater capacity to understand than to speak it, as my grandmother had spoken Yiddish to me as a child and I had answered her in English. Why? I have no idea. That's how it was, and I have discovered it was that way in a great many American Jewish families. The Schiff parents never spoke Yiddish. They communicated in German when discussing something important. Michel spoke English very well, with only a delicious trace of accent. He spoke German and he was learning Italian. I can still hear a resonant male voice speaking on the Asimil record he used: *L'italiano non es difficile por un francese.*

I played French housewife, shopping every morning for our midday and evening meals, which were, however, prepared by the maid, Simone. I had trouble communicating with her at first, but we got better at it. She did not want me in the kitchen, although I was determined to learn something about cooking. She shooed me out. I would have to learn from cookbooks, later on.

We left Paris after three weeks and went first to the Loire Valley. We had so little money that we stayed in fleabag hotels with bedbugs and prostitutes; where they were available, we stayed in youth hostels. Some of them were clean and some were filthy and bug infested. We took trains, buses and hitchhiked. We lived mostly on bread and butter and chocolate, with an occasional piece of fruit.

We went up on the Massif Central. I had a desire to see Le Puy, which was as strange as I had anticipated. It was high in the mountains at the end of a train line. In those days on the French railroads, there were not only first and second classes, but third class, and in this case, fourth class. We changed at Clermont-Ferrand to a crude mountain train that had benches around the rims of the cars and a stove in the center. People brought on dogs, sheep and a goat as we climbed higher into the mountains. Finally we arrived in a town studded with great pillars of black volcanic rock. It seemed as if every woman in Le Puy was making lace and trying to sell it. Some of the basalt pillars had chapels on them. Some had sacred statues.

We were pointed to a sort of hostel in an old orphanage, which stank too badly even for us. We ended up lying on the ground on a mountain above the town. We had traveled all night and we slept where we were with the rising sun beginning to beat down on us. I woke with a high fever, burning up with sunstroke. We had no ice. I had taken a Red Cross emergency course at some point, so I knew what was wrong with me and that I was in danger. We found a creek and I simply climbed in and sat there, lowering my body temperature until my brain was no longer boiling in my skull. Now I always wear a hat or a scarf, for I have had sunstroke twice. My black hair heats up like a stove top.

We took a bus down to the Rhône, even wilder than the train. It bounded and bounced down the narrow mountain road, squealing around the turns. Everybody who got on seemed to have produce or an animal in tow. Dogs, sheep and many goats, rabbits, chickens, a rooster, even a calf. We went hurtling down the mountainside much too fast for the road and pitched high in the air with every rock and pothole. I was too young and foolhardy to be scared. I thought it all marvelous.

I liked the Rhône Valley enormously and would have gladly stayed in one of those towns like Montélimar, where we ate nougat. We kept wandering till we got to Avignon. We played in the Villeneuve, which in spite of its name was a well-preserved medieval ruin. There were not many tourists anyplace we had gone so far (none at all in Le Puy), and we had the ruins to ourselves. Michel lightened up away from Paris. He was once again charming and less judgmental, less instructional. The Rhône fascinated me. It was a fast powerful river like the Detroit River, although not as wide. As a treat, I bought a bottle of Châteauneuf-du-Pape that we drank picnicking.

We went on to the Riviera, to Menton. I know we went to the beach. I know we saw Roman ruins, but for some reason, Nice impressed me more. I thought it charming and livable, halfway French and halfway Italian. I had my first pizza in a restaurant on a date my freshman year in college: here it was street food and cheap. Here when I spoke to people, they did not first correct my grammar but answered me back. I found it easy to understand their melodic French and easy to communicate with waiters and fruit sellers and people standing waiting for buses. We slept in a park one night and then located a youth hostel up on the mountain in Villefranche.

A few days later, we went on to Pisa and then stayed for two weeks in a little dusty pension in Florence, in the studio of a sculptor on vacation. Michel talked of marriage but was not sure. I got caught up in persuading him. What a tangled weave of intentions and fears and unlikely desires. I was far more experienced sexually, and it did not occur to me I could not make him enjoy sex with me, could not waken him sensually. Sex came easily to me. It was years before I understood it does not come so easily or naturally to everybody else. It was the natural language of my body, but not of his. I could give him an orgasm, but I could not really give him pleasure. He doubted the body too much. I should have understood our differences would not only refuse to mesh but grate on one another, but I was too naive, too eager, too confident. I was like a poker player convinced I could bluff my way to the pot on two tens.

His speaking voice was deep and pleasant, as was his singing voice. He had quite a repertoire of songs, most in French but some in Hebrew. I am not a polite person myself—too greedy, too blunt, too much in a hurry—but I greatly appreciate true politeness in others, particularly in intimate situations, and I appreciated Michel's polite manner. Michel was gentle and kind, but rigid in his ideas and expectations. His early life had been chaotic and terrifying. His parents, upon leaving Germany, were not permitted to practice medicine in France; immigrant Jews were barred from the professions. They had to survive as shopkeepers. After the Germans invaded, things grew rapidly worse. He remembered his mother running with him from one of the roundups of French Jews—the notorious *rafles*—and he remembered the clandestine trip to Switzerland, the difficulty crossing the border. His early childhood had been marked by danger and terror.

In Switzerland, his parents were put in a detention camp and he was placed with a Swiss family, where he was forced to practice the Christian religion. He felt that his parents did not love him as much as his younger brother, for Daniel was with them in the camp and here he was, farmed out to people who, if not cruel, were certainly not warm or kind. He had many psychic scars even though he had experienced, comparatively speaking, "a good war," as they said in his family. Close friends of his family were in the Jewish Resistance, as perhaps his father was before they had to flee to Switzerland. They only got in because his parents kept all their passports and papers. They had originally been Polish, gone to Germany for schooling and a better life and then fled to France early in Hitler's regime. They were more like German Jewish families I had met in college than like Polish or Russian Jews I knew from childhood on. They belonged to a very tight group of friends who had gone through the war together, protecting one another. They were people who had counted on one another for their very lives, and they had a strength to their friendship I have only known with a few friends with whom I went through the antiwar movement: someone to whom you can absolutely trust your back, who will not betray you, with whom you take risks and hope to survive, together.

I learned many things in France and with Michel. I learned how Jewish I am. I learned how American I am. These two realizations caused a rethinking of my identity. Michel was extremely French. The things he said oftenest to me were: *One does not do that. One does not do it like that. That is not how it is done.* He had secured a small fellowship at the University of Chicago, since I was to go to Northwestern. We were married upon our return to the States, in Detroit.

My mother in a fit of pique refused to attend. I could not understand what she was furious about. I could have been married in Europe. It wasn't costing them anything. Michel did not believe in Jewish ceremonies, so we were married by a justice of the peace. There wasn't even a wedding supper at a restaurant. My father too acted annoyed. I had imagined that they would understand that a physicist was a reasonably exalted occupation, like a doctor or a lawyer, but neither of them seemed to grasp that. Besides, they mistrusted doctors and lawyers. They acted as if I were marrying a hit man or a pimp. I was embarrassed for Michel, to have to go through this ugliness, and I promised him we need see little of them for the next few years.

Once we married, slowly I became aware that he expected me to put my writing aside like a childish hobby when we returned to France. It took a while for this to sink in, because for the first nine months, I was going to Northwestern up the El in one direction, while he was going to the University of Chicago down the El in the other direction. We lived on Wilson Avenue in Chicago in the Granada apartment hotel—cheap, cheap, twenty dollars a week—between the Friendly Tap and the Backstage Bar, which had a sign out front CONTINUOUS ENTERTAINMENT BACKSTAGE. It was a neighborhood of transients, pawnshops, dark beery bars, check-cashing storefronts, secondhand stores and Pentecostal churches. We were three blocks from Lake Michigan and two blocks from the El. Michel was preparing for his prelims for his doctorate, as well as working on the cyclotron. We got on well. Our time together was precious, perhaps because there was so little of it.

The El fascinated me. It was not a from-above maplike view of a city, nor immersion in traffic of the streets. Instead I sat looking into private lives, glimpses of people similar to those that had engrossed me in our summer sublet on the Lower East Side of New York. Now, however, instead of watching dramas slowly unfold day by day, I caught glimpses of lives, snapshots in passing. Every day I passed from the urban grime and electric bustle of Chicago across a frontier marked by a line of bars and liquor stores flashing neon day and night into mostly prosperous spacious tree-lined Evanston, which was dry. I found the students at Northwestern bland and boring, for the most part. They seemed cast all from the same mold.

Early in our marriage, the super found a tiny black kitten. We took her in. She had a fierce, avid disposition, a great desire to survive, a purr bigger than she was. Since I was writing on Marlowe in graduate school, I named her Tamburlaine, after the protagonist of one of his plays, a fierce Mongol leader.

She was just a cold lonely kitten and wanted to sleep with us, but Michel, who had never had a pet, insisted she must sleep in the kitchen. She managed with her tiny weight to open the swinging door. He put down pans of water—an improvised moat—to form a barrier. She slogged through them to the bed, arriving wet, half drowned and coughing. I felt as if I were a child again, having to endure my parents' ideas about how cats should be kept. This cat never went out, was living in a two-room apartment and I was still weaning her. Why couldn't she take comfort from the warmth of our bodies and snuggle with us? It is not done to sleep with animals, Michel said. We had our first serious fight.

She was a bright cat but confined to our tiny furnished apartment. She had an imperious disposition and liked to be played with, amused. Many evenings we would both be studying, and she would select one of us, usually me, and pull the plug from my floor lamp out of the wall. She had learned that made me put my book down. After we taped the plugs to the wall, she learned to turn off the lights by taking the pull chain in her teeth. When I would sit at the kitchen table working, she would often sit in the chair opposite me, only her eyes and sharp black ears visible over the tabletop.

I worked hard at Northwestern and established a perfect record. My one friend there, besides my professor in Elizabethan drama, was Charlotte, an Orthodox Jew from Brooklyn, also a graduate student. She and I had come to Northwestern to study with Richard Ellmann, the Yeats and Joyce scholar. As he had gone off on a Guggenheim that year to Europe, we found ourselves forced to take a seminar in Keats instead. We made up for our disappointment by reading *Ulysses* aloud together and sharing our reactions to all the critics we ploughed through for our seminar. We once had the police called on us for doing Israeli dancing in the Evanston streets to blow off steam after a particularly boring seminar.

I took my master's degree at Northwestern and passed the exam with the highest score they ever had up to that point. They offered me a better fellowship. I had only to complete the Anglo-Saxon requirement and write my thesis. But Michel and his family saw no reason for me to continue. We had, they said, to get together key money to buy an apartment in Paris. That was, Michel iterated, the way it was done. I liked some of my professors in graduate school, but the scholarship alienated me. I felt as if we were killing the poems we dissected. The work was boring, boring, boring. My head was being stuffed with stale cornflakes. I did not want to be a scholar; I wanted to be a writer. I suspected that if I continued graduate school, I would begin to get ideas for papers for MLA conferences instead of poems or stories. Security lay that way, but not the work I was put into the world to do. I would never be the writer I wanted to be if I continued for my Ph.D., I was convinced. I went to work as a secretary—first to a project studying urban renewal, then at the University of Chicago in the sociology department—to support Michel and the distant apartment.

My desire to write had not diminished, in spite of setbacks, including a friend's losing the only copy of a novel I had just completed. He was saving money by sending it parcel post instead of first class, as I had requested. After that, I would never again have only one copy of *anything* I wrote. I sometimes kept carbons of letters, out of a compulsion to make sure nothing disappeared—which proved useful in writing this memoir, frankly.

Michel's parents purchased an apartment for us, and his mother proceeded to furnish it in the style of her choosing: large formal bourgeois interiors of heavy wood, massive, respectable, depressing. We were living on what I made, and now we were in debt thousands of dollars to purchase an apartment I did not want, because that was what one did. Somewhere in Paris was a six-room apartment we were paying for, that I was expected to go to work to support in France at some extremely menial and ill-paid job, while Michel was off in Algeria in the army fighting a war he opposed. When we returned, he made clear, he wanted to start a family at once. We would visit his parents every Sunday. We would live in that damned flat with its hideous furniture.

What I wanted did not enter into the equation. He simply ignored it, not arrogantly, but backed up by his family. That was the way things were done; that was how it must be. There was only one path, and we must walk it, me several feet in the rear. I had not expected this, in my idiocy. I thought how things were when we were both university students was how things would be when we were married. I thought this in spite of everything I had seen all of my life about sex roles in marriage. I expected it to be different for me.

I experienced something interesting. As a student at Michigan and again at Northwestern, I was highly visible. I was loud, opinionated, noisy and sought as a friend and earlier as a sexual partner. I was known as a poet and a fiction writer and as a political person. I was used to being listened to, argued with, fought, followed. I was used to walking into a party and being instantly noticed.

The moment I became a married secretary, I experienced a loss of visibility. I would speak and no one would hear me. It was as if my voice had been swallowed by the air. I moved through rooms as if on castors, as if in purdah. At first, I rather enjoyed being invisible, although I found no pleasure in being inaudible. I came to resent my nonpersonhood. I got louder, shriller. It did not matter. I spoke, but the conversation went on over my head in waves that broke over me. I was of no more consequence in a conversation than Tamburlaine.

When we moved to Hyde Park, the racially mixed neighborhood around the University of Chicago, where Michel was studying, Tam went with us. Now we had a much bigger apartment, unfurnished in a run-down building. Tam could run and jump and climb up on the ledges and see pigeons and sparrows in the trees outside. She was a lithe cat, completely black. Her eyes were an amazing yellow green, deep, more green than yellow. We had her altered. She was thin, as were we, partly because we had been living mostly on my fellowship and now on what I made as an underpaid secretary. Once we lived on smelt for ten days because it was the cheapest thing on sale and I bought an enormous quantity of it frozen. We ate a lot of rice, and I used food coloring on it to make it more interesting: blue rice, anyone? One night while I was still studying at Northwestern, I invited my favorite professor, a Shakespeare scholar, and his wife to supper. What I served them must have been astonishing, if not frightening. One tiny lamb chop apiece, lots of blue rice, frozen beans and some kind of pudding from a package. After they had left, Michel and I took a walk and saw them in a Chinese restaurant near the El, eating ravenously. They were both very polite.

I had no idea how to cook, but since I was expected to, I soon bought a cookbook and tried. I developed a repertoire based on the inner organs of cows and chickens and seventeen ways of cooking kosher hot dogs. My early attempts were limited by the one cookbook (I now own a hundred), our meager finances and my severely limited knowledge of food, not to mention how little time I had when I got home from work. I went through the usual period of dumping a can of soup on everything to make a sauce. What I produced was barely edible, but we were always hungry, and food was unimportant to Michel. The vet said Tamburlaine was malnourished also, but we could not afford much. I shared my food with her, all I could do. She was particularly my cat, and as my life began to fill me with despair, I cried into her fur. We would lie on the double bed together, its sagging mattress sloping to a ravine, and I would hold her and weep.

Michel and I fought more and more. I began to try to have some influence on the course of our marriage, and I wanted our sex to improve. Michel went to a psychiatrist who told him I was immature sexually if I could not have an orgasm during our brief and perfunctory intercourse, and that I was pursuing what Michel called a chimera. Having had a good deal of quite satisfactory sex, I could hardly argue that I knew what good sex was without hurting his feelings, but neither Michel nor his psychiatrist nor his family could dissuade me of what I knew I desired. I began to realize he had little desire to please me but wanted me to "behave correctly" in all things, including sex. These were the days of the Freudian ideal in which a woman was supposed to come on demand as soon as a penis was inserted, and both partners would go off together in a simultaneous big bang. Always when I tried to talk to him, he would put off the conversation by saying he had some pressing thing in graduate school. He was angry with me but expressed it in withdrawal. He adopted a superior tone, as if dealing with an irrational child who had to be firmly disciplined. The whole last summer we were together, he refused to discuss our marriage at all until he had finished his experiments and the cyclotron run.

I began to have vivid symbolic dreams about freedom, about escaping. I was excavating a tomb, finding a sarcophagus from which the light was pouring. When I opened it, I saw myself inside. I'm alive, I thought as I

sat up. Why had I doubted it? I was writing feverishly, aware that if I succumbed to his wishes, I would soon stop, perhaps permanently. I could
feel my life closing upon me, and I clutched Tamburlaine to me and
talked incessantly of what I should do. I was stifling. In my dreams, I was
in danger of being buried alive; when I woke, I thought my life was narrow as a grave and growing darker. I tried to speak to him in spite of his
prohibition, but he turned away and glowered. He spent more and more
time in the lab. I scarcely saw him. He would come home for supper and
then he would go back. I knew his experiments were consuming, but I
also suspected he found it pleasanter in the lab than in our apartment. I
was a loud demand he wasn't about to meet. The guys using the
cyclotron were a jolly lot, an elite, a club of the chosen who were careless
with the danger. They held occasional parties there, drinking beer and
dancing around the cyclotron.

After one of our really bitter, bitter fights, Tamburlaine pushed out the
screen and ran off into the night. I put up handmade posters on every
tree. I ran through the streets calling her. It was not until a year later I
was walking down Woodlawn Avenue in Hyde Park and heard a cat
meowing loudly. She came running up to me. With her came a boy of six.
Tamburlaine was now his cat. She was sleek, well fed, friendly but not
about to go off with me. She remembered me, but she had given herself
to this family, a professor's family with a nice brick house and a big backyard. She was allowed outside, but the boy said she never left the yard.
Tamburlaine had moved up in the world. I had moved on down.

That summer, I read Simone de Beauvoir's *The Second Sex,* which clar-
ified my thinking and gave me an analysis I could share with no one but
found illuminating. She gave me a way to think about being a woman,
about marriage, about sex roles, about expectations, about freedom. I
tentatively began an affair with a man I met in a writing group, loved him
as I tended always to love anybody I was close to. The sex with the fellow
writer was good and strengthened me, although I did not take the relationship as seriously as I was supposed to. He was southern and much
older. At least he listened to me when I spoke, and he understood I was
serious about writing. Both of us were in a group of Black and white

writers on the South Side who met once a week and shared our work. Several other writers came out of that group, including Harry Mark Petrakis and Robert Coover—but none of us were published yet, all wanna-bes. My lover went out of town to visit his ex-wife and children, and I resumed brooding about what I should do. Then quite simply I decided.

Why had I chosen to be unfaithful? It was partly out of simple sexual frustration, but mostly to force myself to a decision, to pry myself out of a relationship with a man I did love but with whom I could see only slow diminution, the loss of everything about myself I valued.

As soon as the cyclotron run was over, Michel finally agreed to talk with me. It was September in Chicago, almost hot, sticky. We sat in the living room of our apartment. We had a big mission oak table we were keeping for a friend whose husband had committed suicide and who never came to claim it. She disappeared. The big table filled most of the room, with a makeshift couch on one side and plank-and-brick student bookcases against the other wall. We sat elbows on the table, glaring at each other.

"What is so important you have to pester me with it?" he asked.

"I'm moving out. I want a divorce."

He was hurt and furious. He did not ask why. He simply said, "You've never had a better relationship."

"Perhaps not."

"You go on and on about sex, but you don't know what you want."

Ah, but I did. Still, I had no desire to wound him more than I had to for my own survival. He agreed to a divorce, more out of sore pride than any desire for separation. I left him everything, took my few clothes, books and papers and moved into a rooming house. Now I had only myself to support and I began to work only part-time, writing furiously. Everyone I knew thought I was crazy to leave Michel, a handsome physicist with a brilliant future and never likely to have to worry about money, but I knew my mistake had been in marrying him, not in abandoning him.

A friend told me a month later she had a long conversation with

Michel about me and was shocked to learn how little he knew of me, how little he understood of what I wanted. He saw me as an immature demanding American woman pursuing fantasies of fulfillment that did not exist. Never having read the stories or poetry I was writing, even the few things that were published, he had no notion of my work and what it meant to me. To Michel, my writing was a hobby, like stamp collecting. It had no importance, no validity. He knew little about my previous life. What I had told him he could not put into any context that was meaningful, so he simply ignored it. I had done what my mother had done, married into sexual frustration and a complete lack of understanding.

Michel argued fiercely with me for three painful and acrimonious meetings at the old apartment. He considered me a silly adolescent who did not understand what I was doing. He tried to make the divorce contingent upon my going to his psychiatrist or another at the same institute. I refused. I did not trust any psychiatrist, analyst or therapist I had met or with whom I had watched my friends try to solve their problems. I knew the Freudian and official psychiatric line on women like me, and I wasn't interested in becoming the sort of women Freudians found acceptable. There was much good in our marriage, yet it was a box for me where I experienced a gradual diminishing of self. Before I began to make demands that summer, our daily patterns were gentle and harmonious, which after my contentious home life, I valued. We were mostly considerate of each other. But I had learned that trying to write in a corner of my life didn't work.

I had several very hard years in the bottom of Chicago ahead of me, and I deserved them. I should never have come close enough to Michel to hurt him. I carried around a worm of guilt that gnawed at me. I acted nonchalant. The lawyer representing both of us took a dislike to me because of my apparent indifference and attempted to persuade Michel to track me and divorce me for infidelity. Michel did not believe I was having an affair—he had never met my lover—and the lawyer was guessing. I was not indifferent, but rather poleaxed by guilt and motivated by a fierce and consuming desire to be free to write. My attempt to draw my identity from someone else was a complete failure. No wonder Tam-

burlaine had run away from us. She too wanted to be fully alive, to
be free.

A COLD AND MARRIED WAR

Loving you is a warm room
so I remember
how I lived on the moon.
Ash and jagged craters
cold bright place under
a black steel sky.
The stars pierced me
stabbing my secret
aches and itches.
Torture of the witch with needles.
Am I worthy, eyes?
Never. Objects
came out of the silence
bizarre as medals
for unknown services:
chocolate cherries
rolling down from Sinai,
rosebuds pink as
girls' first lipsticks.
When I lay down
head on a rock,
the rock
recited tirelessly
as a language record
my sins and errors.

The months bled slowly
out of us.
The landscape went bald.

The cold stayed.
One morning there
were regulations posted.
Where I had not known
boundaries existed,
first hedges, then stakes,
finally barbed wire.
His cock crowed
I know you not,
repent, and other homilies.
My bones knocked.
Chessboard of dead volcanoes.
I had to go.

The only thing to do
with the corpse
was to eat it.

EIGHT

BOTTOMING OUT

After my divorce, I lived in a rooming house overrun with mice, water bugs (the Chicago equivalent of roaches) and bad smells. There were mice in the cabinets, in the closet, even in the refrigerator. I could not keep cereal on hand. I finally set traps. Every morning I would find one dead mouse in each trap, and every evening when I returned from work as a secretary in the department of sociology at the University of Chicago, I would find two more. I dreamed of a cat, but I could scarcely feed myself.

One morning I was wakened by something thumping against the furniture. I saw a large brown rat wearing a mousetrap. It was mostly uninjured, but the trap had closed around its leg. It was trying to knock the trap off against the furniture. I jumped out of bed, grabbed the rat by the tail with a wad of tissues and tried to stab it with a kitchen knife. I failed. The rat was snapping at me and wriggling all over the place. I ran across the hall and into the bathroom I shared with my floor. All I could think to do was to drop the rat, trap and all, into the toilet. I forgot that rats swim very well. I slammed down the toilet seat, pissed in the sink, grabbed my purse and left, leaving notice under my landlady's door. I found a woman graduate student in the mathematics department who wanted a roommate and I moved that day. I had so little, I only had to carry boxes four blocks in three trips, plus my typewriter and suitcase of clothes. I don't know what happened with the rat, the plumbing or the other tenants. I was out of there.

My roommate, from a tight Greek family, and I began sharing a large run-down five-room apartment over a row of stores on Fifty-fifth Street in Hyde Park. Beneath us was a place that distributed newspapers, so it was noisy in the early morning, but I had never lived anyplace comfortable. I was used to making do and slept on a mattress on the floor. The dining room had a lurid antiwar mural left over from the Korean War, rife with vultures and exploding bombs. It reminded me of the movie of *The Horse's Mouth,* about a mural painter always in trouble with the law. I identified with the con man–artist and his willingness to sacrifice anything or anyone to his painting. I had just sacrificed a marriage to my writing.

Right across Fifty-fifth Street was the Compass, the bar where Elaine May and Mike Nichols, Shelley Berman and countless others had begun their comedy and improv careers. It was my bar of choice until the University of Chicago had it torn down. They were urban-renewing the neighborhood. Our building would be demolished eventually, one reason the rent was low and the landlord uninterested in repairs. We lived in a disappearing neighborhood.

The demolition began across the street. I stopped work on my novel, quit everything except watching the four-story apartment building being eaten by a crane. The crane, tall as a six-story building, opened its jaws and fed. Bricks cascaded in a rising cloud of plaster dust. Timbers, doors, pipes stuck crossways out of the crane's teeth. I thought of it as "she" because there was something delicate about her nibbling; a female dinosaur. The crane operator was white. The men who did the manual demolition were Black. All that remained beyond the fence of varicolored doors of what had been the Compass was a wall inscribed in huge jagged letters MENE MENE TEKEL UPHARSIN, from the Book of Daniel. The real estate powers and the university had decreed that the Compass should go but that Jimmy's, the bar where jocks and frat boys hung out, should endure. After the Compass fell into rubble, all us fringe types piled into Jimmy's, and it changed but not into the cultural icon the Compass had been.

Our apartment wound around a courtyard with a tree of heaven growing out of the roof. We sunbathed there, for it was enclosed on every side, until we acquired a voyeur. I can close my eyes and see him standing or squatting on the roof watching us. We called the police, but the police felt more dangerous than the voyeur. One of them would come upstairs, plunk himself down with his gun clanking and regale us with stories of rapes and murders of young women. We hung improvised curtains and put up with the voyeur.

When Michel, who continued to see me as an immature neurotic American girl, returned to France, I acquired furniture. He had asked me to take the dining room table, since we still thought the woman who had left it with us might return. It was a handsome mission oak table big enough for eight. I was astonished when I returned to the apartment where I had lived with him to pick up the furniture. It was meant, I think, as an indictment: full of fast-food containers, dishes on which some meal had been eaten, pots in which food had burned, trash and garbage. Water bugs and ants swarmed over the rancid food. With the help of my roommate, my boyfriend and hers, I took the table, the chairs and a small desk, then fled. If the state of the flat was supposed to indicate to me that I had not taken care of him properly, the message was wasted, since I wasn't much wanting to take care of anyone. I was barely surviving. I was trying to learn to write the kind of fiction and poetry I needed to write. I was a wee bit more successful in getting poetry published than prose. I did have a couple of short stories accepted by literary zines, but my novels came back as quickly as they went out. I was working part-time so that I could write the rest of the time, but I lived mostly on rice, pasta and potatoes and bought my clothes at rummage sales.

I went on seeing the man I had been having the affair with—saw him steadily for the next year and a half. He bought me a couple of dresses; as his taste was surer than mine had the opportunity to be, I learned a little about how to dress from him. He was fourteen years older than me, a pleasantly ugly man with prematurely gray hair and a great body from roadwork in the Virgin Islands, where he had lived for years until his divorce, and where his ex-wife still lived with their daughters. After growing up in North Carolina, he had gone through World War II in the signal corps in India, Burma and China. In college on the GI Bill, he had developed the desire to write and had also met a young poet he married. In some ways with me, he was replicating that, for I was about the age she had been, and he considered me primarily a poet. But she was far less driven than I was. Our differences became clearer as time went on, as did my writing. He was taking his degree for high school teaching.

The hostility of everyone who had known Michel made it unpleasant to run into them. An acquaintance of his came to visit my roommate one evening while I was collating a story on the dining room table. He picked up a page, read it with a sneer and said, "Jason, Jason. Who ever heard of somebody named Jason?"

I said I had gone to school with a Jason from third grade through eighth, a skinny graceful Afro-American boy who lived not far from me, with a talent for throwing balls and knives. It was insufferable that I should have pretensions to be a writer, a badly dressed secretary who had divorced a graduate student in physics. I did receive encouragement from my boyfriend and other members of that racially mixed group of writers who met in Hyde Park every week. The most talented of us, a very tall very dark man from Trinidad named Clyde with a voice of honey and a lyrical style applied to tough material, had to give up writing to support his family back home. He went into real estate instead. I have always wondered if he ever returned to writing. Without the group, I do not in the least doubt I would have continued writing, but I would have done so more slowly and with more despair. Feedback was essential. The group was run by a couple of would-be literary agents who had taken Henry James far too seriously, but the writers in the group were what mattered. We were a bright underappreciated contentious lot with delusions of grandeur some of us eventually fulfilled.

The other day on the treadmill I was exercising to Dvořák's *New*

World Symphony—I use *everything,* from world music to rock to rap to classical to Shakrit chanting—when a memory remnant surfaced. A bunch of us—Mark Petrakis, Robert Coover, Clyde—were making a recording of Benét's *The Devil and Daniel Webster* for some project of my boyfriend's. There were no good parts for women, so I volunteered to do sound effects. I chose the Dvořák for intro music. I remember making crickets with a pocket comb and using beanbags for footsteps. Clyde was the Devil and Mark was Daniel Webster. We had to stop frequently because we broke each other up. We had a lot of games going in that group.

What happened with the boyfriend was that I began suddenly to write better fiction. I abandoned the made-up thriller I was attempting and began to use my own experience and perceptions. He didn't mind that my poetry was improving rapidly, but when the fiction began to harden and shape, it shook him. Things were not going well with his writing, and for me to suddenly begin to write as well or better turned off his sexuality. I was sorry about that. I liked the sex with him, and I liked the company. I liked being able to talk about writing with someone I was involved with. I had known it would not be a permanent relationship. I was only willing to stay in Chicago perhaps another year, and then I wanted to go to New York or San Francisco. He had no intention of leaving Chicago. He felt that given his ex-wife's health, both physical and mental, he might have to take the children. He was still emotionally entangled with his ex-wife, to the extent that whenever she came to Chicago, he could scarcely relate to me. I respected him for being responsible. The relationship was good for me while it lasted, and it ended without rancor.

What had also hurt my relationship with my writer-boyfriend was that Louise died suddenly. The official line was that she had died of a perforated ulcer, but I heard from a friend in New York that they suspected she had died of a botched abortion. She had been my best friend the first years of college, a real intimacy such as I had never before known. She married someone I had been involved with, one reason she broke off our relationship. Yet there was always a connection. Sometimes all the theatrical animosity would simply vanish and we would talk richly, honestly.

News of her death cut through me, leveling the terrain. I had always assumed there would be plenty of time to revive our friendship. I had always assumed that we would be close again.

Now the time was gone. Now there were no more chances. She was dead at twenty-three and I was paralyzed with grief and guilt. Somehow I should have prevented her death. My grieving seemed excessive to everyone around me, boring really. None of them had ever met her or could understand what she had meant to me, how close we had been, how strongly I had cared for her. I withdrew into silence. Slowly I returned to normal life, but nothing was ever the same again. I have never been able to endure a quarrel with someone I love that is not made up. To this day, I have a compulsion to make things right, because there might not be another chance.

I got a job teaching freshman comp at the Gary extension of Indiana University. The next year and a half were filled with my peripheral involvement in civil rights, attending rallies, demonstrations, various actions around Chicago, attempts at integrating restaurants or beaches. I had good friends in the civil rights movement—indeed, this was one of the times in my life I lived in a truly racially mixed milieu. In Hyde Park, there was a lot of socializing across race boundaries, and that was certainly true in the civil rights movement. It was one of the few good aspects of my life, pretty grim in general. I was poor. I was invisible as a writer. Nobody except people in my writing group gave me encouragement. Once again, I had no idea what was going to become of me, how I would ever get published.

During the presidential campaign of 1960, I was a precinct captain. Most nights I went around talking to "my" voters, laden with literature and my booklet of names. I liked it. I found going into people's apartments and houses fascinating. Here were all these buildings I had passed fifty times, and now I knew who lived in them and what colors their walls were painted and what pictures hung on those walls. My endless curiosity was fed, and I spent longer with most of them than I needed to, getting them to talk with me. My friends all asked me how I could bear to do something like that, but the truth was, I had fun and I was a good precinct captain—rewarded by a brief close-up glimpse when Kennedy came to Chicago.

Teaching at Gary was depressing, because we were in an area like the part of Detroit where I had grown up, and Afro-American students had received little education. We were expected to maintain a 33 percent flunk rate. I salved my conscience by picking out a couple of students to tutor each semester. I brought them up an average of a point and a half, usually from D to B, but it was a gesture, and I knew it. I was a good teacher and they rewarded me by giving me freshman lit to teach, sort of Great Books. I loved teaching Homer, Job, Sophocles. I tried to give them a little extra in every course, because I felt bad about their prospects. Another poet, Henry, taught there, and we became good friends. He was part friend, part lover, part would-be shrink.

I had gone on being close to Nadine after Michigan: she was one of the people with whom I regularly exchanged manuscripts and criticism. She had gone to the Iowa MFA program, where I visited to decide whether to enroll. We spent a lot of time with an Afro-American writer from St. Louis who was also an outsider in the program. He drove a white Caddy convertible he had paid blood for in the ghetto, and it meant a great deal to him. It was in a way the symbol of what he had given up to become a writer, the easy but violent drug life. The guys who ran the writing program told him halfway through his year that they wouldn't renew his fellowship if he didn't sell the car. Why should he have a Cadillac when they didn't? We bugged everybody by riding around in it the whole time I was visiting, but I knew that program was not for me. They simply could not empathize with him. I would fare no better with them, and the classes I sat in on were competitive and wanted to impose a type of writing I had little interest in doing.

After a disastrous affair with a professor, Nadine broke down and her mother put her in a mental institution. When she managed to get out, Henry and I finagled a job at Gary for her. It wasn't much of a job, but I was living on the same thing. We called ourselves the kibbutz. We were a kind of eating club, reading group, writers' support group. Henry ran a little zine we both worked on. He had more money than we did, from his well-to-do family, and often treated one or both of us to supper. Certainly his apartment was far more luxurious than either of ours. He was a moody broody sort of guy, obsessed with a girlfriend he had lost years before, a stocky bearlike man deeply into psychoanalysis and Roethke. He longed to be a lay analyst and lived and dreamed in Freudian. He had a terrific ability to hold a grudge.

Nadine was seductive, sexy, opinionated and apt to take on superior airs. Her father had been a charismatic intellectual; she despised her mother as ignorant, but they were close. Her father had walked out and hadn't helped financially or related to her in years. She had a lot of class attitudes that meshed poorly with her economic situation. She was just as poor as I was but was convinced this was a temporary state. She fell in love as often as I did, but with even more disastrous results, for every relationship filled her with desperate hopes of marriage and security. She was talented and driven, so we understood that aspect of each other very well indeed. She strongly identified with male authority and tended to dismiss other women. I was one exception, and the other was her younger sister, a painter. The sisters had a complicated love/hate relationship, which they transferred to me. Nadine once wrote a story in which I ended up killing myself because I could find neither love nor success in writing. I was shocked and wounded by the story, but after a month or so, I had to recognize it was her best story, because, alas, I was an interesting character and emerged as such, whereas she often had trouble with characterization. No one in her fiction seemed real except the protagonist, who was always Nadine.

I was trying to move to New York. A friend, David Newman, who was working at *Esquire,* offered me a job as a slush editor, but I declined. I repeat that all my friends thought I was out of my mind. But I was afraid if I moved into that world, I would need to succeed in media and that would consume me instead of allowing me to learn to write the kind of fiction and poetry I was struggling to produce. I brought my file of letters of recommendation up-to-date, did the Modern Language Association interviews that December, wrote letters and sent my résumé to every college in and around New York City. I had some interviews that led to two prospects. I was lining up my New York friends to look for anything else that could support me and an affordable apartment. I imagined I would live with a college friend, as I had that summer between my junior and senior years. These plans were about to tear to confetti pieces.

My second fall of teaching at Gary, I met Robert at a party at Henry's house that Nadine, Henry and I were throwing. I forget the occasion, but the crowd was far too large for his apartment. Robert was there on impulse, having run away from his job as a systems analyst with a small computer company in Massachusetts and turned up at Henry's apartment—where floaters often came to rest. Our first contact at that party came when he was lying on the floor. I stepped over him, he grabbed my leg, and I kicked him. Not a promising beginning. I resented him, because he had moved in with Henry and now Henry had less time for me. Henry was another one who found my poetry too female, too direct, too emotional, but at least he was willing to read it. Gradually over the next three months, I came to know Robert and like him. He had a curly Toulouse-Lautrec beard much too big for his face. When he shaved it off, he looked more attractive and vulnerable. At first he was loudly discontent and surly, but shortly he calmed down and began to be himself.

He had grown up in Sheepshead Bay in Brooklyn, in a lower-middle-class family. At fifteen, he had gone off to the University of Chicago as part of their misbegotten Children's Crusade: the program that offered entrance at fifteen to gifted high school students. Small, bookish, bright but completely inexperienced, he got into a great deal of trouble. He received his bachelor's, although he spent more time shooting pool and playing poker for money than in classes. Since he looked about twelve and was only seventeen when he graduated, he didn't develop relationships with women. He thought he would take his Ph.D. in physics (as Michel had), but instead was seduced by Leo Szilard's work in biophysics and became his assistant. When he discovered the UNIVAC computer, which filled an enormous room at the university, he was hooked and became an early computer nerd. He worked first at an air weapons facility; then for IBM, where he developed a language for big machines called EXTRAN—this was the era of FORTRAN. He worked well at IBM but found the corporate culture stifling. He ran off on an Asian trip.

When we got involved, Henry was not pleased and managed to manipulate us into a breakup with the aid of a tape recorder and the pressure and opinions of his other friends, who backed him. He interviewed each of us about the other, edited the tapes and played them for us. He persuaded guys who had known Robert in the past to talk about him in unflattering terms and then gave me those tapes. We both were shocked and mistrustful. Everyone seemed to be jealous of everyone else. Robert resented how much time Henry gave me; I resented how much time Henry gave Robert. Henry was determined Robert and I not become involved. When we started seeing each other again, it was clandestine. We did not let anyone except my roommate know we were intimate. Henry eventually figured it out, but by then, Robert and I knew each other much better and Henry had the crisis of a pregnant girlfriend on his hands.

Robert was a small neat man. He was the smallest person in his family of large men, as he was born with osteogenesis imperfecta and had undergone a series of endless broken bones all through his childhood into adolescence, when the disease finally abated. Most babies with osteogenesis are crushed to death during birth. He was stoical and had trouble believing in other people's pain, perhaps because he had undergone so much himself. He was prone to depression but enjoyed food and wine immensely, and he liked sex. He was bright, not much in touch with his emotions, but curious, open. His features were sharp, his nose prominent. His eyes were a warm hazel. He wore glasses and at that time had his hair cropped close to his scalp. He was slight but not weak, in spite of his bones. He liked to laugh, and he could be reduced almost to tears if something was funny enough.

I liked making love with him, and he liked it with me. He was the first person I had been with since I left Ann Arbor who was into oral sex as well as intercourse, and that was a great pleasure. He was open to trying new experiences in all areas, which again was a thing new to me since college. Most of the men I had been with were fairly rigid in their expectations and their behavior. Robert struck me as not at all that way, and I respected him for that openness. He seemed in a great many ways a good match. He was avidly curious about ideas and experiences and sensations. He was fond of music from classical to jazz. In Chicago, I used to go and hear jazz in a hotel lounge in the ghetto often, and we did that together. At this time, he was fascinated by sports car races. Since I had grown up on stock car racing, sports cars were exotic to me. He had been learning to fly a plane the previous year, but he was in debt now and dropped it. He drove a silver Porsche. I had no idea how expensive that was or what it meant. It was just a little car that both Henry and Robert tended to drive very fast. I never thought about the danger. I remember that Robert's hands on the steering wheel were the first time I noticed them: he had strong and shapely hands I found attractive. He was deft with them, good at putting things together, minor carpentry, whatever was called for—when he felt like it. In his interests and his experiences, he was not like anyone I had known.

As for Henry's situation, it seemed ambiguous and sticky, although I had helped women get illegal abortions while I lived in Chicago. I had, since I had aborted myself at eighteen, kept a record of abortionists with prices, how you contacted them, and other relevant information. Since I almost killed myself and came near bleeding to death, I have been an impassioned supporter of a woman's right to control her own body. It is one of those bedrock issues that determines which candidates I support and for whom I vote. It's still one of the issues I work on fiercely and frequently. That and civil rights were my political involvements in Chicago, although nobody thought of abortion as a political issue then: it was considered a personal shame.

Robert had gotten a research job with someone he had known in college, although we understood that with the usual bureaucratic paperwork at the U. of Chicago, he would not be paid until the end of November. November came and went and so did December, and no paycheck arrived. When it turned out that the job was a figment of his boss's cracked imagination and that the project he had been working on for three months did not exist, he was in financial trouble. He got in touch with his former company and they welcomed him back. However, they would only pay for me to move to the Boston area if we were married. Robert wanted very much to marry. I was less enthusiastic, but I have discovered, once you have been married to someone else, it becomes to a man a litmus test of your commitment to him whether or not you are willing to marry him. I think it was not so much that he was crazy for me as that he had been desperately lonely in Boston. After having fled the small—in fact rather intimate—computer mini–think tank, coming home with a wife provided some justification or rationale for disappearing and reappearing. My presence made it all plausible.

The first time we had a serious conversation about marriage, I found myself saying, "If we marry, I don't want children." As soon as I said it, I was simultaneously startled and illuminated. I had assumed earlier that I would have children, as "everyone" did. But by this time, enough of my friends had had babies for the prospect to be far more real to me than it had been a year or two before. I had watched woman after woman abandon her ambitions and become devoted and absorbed by her offspring. As soon as I had spoken to him, I could think of nothing else for the next several days. I realized I was convinced I would be a terrible mother, as I felt my own parenting should not be replicated. I would either neglect a baby in order to write, or make the baby my "novel" and be an overcontrolling mother, secretly resentful of what I would feel I had sacrificed.

Just before the new semester, Gary suddenly cut me back to two classes, not enough to live on. They had promised me solemnly I would always have three classes, but they were hiring Ph.D.'s and needed me less. I had managed to live and in fact even to save money on my ridiculous stipend, but I couldn't exist on two classes and it was too late to try for a part-time appointment at one of the other schools. It was crisis time. Robert suggested that getting married would solve all problems; I was not convinced, but I was willing to try, because I seemed to have come to a dead end and I loved him. I did not consider that preeminent, for—as I've remarked—I have an affectionate disposition and I found it easy to love most people who cast themselves in the way of my attention. I thought him a good person. I thought I would be good for him.

So a local rabbi at a temple I went to (I didn't have enough money to join, although a friend paid my way for High Holiday services) married us. We packed Robert's Porsche and drove to Boston, stopping for a brief awkward visit with my parents, who were stunned, since I had told them little about Robert. Then we visited his. I was not reluctant to leave Chicago, where I had been poor, miserable, unsuccessful as a writer and altogether down-and-out. No one around me believed I would accomplish anything interesting. I was as invisible as I had been when I moved down from Wilson Avenue to Hyde Park with Michel. We were being thrown out of our apartment building on Fifty-fifth Street, which was finally being torn down. All signs seemed to point to departure. My life was vanishing around me, even as the buildings were reduced to rubble.

A VALLEY WHERE I DON'T BELONG

The first cocks begin clearing the throat of morning—
Who's that walking up on Pettijean mountain?—
rasping their brass cries from outflung necks
as they dig their spurs in the clammy cellar air.
Windows upon the mountain trap the first light.
Their bronze and copper plumage is emerging
from the pool of dusk. Lustily they drill the ear
with a falsetto clangor strident as mustard
raising alarm: I I I live I live!

I stand with a damp wind licking my face
outside this shabby motel where a man snores
who is tiring of me so fast my throat parches
and I twist the hem of my coat thinking of it.

"The rooster, or cock, is a symbol of male sexuality,"
the instructor said, elucidating Herrick.
You stuck me with spiky elbow and matchspurt glance.
We were eighteen: we both were dancers in the woods,
you a white doe leaping with your Brooklyn satyr.

Bones and sap, I rode in the mothering earth
tasting the tough grass and my dear's salty mouth,
open and swept, in a gale of dark feathers.
We owned the poems they taught us, Leda and Europa.
We struck the earth with our heels and it pivoted,
sacred wood of blossoming crab and hanging snake,
wet smoke close to the grass and a rearing sun.

That fruit has fallen. You were burned like a Greek
just before the last solstice, but without games.
I was not there. For a long while I hadn't been.
Now you are my literary ghost.
I with broken suitcase and plump hips, about
to be expelled from this man to whom I'm bound
by the moist cord of want and the skeins of habit,
a hitchhiker in the hinterland of Ozarks.

You hardened to an edge that slashed yourself
while I have eased into flesh and accommodation.
The cry of the mouse shrill and covetous in my fingers,
I cannot keep my hands from anything.
My curiosity has been a long disaster.
I fear myself as once I feared my mother.
Still I know no more inexorable fact
than that thin red leap of bone: I live, I live.
I and my worn symbols see up the sun.

NINE

FLIRTATION IN SAN FRANCISCO

W*e found a small apartment* in Cambridge on Upland Road, over-looking the railroad tracks. It was a gray wooden symmetrical building with a red door: we had the second-floor-right apartment. I have three strong memories of that apartment: the kitchen floor tilted toward the tracks so sharply that anything that fell would inevitably roll toward the outer wall. Second, the heat for our half of the building was controlled by three MIT students, who, when they went home for vacation, turned it off. They were also much too curious about us and had to be firmly, even rudely discouraged from dropping in.

My third memory concerns the first Siamese cat I ever knew. She belonged to a friend from Michigan, Dori, who was going off on a trip. I liked the cat immensely—she was a strong and intelligent presence and had come to know us at Dori's. She took over. She instructed us where she would eat—on the kitchen table only—and where she would sleep—between us in bed. She was an unusually big female Siamese, sturdy, confident. Then, unfortunately, she went into heat. She had two targets of choice: one was me and the other was the Siamese cat in the full-length mirror. We got little sleep that week, but I still liked the cat very much.

We hung out during that period mostly with guys from Robert's small computer company and their wives, but also with one of the few women who worked as a computer programmer there, a woman of Greek descent I'll call Sophia. The programmers were an eccentric lot, well paid and fond of male toys—fancy cars, fancy stereos and actual toys like miniature racing cars. Some were married, some had children, some were divorced already, some were set-in-their-ways bachelors. Some were straight and others were into boho. I began to learn to cook, as Robert was a gourmet. Since we were living at first on money I had saved on my negligible salary and that helped get him out of debt, he insisted I not take a job for those months, but rather write full-time. I was pleased to do so. I remember learning many ways to cook hamburger and hot dogs, since we had little money.

That spring was a particularly happy season. I was writing full-time and making good progress on my novel and new poems. We took little trips to New York, into the White Mountains, into the Berkshires, to Cape Cod. We found each other's company stimulating and satisfying. We also explored Boston, which he had not done previously. We walked in Mount Auburn cemetery and the Granary Burying Ground, bought vegetables and fruit in Haymarket on Saturdays, meat and pastries in the Italian North End. We enjoyed the lilacs and the peonies in the Arnold Arboretum. I was happy and my joy was contagious.

His parents' wedding present to us was to pay off the Porsche finally. Robert considered himself a great driver, but he had caused several accidents already, as I learned later. One Sunday when it had been raining and he was driving too fast, he slammed into a tree. Breaking the windshield with my head, I had a concussion and a pelvic injury that manifested itself in an agonizing bladder that flared up on and off for the next year. I also broke a couple of teeth. The concussion fiddled with my short-term memory. For the next few weeks, I would be fine one moment and dizzy the next. Pain in my head and my pelvis came and went. Robert felt guilty, but having suffered as a child, he was convinced others should endure pain silently. He took the painkillers prescribed for me and gave them to a friend of his who liked to get high on them. For the first weeks, it hurt me to have sex, which annoyed him. It was a bad time. I had been writing the first draft of a new novel that was by far the best thing I had done. I had just worked out the ending the day of the accident. I never managed to remember what I had planned, and I was haunted ever after by the conviction that I wrote a poorer ending than I might have.

At the end of August with the Porsche finally fixed, Robert's company sent him out to San Francisco to work on a project with a large computer firm in Palo Alto. We were told it would take about three months, so we would be back in Boston by December. We moved out, put our things into storage, threw a couple of suitcases into the Porsche and headed west. The Porsche broke down in Fargo and again later on in British Columbia. It never ran well after the accident. Locating a Porsche mechanic each time was a major nuisance.

The first stop I remember vividly is Glacier National Park. I found the rocks magical in their formations and rich colors, red, black, buff and green. It was the first week in September. We took short hikes, saw bears and eagles, then camped. It began to snow. It snowed so hard that the next morning we had to dig our way out of our tent. That night we went to a motel on a Blackfoot Indian reservation and ate in the local restaurant, where I encountered something that has happened many times since: Native Americans assume that I am one of them. When I said I wasn't, they kept telling me I should not be ashamed of my heritage, and I kept explaining that I look like Jews from Kazan, who have some Tartar in them. Suddenly I understood something that happened to me on the way to Yellowstone when I was ten. When we stopped in Cheyenne, Wyoming, I went to use the bathroom, but the gas station attendant, who did not see my parents, told me, "We don't want you people using our bathrooms." I thought he meant Jews. Now suddenly it all made sense. He too thought I was an Indian.

We drove into the Canadian Rockies. The Trans-Canada Highway was two lanes and now it was elk-mating season. First we saw one, then another and then yet another, great confident creatures rippling along balancing their weight of candelabra antlers. Frequently cars and trucks were halted in both directions for a mile or two while a couple of bull elks met in the highway—a convenient empty spot—to bellow at each other and then to achieve thundering collision of bone on bone until one backed down. We went out in a skimobile onto a glacier. I was fascinated with glaciers, both the deep crevasses, the ice caves, the expanse of them and the sense that they were active and moving in their own geological time frame, and the runoff at the bottom of blue-green glacial milk, so cold it made my wrists and ankles ring like glass goblets when I tested those waters. I was smitten with everything I saw.

Driving across the continent in a Porsche loaded with several suitcases, a typewriter and computer paraphernalia, was driving several thousand miles hunched over with my chin bumping my knees. It was a condition of permanent backache, interrupted sporadically by bladder pain from the accident. I was always looking for cranberry juice—an exotic substance in those days which my doctor had told me would help bladder pain. Whenever I found any, I would buy several bottles, but there was little room in the car for even a box of tissues. Still, I was content. I was seeing the world, and I had always been ready to go off traveling at the faintest invitation. I was the navigator, as in my childhood.

When we finally got to San Francisco, we rented a two-room furnished apartment on North Point Street from an amateur landlord who looked like Commander Schweppes and lied constantly: a furnished apartment in which we camped in our sleeping bags among rolled-up rugs that were stored there and without any furniture for the first week. You must not imagine that neighborhood as it is now. The Cannery was not a mall but a tomato cannery. The Chocolate Factory contained no boutiques but made chocolate. Another cannery processed fish. A train ran up the center of North Point until the corner by our apartment and then switched to the street behind. Sometimes in the middle of the night, I would waken, sure a train was bearing down on me. Depending on the wind, the neighborhood smelled of chocolate, fish or tomato sauce. It was mixed racially and economically, Japanese, Chinese, Latino people, a few Afro-Americans and a fair-sized gay contingent. North Beach, the next neighborhood, was still predominantly Italian, and we ate a lot of panettone and cannoli. Up on Russian Hill, there were some expensive houses and apartments. Fisherman's Wharf was still a fishing wharf, although tourists came. We bought cooked crabs there, little shrimp and fish to panfry. Cost Plus was just one warehouse where we found cheap tchotchkes as presents and household furnishings. The washing machine was up on our roof. I would hang my clothes, looking at Alcatraz and the Golden Gate Bridge. Never before or since have I done the laundry as often or as sedulously as I did on North Point Street. I was infatuated with San Francisco. I made love to the city by walking.

Robert worked six days a week in Palo Alto. He was swallowed up by the project and I was free to write and to wander around. I soon began working as an artist's model, and I made friends with painters, poets, jazz musicians, writers—would-bes like myself. I had a whole set of separate friends and a life of my own. A Black jazz musician who lived up on Russian Hill in a room in a rambling falling-apart house where several musicians stayed would drop in on me and talk in a slow circling way about his life. It was from him I learned about Watts, where he grew up. He said L.A. was a city built on a sewer, and the sewer was going to explode. The shit, he said, is just going to bury them. Sometimes he would come with his saxophone and play for me.

Soon my Greek friend Sophia was sent out with her son to join Robert, but she could do much of the work in the apartment she rented—so we ran around the city together, guiltlessly. We made friends with keepers in the big cat house at the zoo, who had their own literary zine. John, who was short, black-haired with a pointy beard, was the friendliest. He wrote Beat poetry and loved the tigers. The lions, he said, were just too tame. There was no challenge. They would fuck at the drop of a hat and you became pals with them easily. The tigers were different. They were pussycats until adolescence and then he could not turn his back on them. They were moody and quick to attack. He admired their unwillingness to adjust to captivity. The leopards were harder to understand and read. He often could guess when a tiger was going to give him a hard time, but the leopards could fool him.

We had friends in the coffeehouses of North Beach. It felt as if everybody we fell into conversation with in a bar or at the Marina or in a bakery turned out to be poets or painters or dancers or actors or musicians. San Francisco had powerful energy. When I was not posing for artists, I wrote five to six hours a day. Afterward, friends came by to visit me or I walked miles or went off with Sophia on some adventure while her son was in school. I climbed every stairway on Russian Hill, on Telegraph Hill. I had the ambition of climbing every stairway in the city. Soon I knew almost as many people as I had in college. I was accepted by some other writers and no longer invisible.

In the evenings, when Robert came home, if he wasn't too tired, we tried restaurants (I was learning to cook, but the kitchen was elementary, just a corner of the living room), visited our favorite bars, listened to jazz, went to poetry readings and foreign films and the occasional opening of some artist we knew through the less successful ones who were friends. Usually Robert worked Saturdays, but sometimes he had weekends off or even a long weekend, when we did all the tourist stops: Yosemite, the redwoods, wine country, Monterey. We went into the hills sometimes for birding, for Robert was an avid life-list man, and had taught me to take an interest. I remember an afternoon in the coastal mountains watching vultures. Sometimes we would go as far as Castroville to bring home a bag of cheap artichokes, which I learned to cook four ways.

We drove down to Los Angeles with Sophia and her little boy. He had been promised Disney as a bribe for being pulled out of his school and hauled off to San Francisco for an indefinite and ever-expanding period of time. In Anaheim, it ashed, to our surprise, as it rains or snows other places. We stayed in a motel and called my brother, whom I had not seen in fourteen years. I'd received letters from him perhaps three times. He had divorced again, leaving his third wife and their two sons, whom I never did meet. Now he was with Lilly, a Chicana widow who had a house in the hills and four children, mostly adolescents, from her marriage. I was struck by her resemblance to our mother. We did not hit it off. Grant appeared with a thermos of premixed martinis and took us on a tour of Forest Lawn, which he thought extremely tasteful. He informed us there were no Blacks in Los Angeles. He was no longer working a dubious real estate business around Salton Lake—that polluted puddle of agricultural chemical runoff in the desert—but was a minor executive at Northrup. We also spent a day with my aunt Ruth, my youngest and favorite aunt, and her new husband, Eddie. That was easy for us—we clicked, we understood each other.

Robert and I developed a serious interest in wine. We tended to be systematic about any new interest, and we began reading about and sampling California and European wines, as well as methodical tasting at wineries. Robert started a cellar book, taking off the labels and writing notes on each wine we drank. We bought our first dishes, a black and white brush-stroke pattern that we found in a Japanese hardware store in Japantown. I was still smoking then, not yet having paid the price for the habit, so we were able to go to bars. The Buena Vista, now a tourist hangout, was then just a neighborhood bar featuring Irish coffee. I knew a pornographer who used his writing to support his passion for Japanese pots. He had a list of synonyms over the typewriter: *tits, boobs, peaches, pears, tomatoes, jugs,* etc. It was all according to a formula: the first sex scene starts on page five or six, then a threesome, then an orgy, and so on. He amused himself by working into the pages between the obligatory sex events (the lesbian, the sadomasochistic) satires on scenes he knew, and one of his recent books featured all the regulars from the Buena Vista. The San Remo was another neighborhood bar where we passed time.

Sophia and I used to sit in the sand at the little beach at the foot of Russian Hill, watching the freighters and tankers, the pleasure boats and the occasional cruise ship or liner. If it was too cold to sit in the sand by the Maritime Museum, we occupied places on the wide cement steps that looked to be bleachers but to observe what unlikely sporting event we never learned. A race of seals, who visited the docks often? The sea lions that populate the area today I never remember seeing there. I loved that disparate neighborhood.

I was utterly infatuated with San Francisco. I had never experienced anything like the light, the pastel houses marching up the steep hills, the grid pattern imposed on the rugged landscape. I was never looking straight ahead as in the Midwest, but I was forever looking up or down or into a far vista. I loved to watch the fog sweep in under the Golden Gate Bridge, the best view being from the roof where I hung my laundry. There was a lightness to the architecture, not just the carpenter Gothic one-story houses that seemed wooden jokes, enough froufrou on them to furnish out a three-story mansion, but the pastels of the buildings. Even the common use of gray on wood or stucco was a pale pastel gray, rather than the stone gray of Paris. The greenery felt to me at once manicured and lush—often trimmed to fit a narrow space but overflowing and ready to fill any vacant spot of ground.

Unlike the months in Cambridge, when everything I remember is with Robert, in San Francisco, most of my memories are with friends, artists I was modeling for, acquaintances I made as I explored the city. I saw far more of Sophia than of Robert. This was my first taste of middle-class life: enough to eat, wine to drink, a reasonably furnished clean apartment. I had never lived in such a place. It was tiny but modern, with plumbing that worked, no bugs, floors that did not sag or have holes in them, electricity that seemed to function very well indeed. I had an American Express credit card: I had never had a credit card. It seemed magical. Soon I had a couple of charge accounts at department stores.

I did not rush out and begin buying things madly, but we had come intending to stay only two or three months, and we ended up living there almost a year. We both needed clothes. I wore the first coat I ever bought new, an intense blue wool. If I wanted a book or a pair of gloves, I could buy them. I cannot overstate how incredible this felt, how luxurious, how delightful. I did not become a clotheshorse or a mad consumer, but I enjoyed my enablement. I did not mind the work I was doing, for ten dollars an hour seemed to me great pay and I was vain about my body. Modesty had eluded me. At that age, I was quite ready to drop my clothes and show off. It was, after all, the thing about me that had been most admired. I had plenty of time to write, and I did.

Mostly in trying to describe how it felt to have crept into the middle class I want you to understand that I felt free. Poverty is immensely constricting. If you feel a pain, the first thing that comes to mind is how much is it going to cost. There is no information available about options. If you go to a clinic, you lose an entire day waiting around, and often nothing happens. You never see the same doctor twice. So probably you don't do anything about the pain except take a cheap painkiller or get drunk. Dentistry options are worse, more demeaning, more painful.

If you need something, you do without something else. You are always trading off getting a winter coat against new boots or against paying an electric bill or eating sufficiently for a while. Nothing is ever simple and nothing is ever quick, except random violence. What you want, you will probably not get. If you do get it, it will be secondhand or cracked or an inferior rip-off that falls apart. The first twenty-five years of my life were unremittingly boxed in poverty. I liked being middle-class, I appreciated being middle-class, although I did not necessarily expect that it would last.

The apartment had a garage on the ground floor, but since it was rented out, Robert kept the Porsche on the street. One night a car slammed into the Porsche at the curb, smashing it up. Robert had it repaired, but he did not like the way it handled, so he sold it. He bought a Peugeot, in reaction. He had endured two accidents with the Porsche, and each had been expensive. He felt this family car, the Peugeot, was more appropriate. It was rather sedate, although it had a sunroof—which leaked whenever it rained, as it does rather a lot in San Francisco. I took driving lessons, so I could help drive back across country. I never became much of a driver. Learning to drive on the hills of San Francisco was a quixotic endeavor with a teacher from Texas who would keep saying when I made a mistake, "Your husband isn't going to like that," but I did finally get my license by some miracle of bureaucratic largesse.

My father stopped to see us on his way up to Redding, where he was working on a Westinghouse dam project for a couple of months. Near the end of his time in Redding, Mother flew out to Grant and Lilly in L.A., who then drove up to San Francisco with her. They stayed only briefly, but my mother and then both my parents remained for a week. I had not been around them much in a few years. I was struck by their relationship, how little interest they took one in the other. They seldom looked at each other. My father put down my mother and she was irritated by him. They had the habit of talking to me or to Robert at once about two different subjects, as if they had become so practiced at not hearing the other, they genuinely did not know when their spouse was speaking.

The apartment house was entered by unlocking a grill—like a gate that filled the space—instead of the sort of door I was used to in the East. It was built around a narrow open courtyard, apartments to the back and front. Ours faced the street, with the bedroom window on the courtyard. Next to the apartment house was a vacant lot where I noticed local people scavenging with baskets or bags, so I went exploring. Wild fennel grew in abundance. I took to gathering it and using it in my freshman cooking. Soon after we moved in, we began to be visited by a male Siamese who lived upstairs with a hairdresser. He would sometimes crawl in our screenless window that opened onto a fire escape, but mostly he would come to the door that opened to the courtyard stairs. He liked to climb in my lap while I wrote at the typewriter. He ate most any leftovers and always seemed to be hungry. He was, I would guess, two or three years old. He was a very passionate and demonstrative cat.

He started to show up at all hours. He was not in love with his owner but fell in love with us, as cats do. He was a seal point, lean, athletic in appearance and extremely affectionate. His owner called him some fake Chinese name like Foo Chow but we called him Oscar because he had demonstrated his fondness for King Oscar sardines when he came in the window during lunch. His wanting to be with us had nothing to do with feeding him, since usually I didn't, but his owner accused me of luring him away with tuna fish. The truth was, he just wanted affection and attention. Oscar had an unusually deep baritone. Further, the courtyard amplified his voice when his wishes were not granted. If he could not enter via the window, then he stood and bellowed in the hall until we let him in. His need to be with me was desperate.

Things went on in this way for a couple of months. The hairdresser was getting angrier and Oscar was getting more insistent on being with us. Finally I went upstairs with a checkbook and tried to buy him. The hairdresser quoted a ridiculous price, something like six hundred dollars. That was more than we had in our account. So we had to shut Oscar out, because we could not take him with us. I tried to work out a way to kidnap him and hide him at Sophia's, but the hairdresser knew we were leaving and locked Oscar inside, where he cried pitifully all day while the man was at work.

A phone call came from Henry. He was publishing the last issue of his little magazine and he had a space exactly 4200 words long that could contain something of mine. He had part of the novel I was working on and he said he would publish an excerpt if I could put one together in the next four days and send it. I did so. He called. He did not like the excerpt (it was later published elsewhere). He put together an excerpt of his own. He began to read it to me. I felt it was disjointed and gave a false impression of the protagonist and the book. He sent it off to me, I read it and thought the same. I produced another excerpt and sent it off special delivery. He did not like that one either. He accused me of lacking respect for him. Everyone in Chicago, he said, thought *his* excerpt splendid. I said, forget it. He said if I did not agree to his publishing the excerpt he had put together out of my novel, he would never speak to me again. I said, *so be it*. Robert became upset, because Henry was one of his best friends. Finally, I capitulated, telling myself it was a very small zine and almost nobody would read it. This was the last time I ever made such a compromise, and I regretted it intensely. I began to feel that Robert would always sacrifice me to a friend.

I had a decision to make. I did not know if I should go back east with Robert. I had made a life of my own in San Francisco. I could always work as an artist's model and I had lots of friends in the arts, far more interesting to me than the computer professionals we dealt with in Boston. There were men interested in me, although I had never let them express it. I had several close female friends. One was the wife of a painter I had sat for, not for money but because he wanted to paint my portrait. She wrote—another Iowa graduate—and we shared our work and our ambitions. Another was a woman I had known at Michigan in radical politics, now living in Berkeley. I liked Berkeley, but I liked my seedy hodgepodge neighborhood in San Francisco better. Robert and I were visiting her during the Cuban missile crisis, when we all were convinced we were on the verge of nuclear annihilation. She served a calf's brain cooked very nicely but served whole and cold, au vinaigrette, and I simply could not eat it. I have never been able to eat brains since, although when I was extremely poor in Chicago, I consumed all organ meats, whatever was cheapest. The calf's brain looked like a human brain to me, and I was too death haunted.

Staying would have meant breaking up with Robert. Our relationship was not particularly close. He had been brusque after I was injured in the automobile accident. My body was almost entirely healed, but I was a little dubious about the relationship long-term. It was not that any of the men tempted me. At that time in my life, I did not give a great deal of precedence to finding a man; they seemed to come along regularly as buses. What tempted me most was the idea of an independent life as myself, not as Mrs. Anything. I felt I had vanished into wifehood in my first marriage, driven into anonymity, and I feared the same thing would happen in my second in a more subtle way.

Still, the idea of being twice divorced by twenty-six was appalling. I felt I should give it another hard try. I loved him, I even liked him, in spite of not feeling close at the moment. In many ways we meshed well. The sex, when he was interested, was vigorous and frequent. He was very bright and we could communicate. He liked food and wine and he was vaguely political. He let me write. Yes, he enabled my writing. He understood how important that was to me. He was not interested in having children. We both had a way of getting fascinated with something and researching it together that was great fun. It meant we were always learning new things. I pondered my decision without discussing it with anyone, least of all with Robert. There are certain critical turning points in a life. I do not know what would have happened to me if I had stayed in San Francisco, but my life would have been entirely different. I would be someone else. I would have spent my life with other people than I did and written other novels and poems and been active in different causes and groups. I considered and considered, marching up and down Russian and Telegraph Hills, savoring my favorite staircases and my favorite vistas. I did not want to leave this place. I did not want to leave the life I had made for myself. Still, I told myself, if things don't work out with Robert, I can come back next year. I took having married Robert seriously, and I had not yet given it my full try. I quietly decided I would stay with him and return east. I would make the marriage work. I would show to my friends and myself that I could be married and make it good. It was important to me not to fail again. I was still feeling guilty about Michel, and I didn't need more angst. Surely I could manage to succeed as a wife.

In the meantime, his boss, Tom, who owned a male and a female Siamese, offered us a kitten from their first litter. We accepted at once. If we could not have Oscar, we would have a little Siamese female. She was waiting for us in a Boston suburb. Tom sent us a photo of the threesome, father, mother and our kitten. She looked almost pure white and extremely tiny.

I made one more attempt to carry off Oscar, who jumped up into my arms and clung to me, but I got caught by his owner as I was trying to sneak him down to Sophia's waiting car. It was hideously embarrassing. He threatened to call the police if I attempted again to steal his cat. After that I never saw Oscar outside. I felt very bad, as if I had seduced and abandoned him, but I could see no way to run away with him. He stayed and we drove across the States, to Boston.

CONCERNING THE MATHEMATICIAN

In the livingroom you are someplace else like a cat.
You go fathoms down into abstraction
where the pressure and the cold would squeeze the juice from my
*   tissues.*
The diving bell of your head descends.
You cut the murk and peer at luminous razorthin creatures who peer
*   back,*
creatures with eyes and ears sticking out of their backsides
lit up like skyscrapers or planes taking off.

You are at home, you nod, you take notes and pictures.
You surface with a matter-of-fact pout,
obscene and full of questions and shouting for supper.
You talk to me and I get the bends.
Your eyes are bright and curious as robins
and your hands and your chest where I lay my head are warm.

TEN

INTERLUDE: PHOTOGRAPHS

I *have a lot of photographs,* some in albums, a lot of them loose and fraying—one of those tasks I put on my computer's To Do list perhaps twenty times a year, to sort and put safely away. Several of the men I have been involved with took photographs of me, some compulsively, and Robert and I shot our cats often and friends and scenery. I sometimes use the camera for visual note taking when doing research for novels—for *Going Down Fast,* for instance, I shot many Chicago sites that figured in that novel. I also photographed some favorite spots that produced poems, like the Getty Tomb and the Sullivan buildings that are the basis for "Visiting a dead man on the summer day." I also used film to record scenes I needed for *City of Darkness, City of Light* and for *Gone to Soldiers* (England and France). Twice I have photographed Prague, the first time when I was there in 1968 on my way back from Cuba just ahead of the Soviet tanks; the second time when I was writing *He, She and It.*

When I was with Robert I took many photographs and also shared in the darkroom work. When he left, he took the equipment, and I never tried to develop or print again. Mostly I take photographs on research trips or when Ira needs publicity pictures. But I also photograph him for pleasure, and the garden, and the cats.

I hate to be photographed. For one thing, I do not photograph well.

The camera spreads out my face, emphasizing the peasant in me. I am not natural before a camera. I usually wear an expression that indicates how uncomfortable and how pestered I am. That is not endearing. Yet I treasure many photographs of others, especially those of my parents when they were young or when they were not so young but I was. I have written poems about some of these photographs. Whenever I look at the few pictures of my mother in her youth that I possess, my sense of how she was cheated of her potential, how she was stymied and stifled and starved of affection and pleasure and knowledge, cuts through me. I mourn her death but I also mourn her stunted and unfulfilled life.

I resemble my mother more as I age than I did when I was younger. Sometimes when I see a particular photograph now, that resemblance will startle and touch me. Then there is the throb of pity and nostalgic loss that lances through me when I look at photos of dead friends—Peter, who took his own life; Teddy, blown up in the town house explosion; friends dead of various accidents and cancers and AIDS, ripped away in youth or midlife. Then the album is a walk through a cemetery like those Italian ones I remember with the photos of the dead under glass in the headstones.

Photos are disconcerting to me because they appear to capture a moment but don't. There are photos of me with people arm in arm whom I cannot name and would not recognize as familiar if I saw them in the street, yet there I am chummy with them, as I am in other photos with friends who turned into betrayers. I feel there should be some miasma floating in the shot, some shadow falling over us, but no, we bear idiotic grins. There are photos in which I appear delighted, when I know I was in misery. There are photos with lovers that look like ads for the joy of heterosexual coupling, when I remember that we were engaged in a terminal quarrel. There are people who were and sometimes still are vitally important in my life, and yet I have no photos of them at all.

Yet for all the lies they tell, I would not do without them, for they do jog memory and they do transport me sometimes into the past. A song from a particular year will bring back the emotions of that year, flooding like alcohol into the brain. A photo doesn't do that, but it can be a way of entering the past, how we looked then, what we wore, how we carried ourselves. In photos of the 1960s, unless they were publicity shots, I am never alone. I am always in a group, a circle, a crowd, a youthful army.

There is a certain snapshot of Ira when we were first involved with each other but still also with other people, and I have only to look at it to remember how hopelessly and helplessly I loved then, never imagining we would be able ultimately to be together as we are. I remember love like the flu in my gut. My love for him now is calmer and surer and stronger, but it is not uninteresting to remember how I felt when our relationship was new and raw.

I have many pictures of my cats Arofa and Cho-Cho, who were both photogenic and early accustomed to posing for the camera. Jim Beam, who was close to psychotic, was also handsome. There are far more photos of him than of his sister Colette, who was my familiar, because he liked to be photographed. He viewed it as appropriate homage, whereas Colette hated the camera as much as I do—as much as I like the result of turning it on others.

I feel often we let our media come between us and experience. People who take too many photos on their travels may not have time and receptivity to experience fully what's in front of them when they are actually present. I encounter people for whom what is recorded on videotape is more real than what simply goes on. Sometimes when I am giving a reading or taking part in an event, I will be annoyed that the video crew and their lights and devices get in the way between the audience and my performance. The record of the event becomes preeminent, while the actual living event is shunted aside. Sometimes we seem to believe what the camera tells us before we believe what we ourselves experience.

I never want to be like that. I do not want even these snapshots to slip between me and my memory and impose what the camera saw for what I felt. So I am sharing some of these photos with you, but take them all with a pinch of skepticism. I am the storyteller. The camera is just a bystander to my life.

We believe strongly in the importance of surfaces. If someone has an almost perfect surface, they must be better than someone with pitted skin or a weak chin or bulbous nose. I do not love primarily with my eyes. I have had lovers who were gorgeous and lovers who were plain, who were skinny and neurasthenic, who were bulky and overweight. I have cared far more for how each of them treated me than for my eyes' pleasure.

I remember a poet I became involved with suddenly, after we had been friends for years. He saved me in a demonstration when I was about to be busted. I believe I used that in *Vida*. Afterward, we went back to the office of the zine we were both working on and fell into each other on the old couch there. It was the best sex we ever had with each other. He was a thick bearish man who liked to make love lying on his side, which was not a good position for me, and I became aware he liked thin very young women, so I gradually withdrew. We remained friends. But what I felt for him that day we made it on the couch could never be captured by any camera. So much of sex happens with the eyes closed and the flesh wide open.

BURNISHING MEMORY

I am learning how to remember
little colored crayon nubs of my childhood,
the sun coming through mason jars
of peaches still scalding from the canner,
the fat chalk the brakemen would throw
when we begged, perfect
for scrawling dirty words on sidewalks.

I save the newly found pieces of memory
like bright exotic stamps carefully put in
to the scrapbooks of a collection.
Unlike butterflies, collecting them
does not kill them, but captured,
saved, they become vibrant.
Soon they grow bigger.

I am building a simulacrum of my life
as untrue as maps. I remember when
I learned those red arteries and blue
veins of roads were just cement
or asphalt, not the scarlet road
I had imagined our car roaring over,
like the first time I heard the phrase "silk road."

So I am neglecting the vast hangars
full of nothing, the tunnels of boredom,
the days leaked out in classrooms
of despair, the banality of dusting.
Instead I build a tower of beautiful
junk, the blue sapphire glass of terror,
the winking red stars of sex, the purple

suns of transcendence, the white
light of insight flashing, the intricate
webs of belief and refusal, the homely
satisfying bricks of friendship, books
and recipes and yes, maps of places
I dreamed into being and inhabited
a season, a lifetime, a glimmering moment.

ELEVEN

A LIGHT APARTMENT
IN BROOKLINE

We found an unfurnished apartment on Egmont in Brookline, on the edge near Boston University and Commonwealth Avenue. Immediately we brought our Siamese kitten home. We were on the top floor of a yellow brick building with a parking lot and garages behind, a six-room apartment: one bedroom we shared, one was his study and one was mine. The rooms were large, light and airy. Robert announced that he would give me five years to establish myself as a writer, because the amount of money I could bring in was negligible and not worth the bother. I was very grateful and worked harder than ever at the marriage. I wanted him to be pleased with his choice.

What he did want was a comfortably appointed apartment—but not with much expenditure—and a gourmet cook. We furnished the apartment mostly out of Sunday want ads. I had six cookbooks by now. This was my period of great bread. I was home and I enjoyed the kneading, the rising, the entire process. I made challah, rye breads, cinnamon swirls, whole wheat, raisin bread, Swedish orange rye: if the cookbook gave the rule for it, I baked it.

I was part writer and part homemaker. I even polished floors and tiles. I was grateful to be given a chance to write and did not notice how much time my efforts to be the perfect wife used up. Still, I was dedicated to my new roles, and my writing career did not seem to be going anywhere fast. I had tried two agents without publishing more than the poetry I sent out myself and an occasional story in a literary journal. My novels were unpublished and seemed likely to remain that way. Making curtains was an escape from despair.

Our seal point Siamese kitten bonded with us quickly and from then on, she slept between us in bed, often on one of our pillows. She was delicate, quick and very bright. Robert named her Arofa—the Tahitian equivalent of the Hawaiian *aloha*. Nobody ever got it right in her seventeen years. She was a tiny kitten who grew into a small lithe cat, never gaining an extra ounce. Her frame was small, but her spirit large: she was fierce enough in her loyalties and her antagonisms to make up for her size.

I had never before had a cat truly mine, that I could treat as I chose. She received a huge amount of attention. When I walked, I took her along on a leash. She went down to the laundry room with me and up to the roof. It lacked the spectacular views offered by North Point Street, but I could see the Charles River and a good bit of Brookline and Boston. I wish my current house had a flat place on the roof so I could climb up and sit there, looking into the trees and over them to the hill and the marsh.

Arofa was attuned to us, alert and intelligent, strong willed but passionate to please. She would never do anything as stupid as jump off the roof or dash into the street. She was easy to train to walk on her leash and stay when commanded. She would taste anything and early developed a desire to have a little wine with her supper, just a lick or two, especially dry red wine.

I believe Robert was pleased with me. We were closer during the couple of years we lived there than we had been previously, or would be in the future. I found the novelty of behaving as a middle-class housewife somewhat entertaining. I worked my way through Julia Child and began to collect other cookbooks, as I still do, although my tastes these days are more for peasant than haute cuisine, and I cook mostly Mediterranean. I discovered a gift for cooking, an ability to grasp the fundamentals of a recipe, then to vary it and make it my own. I do not do a great many things well. I've never been able to muster the energy or discipline to play seriously at cards, chess, computer games. I think basically the peasant in me wants a product to emerge if I spend my time and energy on an operation. It can be a stew or a mousse, a poem or a story, a row of hollyhocks or a cabbage patch, but I want product. I loved to go to Haymarket and the North End and shop for good meat, the freshest artichokes and the crispest greens.

Our apartment was pleasant, although never fancy. No place I have lived has ever been elegant. The furniture is old and comfortable. Rugs provide the glamour. My infatuation with carpets began with an Oriental we purchased at a Sunday house sale. I still have it, in my office. We began collecting interesting items of decor, a few of them from Robert's time in the Pacific.

Robert had been working for IBM after college and had gotten engaged to a young woman with whom he seemed to have a rather chilly relationship. At one point, he felt bored, irritated, trapped—as had happened just before I met him. He had thrown up his job and set off to journey around the world. During the next year and a half, he spent time in Tahiti, New Caledonia, Borneo, Australia, New Zealand, Indonesia, Malaysia. Not long into his wandering, he joined another young man, Scotty, who rapidly became his best friend. They traveled together for a year and a half until finally Robert was recalled home by his fiancée, who demanded that their relationship be resolved, and also by a letter telling him about a new computer company. It would be run by computer types, not business types, and there would be great freedom of hours, of lifestyle. They would take only work they agreed was interesting.

Scotty continued his journey through Indochina, spending some months in Vietnam in 1962. He wrote long letters about the American presence and why he felt the Viet Cong had the allegiance of most ordinary people, especially in the countryside. He determined for Robert and me an early and continuing opposition to that war. Scotty went on to Japan. In photos, the two men resembled each other, both small, wiry, wearing glasses, with brown hair and a similar expression of guarded curiosity. Scotty had been the perfect companion for Robert.

Robert broke up with his fiancée and went to work for the new computer company, which he hoped would be more compatible with his creativity than IBM had been. They promised him freedom and that he could take leaves of absence between projects when he desired.

In Japan, Scotty began learning Japanese in an intensive course and studied Zen with a monk. He urged Robert to bring me and join him in Japan, which Robert planned to do the following spring. I am sure I was no more real to Scotty than he was to me, but he was very important to Robert, who viewed him as his other, better self. Scotty's letters came regularly, keeping us posted on his progress with Japanese kanji and Zen. I would never be the ideal traveling companion that Scotty had been—up for anything, ready to sleep on the deck of a junk or roll up in a sleeping bag in a doorway, ready to slog into the jungle and be sucked by leeches, ready to eat anything at any time and try to like it. Going to Japan to be with Scotty was not negotiable.

The worst aspect of that time in Brookline was being invisible as a writer. I can't forget the despair and hopelessness of those years, but I never stopped writing. My friends from college seemed to be leaping forward. Victor and Padma were hooked up with *The New Yorker;* David Newman was working for *Esquire.* Eric got his Ph.D. and went to work for IBM. Nadine, however, was locked up in a mental ward again.

I believed in myself, even if I was a minority of one. I had space and time to write, and I finished the third draft of the novel I had been working on, wrote a great deal of poetry that slowly but surely was getting published. I found the apartment luxurious—all that space only for me and Arofa during weekdays. She sat with me while I wrote, although at this stage of her life, she was too young and rambunctious to be the perfect writer's cat she would grow into. I played with her, rough and tumble games, games of skill, of leaping and climbing and chasing. We often took her with us when we went out socially. When we climbed Mount Monadnock, she climbed it with us, on her leash. No wonder she was a bright cat: she had the equipment and constant stimulating experiences.

The apartment, full of colorful Indian cottons and oak furniture, felt warm and open. We continued the study of wines we had begun in California. In those days, this was an easy matter. It was possible to drink great Bordeaux and great Burgundies for five to seven dollars a bottle. We found hundred-year-old prephylloxera Madeiras at four to five dollars a bottle. Our social life as a couple was typical of the times. Wives made elaborate dinners, husbands mixed and poured drinks and talked shop. My interest was more in the planning and preparing of the meal than it was in what transpired after the guests arrived.

In spite of not having a job, I did not write as rapidly as I had in San Francisco. I did not work weekends, because we often went off on excursions or entertained or were entertained. Guests came to stay with us. Gourmet cooking and shopping for it took time. All of this was interesting, but I kept having the sense I was not getting done what I should. I carefully resumed the discipline I found in San Francisco, and every day I worked for several hours straight. I was sure if I knew other writers and could exchange work with them, I would write faster and better. I sent writing through the mail to friends in New York and Ann Arbor, but their feedback could take months to reach me. I was convinced I needed closer stimulation.

Early in 1963 Henry—at whose apartment we had met in Chicago— arrived to visit and then to stay indefinitely with his younger wife, Sylvia. Before they arrived, I was excited and happy. I wrote thirty letters trying futilely to find Henry a job in the Boston area. He had been working for the post office but wanted to resume teaching English. I was delighted at the prospect of dealing with another writer regularly and having someone to exchange poems with, doing mutual critiques. Whatever I had lacked in Chicago, I did belong to a group of writers. Here nobody understood what I did or took an interest.

Henry arrived coldly angry with me. If I had admitted to being unhappy with Robert, he would have accepted the marriage, but I was absorbed in my life, narrow as it was. My poetry was rapidly improving, and so was my fiction. I was gradually learning to do more of what I wished I could. I just needed feedback.

He liked best to have long late-night sessions probing motives and rehashing Chicago. "You've sold out," he told me. "Sold out for bourgeois comfort. You're a kept woman." He jabbed at me, smoking cigarette after cigarette, stubbing the butts into ashtrays soon overflowing, into glasses and cups. Since he was also being "kept" by Robert at the moment, this hardly seemed fair.

"You live by the clock. You want to write us into your social calendar."

"I can't write a novel in odd moments. I have to put in hours every day."

He felt that my authentic self was the poor, needy and lonely woman he had been drawn to in Chicago, and this new competent and disciplined self was inauthentic. Since I pretty well liked bourgeois comfort, that accusation made me uneasy, but when I married Robert, he was deeply in debt and his prospects were wobbly and uncertain. I had little motivation to rehash Chicago. I was aware I had kept my burgeoning affair with Robert secret from Henry, that I had not been open or honest. I felt I had escaped Chicago with what I needed, the base of a good relationship, and there was little I wanted to subject to Henry's revision.

"You have shut all uncertainties out of your life." He thundered at me like an Old Testament prophet, like Ezra. Repent Ye Whore of Babylon. "You don't care about anybody else now."

Sylvia did not like me any more than she had in Chicago. However I spoke with her was wrong. I said the wrong words, used the wrong tone, ignored her or patronized her or pushed myself on her. She was in a difficult position—she was years younger than any of us, much less educated and experienced and dropped into a strange town where she knew no one except her brother, whom Robert had brought into the computer company as a trainee.

The situation with them grew tense. "You're fooling yourself," Henry said. "Love? You don't feel love for *him*." I had to be pining for Henry, and if I contradicted him, it was because I was in a state of denial. Sylvia was sure I wanted Henry. I had been close to Henry and dependent on him in Chicago. I had never loved him as I did Robert, but there was no way to convince him of that. I was rather annoyed that I had to try, daily, nightly, endlessly. He kept saying, "You're suppressing your true feelings."

My true feelings were that I was tired of cooking for them, cleaning up after them, having them in my space, experiencing their lack of respect for my work time and my need to concentrate. My true feelings were close to a desire for strangulation. This was the period when my zeal for housework dissolved and it has never returned. Finally I said to Robert that I was going to New York to stay with Vic and Padma Perera, and I wouldn't come back until the Chicago party had decamped. I took the next train to New York. Vic was a Guatemalan Jew and Padma was from India, but both wrote in English and were heavily involved with *The New Yorker*. I took the train to see them regularly, but this time was open-ended, and they were a little nonplussed. Robert called me forty-eight hours later to tell me Henry and Sylvia had cleared out. I was sorry I had lost a friend, but I was desperate for privacy, tired of being psychoanalyzed by an amateur and sick of being a target.

In July we went up to Maine for a total eclipse of the sun that we viewed from Great Moose Lake. Robert found the Maine woods boring—too much the same—but the eclipse moved both of us. I found it magical and holy. The extraordinary darkness with the effect of sunset all around, the whooshing in the trees, all lodged in my deepest imagination. That image of the sun occluded but with its mane of corona flaming out has asserted itself in my poetry several times. I can close my eyes and see it. I know a woman who pursues eclipses. She has enough money to go to as many as she pleases. I am not sure if I would do that, if I could. That experience feels so vivid and complete to me, I don't want anything to compare it to.

I am one of those people who remember exactly where they were when John Kennedy was assassinated, partly because of what followed. We were both home packing, for we were about to spend Thanksgiving with Robert's older brother, a statistician working in Schenectady in upstate New York. Then we were to see a friend of mine from Michigan, Eric, with whom I had edited the college literary magazine. Now he was working for IBM in Poughkeepsie, so he and Robert had more in common than most of my literary friends. We were stunned by the news. We didn't own a TV, but the woman across the hall did, and we watched the news on her set.

We drove to Schenectady with the car radio on, scarcely able to believe what had happened. I had worked on Kennedy's campaign in Chicago and had been struck by his impact on a crowd and the electricity that came with him into a room. I had mixed feelings about him as a president. I had found the Cuban missile crisis terrifying—machismo out of control—and I didn't think he was doing what he could on civil rights. I was appalled by our Vietnam policy. But I surely preferred him to Nixon 100 percent. It was one thing to have mixed reviews on his presidency and quite another to accept his assassination. It was a turning point in modern American political history, assassination as a recall device or a way of preventing someone with whom you disagreed from continuing or gaining power.

We arrived at his brother's house in a state of mild shock. Sandy was about ten inches taller than Robert and treated him with an air of jocular contempt that set my teeth on edge. We were walking in with our luggage when Sandy said, "Hey, isn't that too bad about your friend Scotty. What a huge accident."

That was how we learned that Scotty, along with several hundred Japanese, had been killed in a hideous railroad accident, when a crack express had cut right through a local train carrying commuters. There were two Americans among the six hundred or so killed, and Scotty was one of them. It had been on television.

I don't believe there was any malice in Robert's brother, only a lack of empathy, an inability to understand that Scotty and Robert had been intensely close and that Robert cared for him very deeply. Robert went into emotional shock, a zombie numbness I found terrifying. I had to get him out of there. He did not sleep at all but lay rigid that night in a kind of catatonia.

We spent the next couple of days in Eric's small Poughkeepsie apartment or in bars. We drank a lot and finally Robert was able to talk about Scotty. Scotty and Kennedy were somehow confounded into a dead martyr. Everything was changed for Robert, even as everything seemed to change in American politics. He was never able to cry, but finally he was able to talk. In my memory there is no snow but the light is gray, the wind is raw and always it is overcast and dank. All the bars we drank in blend into one dim hole where we cram into a booth. Eric was gentle and understanding to Robert. The days felt interminable and all I could do was hold him when he let me and try to get him to express his grief.

That winter we went to Ann Arbor and talked with political friends about Vietnam and the situation in the country. Afro-American friends were optimistic about Johnson, but I was less persuaded. I had been going to Ann Arbor a couple of times a year, but this time Robert went with me, because Scotty's death had made him feel he should do something political. My friends were starting Students for a Democratic Society, which grew into the largest and most visible antiwar and New Left group in the country—although at the time none of them knew that was what they were doing.

Ever since Scotty's death, Robert had been talking about going on an extended trip. He abandoned the idea of Japan. I suggested Greece. I was fascinated by Greek mythology, both the more conventional approaches and Jane Harrison's study of the chthonic elements. I am still an archaeology buff. In December, we began learning demotic Greek with the intention of leaving in the spring. I knew enough about Greek culture and politics to know that we had to learn demotic, not the artificial "purified" Katharevousa that was never the language of ordinary people. In January, Robert booked tickets on a Greek ocean liner sailing out of Boston, the *Vassiliki Frederiki*. We had a small private cabin well inside—not even a porthole. We were scheduled to depart in March.

Two weeks after Robert bought the tickets, we had a phone call from his mother. His father had met with an accident. He took the commuter train every day between Yonkers and Manhattan. That particular day while returning, he had dozed off. He wakened as the train was in the

Yonkers station and leaped out of his seat. The train was already beginning to pull out as he jumped off. He fell beneath the train and struck his head. As he lay unconscious, a second train ran over him and severed his legs.

I got on better with his father, the vice president of an engineering company, than I did with his mother, a housewife who had been a grade-school teacher until she had children. I could talk opera with the father. One of my Chicago boyfriends had been enamored of opera. We had gone to *Turandot* together and to *Don Giovanni* and *La Bohème*. We saw Robert's parents a few times a year, usually for an evening when we were in New York. It has always been the case that I have found the fathers of my husbands easier to please than their mothers. Although in general I get along with women better than with men, the same dynamic doesn't apply with in-laws. My fathers-in-law would get a twinkle in their eyes with me and there was always some rapport.

We drove to New York at once. Robert's father lay in the hospital bed, gray-faced, legless and in a coma, his head completely bandaged. Robert spoke to the doctors. He had enough scientific background—as did I— to understand that his father's brain had been largely destroyed, and he could not possibly regain meaningful consciousness. Robert's mother refused to accept this. She was buoyed up by stories of people who awoke from comas after days or months, and one of the nurses encouraged her belief. Robert found the sight of his helpless father being kept in a vegetative state on machines close to intolerable. Robert was at odds with his mother and the rest of his family, as was I, because we understood that his father was already gone.

Robert began to say to me that he was going to Greece regardless of what happened. He insisted we continue studying Greek and making preparations. We would leave our apartment as it was. One of his colleagues would take Arofa. We were leaving on the *Vassiliki Frederiki* as scheduled. I foresaw a terrible collision between Robert and his mother. It was fortunate for Robert that his father died just before we were to sail.

Every few years, in the time I was with Robert, he would grow seriously and vehemently unhappy with his situation. Often he dropped relation-

Arofa, Brooklyn, 1966.
Photograph by Robert Shapiro

ships completely, dropped projects, groups, commitments. Sometimes he left a job. Sometimes he left a city or a state or the country. It was his way of dealing with expectations that could not be met, with disappointments, with an intolerable feeling of being trapped. I would think twice now about going off for an indefinite period of time and leaving any animal in someone else's care, but I understood little then of how seriously a cat can take the departure of its person. Arofa was only a year and a month old when we left, and we assumed she would easily adjust to the people she was staying with.

Greece was my idea, and I liked it much better than Robert did. For the first time in his life, he developed serious allergies. He would not be free of them while we were together. I thought it might have something to do with being unable to mourn his father, whom he would not discuss. That was only a cheap guess. We had been close in Brookline, but in Greece, we were often distant. He was constantly comparing traveling with me to his backpack adventures with Scotty. Those had been realistically narrated to me when I first met him, but by now, they shone with the radiance of loss. The disagreements and discomforts vanished into the mythology of the perfect companion—which I was not. I liked comfort more than he did. I spoke Greek better and more readily. I could explain to the Greek peasants and shepherds and fishermen what I did—a poet was comprehensible. A systems analyst was not explicable in demotic Greek or probably in any form of Greek in 1964, and he often felt alienated. My knowledge of the mythology, history and archaeology made the landscape, ruins and artifacts meaningful. I had been dreaming the Mediterranean since I was sixteen. He was largely indifferent to the landscape, and increasingly to me.

Still, we had our adventures. We ferried to Crete and fell in love with it. Crete was wild then, not a tourist destination. We met and visited a peasant family in a little village called Ano Moulia in the mountains—Crete is a long skinny island that goes up to a ridge pole of mountains from sea level and then down again toward Africa. You pass bananas growing in the morning, and by noon, it's snow-capped peaks. We met the mother of the family on the road and gave her a ride in our VW rented in Iraklion. We came to know the family well. In that little village with the well at one end and the latrine at the other, I contracted a periodic form of paratyphoid that would not be recognized nor dealt with for months.

When we left Rhodes for Mykonos, a storm came up. The wind was howling, the ship was pitching and rolling and heaving as if about to break in two. The deck passengers had long since taken shelter in the salon, for waves were breaking high over the decks and sometimes we seemed entirely underwater. We came to know two Australian women when one of them passed out on me. They were deck passengers who had come inside. They were bold, up for any side trip, raunchy and delightful. Soon most of the crew was seasick, and so was Robert. I have no idea why I did not become sick in that storm. I was certainly frightened, but after a certain point of alarm, I tend to get hard and steely. When events pass into real danger, I turn clear and focused.

My father's side of the family, to which I feel so little connection, may have contributed something to me besides glaucoma: they were seafaring men. I saw a plaque in Canterbury Abbey to a Captain Piercy lost at sea. I was once told that a great-grandfather Piercy was accused of piracy. Perhaps in my own private mixed gene pool, there is something that makes me less prone to seasickness. At any rate, there were only five crew and me standing as the storm was at its peak, and I was pressed into service helping to batten things down, stow flying furniture and help those who thought they were dying.

At two in the morning we arrived off the harbor of Mykonos. The ship signaled and a little fishing boat chugged and bounced out. We were still bounding wildly, but passengers for Mykonos, including the two Australian women, Robert and myself, had to climb down a ladder. Then they threw our luggage on top of us, almost capsizing the fishing boat, and steamed away.

The next day, we were covered with livid bruises, from the luggage landing on us and probably from being flung about in the storm. On Mykonos the sun was shining in the morning from a sky as blue as hope and the light was creaking bright and dry on every windmill and dovecote adorned with the horns of the great goddess. Together the four of us walked and walked, picnicking and glorying in our survival. We heard that two boats had gone down in the storm.

I had begun collecting old Baedekers in San Francisco. For a couple of dollars I found guidebooks to the Austro-Hungarian Empire, to Bohemia, and to New York in 1890. They were far more detailed than anything produced since. But sometimes our information was a bit out-of-date. In the Peloponnisos, we spent four hours climbing the Akrocorinth, a great rock that sits over Corinth, crowned by the ruins of a temple of Aphrodite. We climbed hand over hand in the broiling sun, running out of water halfway up. It was a hard scramble, but we knew we would be rewarded by a great view from the deserted summit. When we reached the top, exhausted, the first thing we saw was not Aphrodite's temple, but a bus disgorging German tourists. A road had recently been built from the other side to the summit. A kiosk was selling refreshments and a sign advertised orange soda. We quenched our thirst and got a ride down.

Nearby on Greek Easter a middle-aged man (probably thirty-five and prematurely old from hard work) flagged us down on the road and brought us into his small house—little more than a two-room hut—to share their meal. They had killed the Paschal lamb, roasted potatoes with it and field greens. Since they had no refrigeration, it was a matter of eating the whole thing. It tasted great, but we got into trouble with the family patriarch. He had been in the States for twenty years in his youth, although he spoke little English by now, an enormous imposing mustachioed barrel of a man with bushy white hair and leathery skin and a tendency to bellow. He explained he had worked on the great bridge at what sounded like You-frens. We had no idea what he was talking about, and he became instantly suspicious of us, saying we could not be Americans if we didn't know about the great bridge at You-frens. I asked him to write it down (in Greek). Then I pretended to recognize it and asked him how hard it had been to build such a wonder. By then I had figured out he had worked on a railroad bridge in California. To him, it was one of the great engineering marvels of all time, and if I understood him correctly, two men had been killed in its construction. Stuffed and having reassured them we were real *amerikani,* we drove on. The next day, we ate at a castle in the bay, a former retirement home for executioners where the food was not nearly so good.

We were often traveling in extremely poor districts. Yet the American military presence was striking. The village women went about in eternal black, carrying bundles of sticks on their backs, but all the shepherds had transistor radios and listened to rock music, and the village boys who had gone into the army had the newest, fanciest weapons and trucks. Everywhere in Greece we found lean hungry half-feral cats who responded to a bit of food and a pat with utter ecstasy. I felt guilty before them and wondered about the cat we had left in Boston—but at least she would be sleek and well fed and pampered.

We went north to Epirus and stayed in Ioannina. Now we were to cross the Pindus Mountains—the backbone of this part of Greece—on the highway indicated on our tourist map. After we had been going for a couple of hours, it became clear that yes, someday there might be a highway, but at the moment we were on a one-way journey—there was no way to turn around—on what deteriorated into an unpaved road and then a cart track and then little more than a shepherd's path. Our car climbed boulders and forded gulleys and gushing streams. We went up and up and up past the tree line and then we ingloriously bumped down the other side. When we finally got to Thessaloniki, the VW Beetle was half destroyed. Our best times together were when we found ourselves in trouble. The sightseeing bored him, and then so did I.

Three months after we had come to Greece, we returned to Boston.

We were out of money. Robert was an extremely good poker player, and he managed to win enough on the trip back to tip everybody and pay what we had to—enough to get us home. Poker was one of his great useful gifts. Robert could do a great many things well. It enabled us to improvise when others had to plan. There was a streak of adventurer in him that meshed well with me.

We picked up Arofa immediately and were stunned. For the last month, she had refused to eat. She was skin over muscle and bone. Her eyes were glazed, but then fierce again. She recognized us immediately, and as soon as we got her to the apartment, she began to eat. She had gone on a hunger strike to bring us home. She was convinced it had worked. She was very happy.

AROFA

My little carry-on baggage,
my howler monkey, my blue
eyed sleek beige passion,
you want a monogamous relationship
with me. Othella, if you were
big as me you'd have nipped
my head off in a fit.
Gourmet, winebibber, you fancy
a good Bordeaux as much
as schlag, but would rather
be petted than eat.
You play Ivan the Terrible
to guests, you hiss and slap
at them to go away. Only
an occasional lover gains
your tolerance if my smell
rubs off on him and he
lets you sleep in the bed.

When I travel you hurtle
about upending the rugs.
When I return you run from me.
Not till I climb into bed
are you content and crouch
between my breasts kneading,
a calliope of purrs.

When I got a kitten a decade
and a half ago, I didn't know
I was being acquired
by such a demanding lover,
such a passionate, jealous,
furry, fussy wife.

TWELVE

HELLO CHO-CHO

*A*rofa was overjoyed we were back, but her pleasure took the form of being increasingly demanding. I read books on feline behavior while trying to get back into the novel I was endlessly rewriting. It was always coming back with letters of almost-made-it but no cigar. The solution to Arofa's boredom seemed to be to give her a companion kitten.

In early August, we went down to the Animal Rescue League. I hate those shelters that kill unwanted animals for the general public. I give to no-kill shelters. I know they are a luxury, but when you go into them, the atmosphere is completely different. The cats in the disposal shelters know what faces them: they know it very well. A tiny fluffy black and white kitten reached out of its cage and grabbed Robert by the arm. He named her Cho-Cho—*butterfly* in Japanese. He had just begun the study of Japanese when Scotty was killed. Cho-Cho-san was Madame Butterfly in Puccini's opera.

It turned out that Cho-Cho was sick—she had distemper, and Arofa, even though she had shots, caught it. The vet said that both cats would die. I force-fed them baby food mixed with water every two hours during the day, and set the alarm for the night feedings. They could not keep much down, and this went on for a week. I was so exhausted I could barely speak or function, but on the eighth day, they both ate a little tuna in water. I swore to them that if they would only live, every Saturday they would have tuna as a treat. To this day, long after Cho-Cho and Arofa have died, all my cats get tuna every Saturday morning. With five cats splitting a can, that isn't much, but they enjoy the ritual. I swear to you, although it defies logic, that at least one cat always knows when it's Saturday morning and she's entitled to tuna.

Cat and kitten slowly recovered. Cho-Cho may have been brain damaged by her early illness or she may just have been genetically predisposed to stupidity. Fortunately, she was beautiful. She grew into a long-haired tuxedo cat, probably a Maine coon to judge from the plume of her tail and her extraordinary ear and leg tufts and her gorgeous ruff. She was beautiful, vain and about as smart as a footstool. She was given to panics (thunder, loud noises, the vacuum cleaner) but at other times was placid in the face of things that should have alarmed her like strange dogs. She adopted Arofa as her mother, and Arofa tried to teach her manners and cat behavior. Her mew was a tiny high-pitched cry that only grew into a magnificent dramatic contralto when she was angry (and when she went into heat before we had her altered). Cho-Cho was far more attached to Arofa than Arofa to her, although they slept curled together. Cho-Cho was the cat visitors liked, because she circulated from person to person asking to be petted, and she was extremely pretty. Arofa developed a hostility toward visitors. She would bite guests if they tried to pet her, apparently believing any outsider might carry her off and imprison her for months. She had been a friendly kitten. Now she viewed every person who was not Robert or myself with intense suspicion.

Both cats were so photogenic that we took many photos. In the albums of those years, there are pictures of friends, some of each other or our travels, and many shots of Arofa and Cho-Cho playing on a ladder, watching the snow through the window, chasing toys or flies, curled up in a variety of positions. Cho-Cho slept on her back with her four paws in the air and her head flung back, as Malkah sometimes does but only when she is right next to me.

Cho-Cho never grew out of her kitten awkwardness. She was the only cat I have ever known who could run into a room and trip on the rug.

Arofa never broke anything unless she was angry. If we had gone off on a trip without her, often when we returned she would wait till she had our full attention, and then carefully knock a vase or a glass to the floor. Cho-Cho was always breaking things without meaning to, then looking astonished. She had such a sweet innocent face, it felt unfair to punish her for klutziness.

Some of my friends began to have children. Among the writers, mostly the men went on with their work while their wives cared for the offspring. Among my female friends, having a baby seemed to spell the end of whatever they had been doing previously. Robert did not want children, and neither did I. He wanted to be free to travel, and I wanted to be free to write. This further cut down on what I had in common with female friends—that and the fact that everyone seemed to come in couples, and few of the women besides Sophia were motivated to pursue female friendships that did not involve children or their husband's careers.

That year we went several times to Ann Arbor, where the VOICE chapter had been founded—the precursor to Students for a Democratic Society. The Port Huron Statement, that ode to participatory democracy, was our credo. I took the train to New York to see my agent and friends, to take part in an occasional demonstration against the war in Vietnam. I made new friends in Brooklyn, the writer Sol Yurick and his wife, Adrienne. Robert and Leslie Newman were living in a fancy apartment and trying to break into writing for the theater. Robert began to accompany me, as he found some of my new and old friends interesting. He was increasingly restless in Brookline.

Robert always said he worked best alone, but I did not over the years observe that to be true. When he worked alone, after a while he would begin to feel isolated and finally desperate. He seemed to work best not in a group, but with one other man. Around this time, he began working with a mathematician named Tole (pronounced to rhyme with Jolly) who lived in Philadelphia and was with a company based in New Jersey. Tole was a tall charismatic man with many interests. Born in Riga, Latvia, as a teenager he escaped from the Nazis. His mother got out ahead of him, to spend the war in Indonesia, where she learned Balinese dancing. He did not see her for years. He had no accent, a great deal of intelligence and charm. He, his wife and his two daughters lived in a rambling turn-of-the-century house in the Germantown neighborhood of Philadelphia. Their third daughter had been murdered. His wife had leukemia and grew sicker and sicker. After Robert began working with Tole, he was always going down to Philadelphia or Tole would come and stay with us. Robert and he would work, I would make dinner, we would socialize, Robert would go to bed and Tole and I would talk on for an hour or so. Tole was intelligent and read some literature and was knowledgeable about music, which made him more interesting than most of the people we dealt with socially. I was starved for communication. From college on, I wrote very long letters to friends, which I doubt they bothered to read. I was trying to fill in gaps in my life with friends located elsewhere.

Going to visit Tole in Philadelphia was bizarre and amusing. Around this time, he discovered the Beatles and began to proselytize everyone he knew. Taking their music seriously was a heretical view when they were considered teenage bubblegum music. At his house in Germantown, interesting music was always playing and interesting books lay around. His wife was now bedridden. His daughters, in grade school and middle school, took over the cooking. I especially remember breakfast oatmeal with half a jar of jam cooked into it.

I look back at myself then and in some ways I am the same person and in other ways, so different I have to work hard to cram myself back into my mind-set. I certainly loved and trusted Robert. Socially I was some-times stimulated and sometimes bored, but my major frustration was being unable to break through with my writing. I felt that Robert was deeply committed to the marriage and I certainly was. It never occurred to me to regret I had not stayed in San Francisco. I was proud of our funky comfortable light apartment and proud of Robert and our life. But I could not ignore signs of his discontent. He had rarely been happy since Scotty's death followed by his father's. His company had not turned out the way he had imagined it. They took on more and more contracts for money rather than scientific interest, and an increasing number were for the military. Crisis followed crisis. Because of too many contracts,

Cho-Cho, Brooklyn, 1967.

they had hired people without experience or talent, and the workplace was no longer an exciting ongoing seminar. It was just a job and a hectic one with too many overdue deadlines.

Around this time, the company was acquired by Tole's larger company. The upshot was that Robert managed to get transferred to New York. In the spring of 1965, we packed up the cats and our household. We found an affordable apartment in Brooklyn near Prospect Park in the area properly known as Adelphi, but usually considered part of Bedford-Stuyvesant.

We moved into a recently renovated town house, one of three owned by brothers. The basements were connected, as it had been one large house owned by the Pirie family, for whom a department store in Chicago was named. Robert had become fanatical about storing wine and bought a gas refrigerator which the brothers agreed could be installed in the base-ment. It was to avoid vibration while keeping wine at forty degrees. When the row houses were one mansion, Teddy Roosevelt had shot billiards in the carriage house in back, now full of the garbage of the ages. Between the rickety carriage house and the terrace of the ground-floor apartment was a small plot of land soon to become a battleground.

We became very close to Sol and Adrienne Yurick, who had just had a baby girl, and joined their circle of friends. Sol was a brilliant charismatic man with a dark beard, dark intense eyes, smoking incessantly and given to bodybuilding. When I had first met him, he had been unpublished except for a couple of stories—much like me. In the meantime, we had gone through all the excitement and disappointments with him of editors' flirtations and ultimate rejections. Robert and I read his novels in their various drafts and gave criticism, and he had read my work. Then *The Warriors* was accepted and there was even movie interest, although nothing came of it till years later. Then *Fertig* sold. Coover too was beginning to break through. I felt like the only failure in our small group. However, now I had regular contact with other writers and as much stimulation as I could reasonably endure. I felt if I could only find some way of opposing the war I would have all my ducks in a row.

The Brooklyn Botanic Garden was nearby. Many afternoons we walked there with the Yuricks, Adrienne pushing a carriage and then a stroller. We ambled under the allées of cherries in blossom drifting down, later the rose garden trellises arching over, blessing us with a litter of fragrant petals. The Japanese garden reminded me of the one in San Francisco where Sophia and I had spent hours. The Botanic Garden was a necessary relief to crowded dirty streets of brownstones where fires broke out every night and fights spilled into the streets.

Just as important as the Yuricks, on the ground floor were a couple, Felice and James. Felice and I were inseparable. We were both attracted to the burgeoning youth culture and began to dance together. We made friends with a Puerto Rican folksinger and her circle. She was bisexual and flirted with all of us. Felice and I wanted to oppose the war. We went to a demonstration sponsored by SDS in Washington and right afterward, we both joined. Although it was primarily a student organization, it seemed more compatible than anything else we could find. We launched what we called MDS—Movement for a Democratic Society, an adult chapter in Brooklyn. Our MDS became notorious because we started our meetings by eating together. Student meetings never started with food, but with grim speeches in cold church basements.

Felice and I were the same height, both of a body type much admired then. Now we would be urged to diet. We had womanly bodies, with busts and hips, well-defined waists, good muscular legs. We liked the same music—the Beatles and Bob Dylan. Motown, lots of R and B. We loved to dance. We needed something bigger and more political to connect to. Felice was far more seductive and flirtatious than I was—or am—and we were enchanted with each other. She was, I think, already growing bored with her marriage to a tall bearded man who worked in nonprofit radio and reviewed equipment and discs for high-fidelity magazines—as popular then as computer zines now. He had been born in Austria and had what I can only describe as a European sensibility: more formal, more restrained, cooler, with a knowledge of and appreciation for culture other than pop. In some ways, he reminded me of Michel, but he had a deeper understanding of the arts.

The rooms were small and narrow, but I had a study. Robert turned his into a darkroom, as he had become fascinated with photography. He had an office on Thirty-fourth and Seventh Avenue in a big old building where his company had taken a floor. This apartment was perhaps half the size of the Brookline apartment, darker and far noisier, markedly so in the summer. In my study, there was a fan that fit into the window. However, the fan swiveled. Cho-Cho figured out how to turn it, slip out and go down the fire escape. There were two problems with these nocturnal forays. First, she got into fights with neighborhood cats and had to have an abscess treated; second, the Indian couple who lived on the floor between us and James and Felice hated cats and threatened to kill her. She miscounted the floors—most cats can count up to five or so, but not Cho-Cho—and sometimes slipped back into their apartment instead of ours. We had to replace the fan with an air conditioner so that she could no longer sneak out.

The tiny yard was disputed space. A couple in the next building took to barbecuing in the yard, which filled all our apartments with noxious charcoal smoke as well as loud banal cocktail party chatter. To preempt the space, Felice and I started a garden, a few tomato plants, bush beans, marigolds, herbs. It was my first adult garden, the casual beginning of an obsession. We grew moonflowers on the fence, whose rich scent came out only at night. I spent far more time than Felice fiddling around in it, bringing the cats down with me. By now, Felice and I did our laundry together. One or the other cooked, and we all ate up or downstairs. They acquired a stray, a big brown tabby of amiable disposition who got on very well with our cats. Even Arofa cuddled with Sebastian and played with him up and down the narrow rooms and over the furniture. He was the size of both our cats put together, but he never dominated them, deferring to Arofa, who ruled the house.

Robert's mother had moved into an apartment on Long Island where we saw her every two weeks for supper. The relationship between Robert and his mother was neither easy nor close. He said little about himself in her presence, only mentioning achievements. She was lonely and bitterly unhappy, with a sense that life had betrayed her by taking her husband.

Felice and I were moving cautiously around the edges of what was becoming known as "the movement." When I look at my daybooks, I see that we had people over, went out to eat, went to hear music or see films or theater or went to meetings six nights out of seven. Often there are three appointments on a given day: lunch with someone, something in the afternoon or early evening, and something after that. No wonder my writing was proceeding slowly. Our social and meeting life ate up the hours.

I went to work for *Viet Report,* a periodical that covered all the information available on what was really happening in Vietnam. It was rather intellectual, and I was treated as a typist and phone answerer. I felt as invisible there as in much of the rest of my life, although the first-person reports of atrocities filled my head with nightmares. I gave my first poetry readings since college, mostly on the Angry Arts flatbed truck and at colleges, public libraries, wherever. I met Grace Paley at those antiwar readings and Robert Pinsky. At first I was so terrified, I had to memorize my political poems, because my hands shook too much to hold the paper. But delivering poems over hecklers and sometimes violent attacks makes for a performer who can project and emote. It was good training. I began to have a very small reputation and was interviewed by progressive newspapers and magazines. I was meeting other poets, giving readings with them occasionally, and included in anthologies. In 1966, I put together a collection of poems and sent it around. Around this time, I met the editors of *Hanging Loose* magazine, who were publishing me regularly. Soon those four poets—the editors of the magazine—and I regularly read together.

That winter, Robert was in an accident in Tole's car. Near the New Jersey office, an oncoming car skidded on ice and hit them head-on. Robert had a mild concussion, sore ribs and a torn ligament in his leg that laid him up for some time. Unfortunately, a couple of days after he had gone to bed sodden with painkillers, a friend was leaving the country. He had a rabbit that Sophia had offered to take. Sophia and her son arrived on Saturday. That evening, she and I went into Manhattan to fetch the rabbit. Once again, I was putting everything ahead of my writing.

When we arrived, I found my lackadaisical friend had neglected to do anything about his cat, Jane. Sophia said she would take care of Jane and the rabbit. We returned with the rabbit and two cats to the apartment where Robert was sleeping. Then it started. Parades of animals. Animals on every chair, flights of enraged and frightened cats, pursuit of cats by sex-crazed huge white rabbit, dropping little raisiny turds all over the carpets, all over the floors, in the closets, in my shoes. Yowls and hisses and busy white rabbit, big white rabbit, tireless hippity-hopping white rabbit eating and shitting little raisins everyplace and always after the cats. At one point Robert woke from a deep concussion-shaded sleep and screamed, "There's a rabbit in my bed!" There was.

Robert's leg healed slowly. He felt isolated and disconsolate. He would complain that no one understood his work, that it was too obscure. I reminded him that he made no attempt to explain it. That is never easy for scientists. A friend of mine who won a Nobel Prize in genetics has something of the same habit. When I first met him, I asked him what he did, and he told me he raised fruit flies. Robert had a coy somewhat condescending attitude when asked about his work. He was ambivalent; he enjoyed his work, but he resented it. Every so often he would withdraw from everyone, including me. He would not talk but would shut the door of his room and play the flute. He had an expensive silver flute but played it badly. It was agony for the cats and me, when he withdrew and tootled disconsolately all day. I had ways of trying to break through (food, sex, flattery, confrontation) but none of them worked when he was not ready to let them.

I became friends with a poet who was studying at Iowa, an old friend of Felice's. His girlfriend had been going to school in England. She had grown up in a colony of once-German Christians—the Christian communist sort of community that shares everything and scorns the state and war and money—now settled in the jungle in Paraguay. She was strongly opposed to the war in Vietnam for religious reasons and had, during a church service in a cathedral, thrown sheep's blood on the prime minister. She was wanted by Interpol. We hid her for a few months.

Once when she got stir-crazy from being confined to our two apartments, Felice and I took her to the Bronx Zoo, to what we hoped would be a safe and pleasant outing. It was fine in the monkey house. She told us which kinds were good to eat, which seemed callous, for monkeys are too childlike. The danger came when we entered the reptile house. When she saw the big boa constrictors, she broke down and began to weep. Her family captured them as a way of making a living for their colony, and some became pets. Suddenly she was dreadfully homesick and dangerously visible, attracting attention, a tall woman with long blond braids, a bit like Brunhilde, leaning over the pit of somnolent huge boa constrictors, crying her eyes out and calling to them. We had to get her out fast.

That fall, Felice and I shopped for the new minidresses and shortened our old dresses. That is, Felice did the sewing. She was amazing with making over dresses, sewing curtains and covers for our bench. I would start a project, knowing what would happen. She would watch me ineptly poke at the cloth with a needle, stabbing myself and making wild jagged stitches. Then she would take it away from me and finish it, quickly and well. Ah, those were the days. Now if a button needs sewing on, it sits there for six months before I manage it—sloppily.

In December, Felice, James, Robert and I went out to an SDS conference and then to Iowa, where our poet-friend was in graduate school and active in the SDS chapter. We came back through Chicago, where I needed to do on-site research for my next novel. I had thought we would stay with friends of mine from Chicago, but they—both academics, and moving up in their careers—were appalled by the idea of me arriving with two friends to sleep on their floor. This was the first time I alienated old friends with my new movement lifestyle. It was not the last. Basically that year and the next, all my old Ann Arbor and Chicago friends bailed out when I arrived, en masse or just my new hyperpolitical self. I was becoming monomaniacally engaged. Images of the war and of atrocities haunted me. I could not get them out of my mind. I was more impassioned about politics than about my writing. The war had to be stopped, and any moment not devoted to that end produced guilt. Villagers were dying, and in my waking and sleeping mind, they burned alive, soldiers on both sides lay maimed and broken, young men were being drafted and it was all wrong: they were dying for a lie. I could smell bodies burning in my sleep.

Felice and I finally found niches. Felice became involved in the coalition group called generally Mobe, or the Mobilization, that organized big demonstrations in New York. She was suddenly well connected and useful. I had been running to Ann Arbor regularly. As a project of our MDS group, we brought two brilliant committed young men, Mike and Peter, from Ann Arbor to New York. They were going to do power structure research, and I would learn how to do it with them. We had to figure out how our country had gone so far astray as to invade a small poor country where we maintained in power a corrupt and unpopular regime at huge cost to ourselves and far worse cost to the Vietnamese. It was a situation in which the more I learned about what was really going on, the more I needed to try to change it.

Robert was becoming tight friends with an underground filmmaker, Popov, a programmer in the New York office. Because of noise in the apartment—radios, sirens, fights, TV—I began going into Manhattan with Robert and writing in an empty office. I too got to know Popov and through him, a whole network of young people in the underground film scene or the happenings scene. What finished me with happenings was an event where a live chicken was bashed to death two feet from me, so I was splattered with blood.

Popov was always falling in love, then becoming disillusioned and dropping the woman. He went through half my friends in the time I knew him. The woman would never understand, because he didn't seem a casual seducer. He came on like the love of her life. Then in a week or a month, he woke up, saw she wasn't the complete answer to his fantasies and vanished. As long as I could put up with this, he was a charming companion. We flirted endlessly and we argued and chatted and told stories. He was a fine raconteur, observant of others, being small, slight of build and something of a con man. He did not like to work too much or too hard, so he had perfected ways of sneaking out of the office while appearing only to be away from his desk. Always work was spread out and his coat on the back of his chair, even when he was off in the Poconos hiking or in some new sweetie's bed or south of Houston at a shoot of someone's indie movie. Robert was fascinated by Popov's life, and we spent a great deal of time with him, Robert more than I. It was interesting for me to watch Sol and Popov together, for everything about them—from their philosophy of life, what was important to how to get it, how to present themselves, how to respond to trouble or danger—was at odds. I called them the champion and the hustler and enjoyed their sparring.

At a party up near Columbia given by an ex-girlfriend of Popov, my relationship with Robert changed permanently and my own sexual life for the next fifteen years as well. I opened the door of a bedroom, looking for the bathroom and found Robert with another woman, the ex-girlfriend whose party it was. Her blouse was off and her small breasts stuck up as he caressed her, the light from the bedside lamp illuminating him. His pants were unzipped. They were not yet having sex but clearly more than halfway there. That night he told me that he wanted an open relationship. He could no longer endure being involved with just me; it was not interesting enough. To remain sexually alive, he needed to have adventures with other women.

It took me a while to formulate a response. I was devastated. He kept insisting the marriage was not over, but he was just making sure it would last by meeting his needs. At that time, men's hair was growing longer, women's skirts were growing shorter, rock music pounded everywhere and the world seemed in a springtime of desire, of possibilities opening like new leaves in the ferment of new ways of doing everything. He was fascinated by all the apparently available women he met, especially through the independent filmmaking world. I ran off to Felice to tell her how my life had unraveled. I had not cried with Robert, but I cried in Felice's arms, and she comforted me. She suggested a positive spin, seeing it as liberation and wondering if she could talk her husband into the same thing. For the rest of that weekend, Robert and I argued without reaching an agreement. Walking in on him shocked me: I had not seen it coming. Actually I had never had the experience before of a man I was involved with going after someone else. I had never been cheated on; but I remembered that my last summer with Michel, when he would not talk about our marriage and I knew it was over, I had entered a relationship with another writer. I felt this was a payback, in that realm of the psyche where old bad deeds gather interest.

Finally I said that if he wanted it, then we would have an open marriage. We sat at the kitchen table. How many important and devastating scenes in my life have occurred at kitchen or dining room tables. I told him that I would not be interested in one-night stands. "If I make relationships with other people, they will be real relationships, they'll be loving and committed." He said, *fine*. I don't think he believed that I would become involved with anyone else, not really.

I became even closer to Felice, a conspiracy of two. I had no idea how to respond to what had happened. I don't remember the young women Robert was involved with that spring and summer. They came and went like movies that play for a week or two, then vanish. I remember only my intense frustration.

A correspondent from a British radical newspaper came to interview me in Brooklyn. I was so thrilled, I made him a sumptuous lunch. First course was an artichoke with hollandaise sauce. Since my original encounter with an artichoke in Paris at the Schiff flat, I had developed a great fondness for them. The Brit had at it without breaking his stream of anecdotes of famous people he had interviewed and scenes he had witnessed. He took a knife and fork, sliced the artichoke and ate it whole, choke and all, before I could say anything.

I realize in looking back that he was interested in me, but I didn't notice.

Although I was presumably open to relationships to balance Robert's adventures, I was out of practice and probably reluctant. I did not notice half the time if men were interested; when Felice wasn't there to point them out to me, I would miss the cues. I had thought I was done with all that. Robert's idea was that we should not even say we were married, as marriage was an inconvenient state if you were looking to pursue other people. He took off his ring. They were handsome rings of white gold over a silver base—what the jeweler who made them for us called a marriage of metals. A sign was carved into the ring that showed oxidized black against the white gold, a Japanese character for love. I still wore my ring, although occasionally friends or lovers in the next years would ask me why: it was a warning that I had a prior commitment, that I was not unattached. I might add commitments, but I was not about to let go of my older ones. I would try to live that way. I thought, when you get a second cat, you don't stop loving the first. Why shouldn't it be that way with people? But it was all hypothetical. I had more friends than at any time since Ann Arbor, but usually the men were involved with women I knew or gay or primarily friends of Robert's and not about to launch an intimate relationship with me.

What the change did was bring me into a much closer relationship with Felice and other women friends. I was no longer quite married but sort of semiattached, semidetached. I went through a period of restive insomnia. Somewhere in my mind I felt I must have been asleep not to have noticed what was happening with Robert, so perhaps I was afraid to sleep. Felice and I hung out with her musician friend on the Lower East Side; we went to demonstrations together in New York and in Washington; we went to meetings, we joined groups and worked together; we did all our wifely chores together; we conspired and confided and plotted. We experimented with drugs, cautiously. We attended *Marat/Sade* and rock concerts. Felice was restless in her marriage, for she complained that her husband was settling prematurely into middle age. She alternated between tremendous energy and the conviction she could accomplish anything and periods of sulking withdrawal and collapse. I learned later that her mother had been diagnosed bipolar, what they called then manic-depressive. I was certainly closer emotionally to Felice than I was to Robert, who was wrapped up in his work and his adventures. Robert and I got along, we did things together, we talked amiably, we made love, although not as often. We had the same frenetic social life we had kept up since moving to Brooklyn. But if I had something intimate to say about my feelings, my desires, my fears, I ran to Felice. I trusted her more than I trusted him. She envied my writing, but I admired her greater facility to get what she wanted from people. I thought her much more competent in daily life than I was.

Slowly I began to emerge a little as a writer. I had a story in the *Paris Review* and another in an anthology, *The Bold New Women*. During this Brooklyn period, Arofa became a writer's cat. She spent hours with me when I wrote, but she no longer interrupted. Sometimes she would sit on my lap while I typed and sometimes she would sit on the window ledge or the desk, watching. She was almost always with me, but unobtrusively, for she knew when I took a break she would get first-class attention. Despairing of the autobiographical novel ever being published, I began a new novel, set during urban renewal and the beginnings of Black Power in Chicago. It was more overtly political and far less feminist than my previous novel, drawing on my political experiences in Chicago. I also used my earlier passion for the blues. It was a different kind of novel than I had written before, in alternating viewpoints, with several important male characters. It progressed slowly because I was involved in so many other things, but it went forward with a kind of surprising authority, because I knew very well the material I was writing about. I gave poetry readings and moved over to a more professional literary agent, whose willingness to try to sell my work lifted my spirits. My situation as a writer no longer felt entirely bleak and without hope. The glacier had moved a bit.

CHO-CHO

At the Animal Disposal League
you reached through the bars
avid to live. Discarded offspring
of Maine coon cat,

your hunger saved you,
fuzzy and fist-sized.

Now you are sunny, opaque,
utterly beyond words, alien
as the dreams of a pine tree.
Sometimes when I look at you
you purr as if stroked.
Outside you turn your head
pretending not to see me
off on business, a rabbit
in the marshgrass, rendezvous
in the briars. In the house
you're a sponge for love,
a recirculating fountain.

Angry, you sulk way under
a bed till dragged out whining,
you permit yourself to be
captured and saved. You blink
then your goldengreen eyes
purr and collapse on your back
with paws up and your snowy
white belly exposed all curls
to the plume of your tail.
Ravish me, you say, with kisses
and tunafish because I know
how to accept pleasure. I am
your happy longhaired
id, taking the moment as I
do your finger in my mouth
without breaking its skin,
or eviscerating it instantly
like a mouse.

THIRTEEN

MANHATTAN TRANSFER

*P*eter and *Mike* from *Ann Arbor* along with some people already in New York, including me, founded the North American Congress on Latin America—which incidentally is still flourishing. I learned power structure research: who actually owned corporations and banks and ran them; how government and industry and other institutions—universities, foundations—interconnected; how the interests of important industries and corporations influenced government policy—starting with the invasion of the Dominican Republic. NACLA actually had a place for me and real political work I could do. Soon we were busy researching CIA penetration of cultural and educational organizations and feeding that information to sympathetic journalists, one of whom was speedily fired as a result of our work. I was good at power structure research and more important, I could write up our findings so that people in the larger movement could understand them. But this kind of work made me paranoid. I was a little crazy while I was doing it, fanatically political, and I developed an intense hatred for certain powerful people. It was the kind of work that, long term, required someone less emotional and less imaginative than myself, in order to do it well and not become mired in nightmares of the misuse of power and the suffering of millions of those upon whom corporate and governmental decisions were visited.

Felice was increasingly dissatisfied with her marriage and her domestic life. She condemned herself for marrying too young. She felt her husband was insufficiently open, insufficiently political by our new standards, but most important she had lost sexual and romantic interest in him and was fascinated by the radical longhaired young men she was meeting. She wanted out. I was as upset as her husband, because while she was leaving him, she was also leaving me. We would be friends, but we would not live our lives in common in the same daily way, would not eat together, share clothes and our quiet moments, household tasks and late-night mull-overs. I wondered whether, if her husband had been willing to try an open relationship such as I was striving to make work with Robert, she would have stayed. She did not deny she was leaving me as well as James, but insisted she needed more freedom from both of us. I was puzzled and shocked, for I did not see how our friendship confined her. I felt there must be something deeply wrong with me, that first Louise, then Robert and now Felice, the people I had been closest to, all felt the need to withdraw at least partially. She left for Manhattan and took Sebastian with her.

Half the people we knew were in open relationships by now. Those who weren't were either older married people (and many of them also were trying experimental openness) or had no relationships to be open about. We had contempt for the standard pattern of serial monogamy, discarding one partner when you were attracted to another, and we believed in honesty, not in having clandestine affairs. We believed we were making a new world in every way, on every level. Nothing could be taken for granted. We considered the nuclear family an abomination and a prison, a breeding ground of bad attitudes. We were going to do much better, starting right away.

Felice became involved with a painter active in Angry Arts, an attachment that lasted a few months. I was immersed in NACLA. I worked closely with a woman from the South whom I grew fond of. Call her Ceci. Of course Popov fell in love with her, had a brief affair and dumped her. I was getting sick of this. He was forever finding excuses to touch me, flirted endlessly, once in midnight intensity blurted that he loved only me. I did not for a minute believe him, but I decided he would do for my first outside relationship, as a foot in the waters of affairs. Felice encouraged me. He fled. So much for that. I was everybody's mama. I cooked for half the people we knew, stayed up all night listening to their problems, held their secrets and their hands, nursed and analyzed and played matchmaker. I was a general resource for everyone but myself.

Felice and I produced the SDS radio program on the Pacifica station for some months. We discovered at once that we shared a dreadful mannerism: an apologetic feminine giggle that undercut the seriousness of what we were saying. Neither of us had ever been aware of this little laugh that said, don't take me seriously, don't mind me, don't crush me. We both went to work on getting rid of it. I also noticed my voice rose into a meek breathy treble when I was nervous or excited, and I practiced to rid myself of that habit—which improved my reading style. I was working on the Chicago novel, which now had a title, *Going Down Fast,* but everything else came first, my political work, fussing over friends, taking care of Robert and everyone else. I completed a draft, but revisions crept along.

Then in the summer of 1967, Wesleyan University Press accepted a book of my poetry that became *Breaking Camp*. They did not bring it out for almost two years, as it made its slow way through the prepublication process. Suddenly I was no longer an unpublished author but a soon-to-be-published poet. Whenever I had a poem accepted by a zine, my bio said that my first book of poetry was coming out from Wesleyan in spring 1969. In the interim, I took out the weaker poems and put in newer, stronger poems. I cannot overstate how much that acceptance meant. I had been calling myself a writer but had no credentials. Now I had them.

Robert told me one morning he wanted to move into Manhattan. Where we were living was becoming untenable. I had gotten along with our neighbors in the Afro-American and Haitian neighborhood until recently, when things got hot and nasty. The racial tension ratcheted up to the breaking point. Walking from the subway to the apartment was navigating a minefield. Guys from the block would slam into me and once knocked me down. Police helicopters hung over the buildings just above roof level, deafening us and making everyone half crazed with the noise. We knew we could not stay.

We had not been apartment hunting long when we stumbled into a big six-room apartment on Ninety-eighth and Broadway, on the fourteenth floor. It was light and just as big as the lamented Brookline apartment. It was forty more a month than we were paying, and we would have to rent a parking space in a garage as well, but I was going to NACLA almost every day, a long subway ride, and spending a lot on cabs coming back to Brooklyn late at night. We took the apartment but before we moved in, sanded years of crud from the parquet floors and refinished them, a hideous job I would never undertake again. Now I lived within easy walking distance of NACLA. Ceci and I, keepers of the database, were only two blocks apart. We did our political work, we danced, we often ate together, we gossiped and commiserated and played with the cats. She was a good friend but never the intimate, quasi-sister of my dreams that Felice had been and sometimes still was.

I worked closely with a tall somber young man, Peter. He was extremely bright, extremely unhappy, lonely. I played an older sister role with him socially, but in researching and writing, we were equals and a powerful and dynamic team. He semi-lived with us, but he was also close to Felice, to the Yuricks. I had never before collaborated with anyone the way Peter and I researched, wrote and presented together. It was electrical. Peter was large boned with dark brown eyes and hair. He was pleasant-looking but did not think so. He was riddled with self-hatred and self-doubt, awkward, a brilliant overgrown miserable boy. He was always being taken under someone's wing and then feeling betrayed, undervalued. I was sure our relationship would be different.

I can only try to convey what it was like in New York in the movement from 1966 to 1968. Sometimes it was like a medieval fair. Central Park would be filled with people in bright costumes, tiny miniskirts like flags, long dresses of velvet, patchwork, costumes put together of upholstery material or quilts, jugglers, musicians, people dancing, street theater and puppet shows. If you had food, you shared it, often with strangers.

"There are no strangers" was our motto, before the Nixon administration made that nonsense by sending infiltrators and agents provocateurs into the movement to help make it nasty and dangerous. People made a big distinction between hippies and politicos, but we overlapped.

Nonetheless, there was danger then from the drugs that freely flowed from hand to hand and burnt out people's brains or rendered them paranoid. Danger from the police attacks on demonstrators, from being clubbed or gassed. Danger from the real possibility of going to jail for taking action against the war. We were paranoid about having phones tapped, being followed, all of which was real, as I discovered when we took my old desk apart to move it and found a bug in it. Long before that, the Dominican super warned me about a mail cover, about a live tap. Danger from the obscene drawings and death threats from the militia, the armed right, that came in my mail.

I was alone only when I wrote. This was life with the intensity dial turned as high as it could go. Intense friendships, intense sex, intense politics, intense pleasures and intense terrors. It was life lived fully in public. Privacy was a momentary thing. It was community as I have never experienced it before or since. It was living with passion. It was a wild searing hope for a better world that seemed almost within reach if only we worked harder, pushed harder, took more chances. It was the illusion that the world was changing, had changed, that we were everywhere and would prevail. The world was indeed changing, but not in ways we envisioned.

Twiggy might be the official fashion ideal, but R. Crumb's zaftig women were far more liked by people I knew. There was a general tolerance for different body types. We placed far more emphasis on values (although hardly what's called family values now), character, courage and trustworthiness. Anybody could get laid, and did. If you were hungry, somebody would feed you. If you needed a place to sleep, somebody would provide a couch or a spot on their floor (often me). If you needed to be kept hidden, you would be. Hitchhiking was as common as taking a bus. We all picked up hitchhikers. (I try to remember when I stopped. Around 1980? I never pick up hitchhikers now. Like every woman I know, I would be afraid to.) It was in so many respects a different world.

Arofa and Cho-Cho liked the new apartment, though they could no longer go out. It was twice the size of the Brooklyn apartment. Off the left of the big foyer was a narrow hall leading to our bedroom and my office, with an elderly black daybed in it for guests. Straight ahead off the foyer were the enormous living room and dining room, connected by a broad arch so that they were almost one room with windows on three sides. The small dark kitchen came off the foyer on the right side. Beyond were a maid's room, where Robert kept our wine and a guest bed, and a smaller bathroom. There were wide window ledges for the cats to sun on, high ceilings offering places to climb up and leap down, a loop from the living room through the dining room through the kitchen and back to the hall again where they could chase each other, marvelous shiny floors to skid on, myriad places to hide. It was the ultimate cat apartment as well as the ultimate party apartment. I gave a great many parties. At big parties, I liked a mix of political, arty and literary, academic and unclassifiable people with a lot of food and drink and dancing, always dancing. A lot to drink then meant wine and beer. None of the younger people drank what they called booze.

I remember a birthday party Popov threw for me at his Riverside Drive apartment. A rumor had gone through youth culture that smoking banana peels could make you high, so a friend arrived with a case of bananas. We were drying the peels and baking them in the oven so people could smoke them. That left a lot of peeled bananas, so I sent Peter out for rum and started making banana daiquiris. People were soon saying that smoking the bananas was great. Everybody got silly and loose. I realized that the bananas weren't doing anything, but the daiquiris were. People had so little experience of drinking liquor then that it did not occur to them that they were simply getting drunk.

The cats liked the space, the airiness, the sun. About another change, they each felt differently. Having a big apartment during the late 1960s meant that you put people up. We always had other people living with us: sometimes one person, sometimes a couple, sometimes several people, together or separately camping in our guest room, the dining room, the living room, my study. Some people stayed a night or two. Some much longer. We had one couple with us for several months, Jeff and Alice who came to New York from Texas to start an alternative newspaper (which I named *The Rat*). My mama aura grew. Our dining room table had extra leaves, accommodating up to twelve. Usually there were at least eight for dinner. I grew accomplished at stretching food and cooking stews, casseroles, pot roasts, hearty soups. Truly, it didn't take as much time to feed eight on lamb stew as it did to cook a gourmet meal every night, as I had in Brookline. That was lucky, because I had little time. Robert liked having a crowd always around us, for he never felt lonely and always there was someone to talk with, to go to a movie or a bar or on a walk.

Robert was always a very generous man, generous in giving to me, to others, in sharing whatever we had with friends and people who needed something. It was a wonderful characteristic. He was certainly the most generous man I have ever been with, and I admired that. It was one reason we were able to live in such a wide-open way. He never begrudged what he had that others needed, and he enjoyed sharing. He also had an endearing silly side. I remember once after a bottle of champagne, he was playing cat and crawling around the apartment with Arofa, who was delighted. She showed him all her favorite places and he shared them with her.

Felice and I became involved in 1967 in the first feminist organization either of us had ever heard of, a group of SDS activists who met regularly, somewhere between a women's caucus and a consciousness-raising group. We discussed our lives, politics, male chauvinism in and out of SDS and wrote little position papers. We did some actions I no longer remember. They merge for me into later WITCH actions (Women's International Terrorist Conspiracy from Hell) and those launched by the Women's Center. But this group was important to me because we met *as women* to talk about women's issues. Our group was not greeted with enthusiasm by the men we knew, but we needed one another, desperately. It was the first time I had ever talked with other women politically about being a woman, and although it was tepid in its actions compared to the women's groups I would be joining soon, it broke ground.

In August I met one of the leaders in the regional SDS office, who was already in an open relationship with Felice. By October we were in love, and finally I had some emotional and sexual counter to Robert's adventures. Of course, with any political man, there is always another agenda. I had experience organizing off campus. Hardly anyone else did, and that was what he was interested in. He wanted me to work with him and gradually pried me out of NACLA and into the SDS regional to do just that. We worked together for the next year and a half and were lovers for that long. Both involvements blew up at the same time in 1969. I called him Goss. He had hair as black

Marge Piercy, Manhattan, 1968.
Photograph by Robert Shapiro

as mine and eyes as dark. He was lithe rather than muscular, sensual, charismatic and accustomed to charming women. He began relationships easily but tended to let them lapse. Ours was his only other involvement besides Felice that endured so long. I probably cared more for him than he for me. He was moody, as changeable as Felice—sometimes sunny and able to throw himself thoroughly into cooking, feasting, lovemaking, playing—other times lost in a maze of Marxist jargon and academic quibbles, sometimes in dark hateful moods when sourness leaked from every pore, sometimes willing to sacrifice anyone to his political goals. He was a natural leader but was not always as responsible in that role as he should have been. He would push less experienced recruits into situations beyond their capabilities or understanding—acting as spokesman, leading a demonstration—and they would get burned, would fail and feel guilty.

I can still remember my intense feelings climbing the rickety, dirty stairs on East Twelfth Street to their small tenement apartment with the bathtub in the kitchen, simmering with passion, anxiety, hope, fear—a seething kettle of emotions. Sometimes everything was good and we were a strong trusting family united by our ideals, our practice, our caring for one another. Sometimes he was evasive, sometimes she was, sometimes I felt deluded, manipulated, used. Sometimes we fought and it hurt; sometimes silence was between us, among us like a judgmental fourth person. Sometimes we just clicked into perfect synchronicity. I can remember Goss bopping around the kitchen making what he called "brown eggs" with burnt butter poured over them. I can remember Felice and me with our arms around each other sitting on the floor at meetings, nursing our bruises from one demonstration or another, speaking as one joined mind and body. Whatever it was and was not, it was real, powerful, often satisfying. For the next seven years I would seek to recapture that tight sense of being one organism together and would put up with many rough passages in an attempt to do so.

Once I had one additional relationship, I found it easy to start others, less serious and less demanding. At one time, I was involved with five people, but I found that exhausting and changed several of them back into friends. My first extramarital involvement was the most committed, and as long as it lasted, it was sometimes my major emotional relationship. I truly loved him and we shared more of our lives than I was sharing with Robert. My relationship with Felice also turned sexual at this time, but the first thing she said to me when we disentangled our limbs was, *Don't tell anyone.* That made me feel rotten. The sexual component did not last because she was too ambivalent. She became involved with Robert instead. She wanted me to desire her more than to make love to her. Elements of power and manipulation were involved. I felt almost as if she were counting coup. If she knew I was interested in someone, like Popov, she would immediately flirt heavily with them and have a quick affair. I became increasingly aware of that pattern. I did not care for her less, but I felt warier. Her relationship with Robert was hot and heavy for several months, during which Robert paid her rent (and Goss's): money he made playing poker with a group of well-off men. Again, Robert liked to share, to help. He really cared for Felice. Then abruptly she broke it off. He was desolate.

At that time, he was interested in group sex. I tried it with him twice, but I did not like it. I could not reach orgasm that way, and it felt weirdly mechanical and performance oriented. There seemed little intimacy in the tangle of bodies. After the second time, I would not do it.

The main advantage for me of an open relationship lay in how other people related to me, politically, personally, in friendship or in a sexual way: I simply was not a married lady in the eyes of the men and women I met, and that was a great advantage in working with people then. Married people were a little mistrusted, for they were considered conventional, perhaps *bourgeois*—the curse word of the time—certainly less committed, less open, less available. Everybody's private life was considered fodder for discussion. If we were closer to one another than I am to anyone except Ira now, we were also nosy and judgmental. All decisions—the way you dressed, the way you spent money, how much money you had to spend, what you ate and drank and smoked, how you behaved in every conceivable situation—everything was the stuff of group discussion, of sessions in which everyone's behavior or choices were up for scrutiny and painful dissection—criticism, self-criticism sessions. I had to defend my choice of not getting busted at Columbia so that I would be able to leave the country that June to go to Cuba, where I had been invited.

We knew more people in a personal and political way than I can now imagine. Cho-Cho generally enjoyed the coming and going. She would seduce even the most dog-oriented guests. Arofa liked Felice, but hardly anyone else was acceptable. Several times she bit someone for being in my bed. She was possessive and territorial, and they were interlopers. During this period of intense and all-consuming political activities and multiple intimate relationships, I could work only by getting up before everyone else. That meant simply going without sleep, because we had meetings or events every night. Seldom did I get into bed before midnight, if then.

By waking at six, I could have a few hours before the phone started ringing, before guests were looking for breakfast, before people started coming to the door, before demands and meetings and demonstrations and deadlines. I rewrote *Going Down Fast* that way and tried to get my agent, Peter Matson, to circulate it. He was reluctant but finally did so, and the first place it went, Trident, then a subsidiary of Simon and Schuster, bought it.

I could not believe it. I had a book of poetry in the process of publication, and now I had sold a novel. I found that this news struck people quite differently. Sol and Adrienne were delighted that I had finally broken through. None of the people I was involved with intimately were pleased. They all saw it either as selling out or as somehow differentiating myself from them, except for Robert, who was astonished. I realized he had never really expected me to sell a novel. He kept saying not to believe it until I had a signed contract in hand. But I did believe it. I had not needed the five years he had promised me. I was beginning to be self-supporting as a writer: I was giving free readings still, but I was also being paid for performing at universities, libraries, conferences. People would actually pay to listen. My poetry was in demand for benefits, and I began to be asked for poetry for publication, instead of submitting blind.

That fall, I read at the West Side YMHA with another poet considered at that time up-and-coming. James Wright, whose poetry I loved, was to introduce the two readers and moderate the discussion supposed to follow the reading. I was intensely excited. My oldest fantasies seemed to be finally reaching fulfillment. I felt as if an immense stone I had carried for years inside my chest had melted away and I was freer than I ever had been. I was not deluded. I was not insane. Some people actually wanted to read or listen to my work, and I was getting paid for it.

That evening of coming out publicly as a poet turned into a nightmare. My lover Goss, who was jealous of my writing and its importance to me, stood up and made a speech about how this was a hierarchical event in the service of the establishment. James Wright made a derogatory comment about Bob Dylan, at that point a total icon-saint of the movement and of just about everyone in the audience under thirty. It turned into a brawl. For years people spread the story that I had insulted James Wright and brought a gang of hoodlums into the Y to disrupt. This event I was so thrilled about was a disaster that haunted me. I sat up there feeling exposed, miserable and helpless. I felt guilty that I had been pleased to be asked to read at the Y, ashamed both of the scene my friends and their allies were making and of my own inability to control or even affect the situation.

I have never been so intensely involved with other people as I was then. I was either hugely happy or thoroughly miserable. I was uncentered. My writing had been pushed to the side until my novel sold, and even after that, I had to fight for work time and generally only got it by giving up sleeping or eating or whatever else seemed inessential. I burned with energy. I could lead three or four lives simultaneously, I believed. I could try to satisfy the needs of everyone around me, write successfully and organize full-time in the movement while carrying on a multitude of consuming relationships. I could do it all.

I began to have health problems. Besides my smoking, I had been gassed in demonstrations. I was coughing all the time, suffering a raw throat. Codeine terpin hydrate was available without a prescription. I don't have an addictive streak, so I never became dependent on it, but when I was sick and I had to attend a conference or chair a meeting or write a pamphlet, I used the stuff to get me through. I thought of myself as an unlimited resource and used myself accordingly. I imagined I could push myself twenty hours a day forever.

I still had not learned that sex and my body were not panaceas. Peter, with whom I was working on certain projects in spite of being an off-campus organizer with Goss, became very jealous of Goss. We had a friendship and a work relationship, but not a romantic or sexual connection. He not only made scenes about Goss. At the regional SDS conference in Princeton, I was dancing with a pleasant young man whom Peter attacked, physically. A few days later, he became so angry at what he saw as my flirting with another man that he threw a large standard office typewriter across the room. He was a big man and his temper scared people. Peter's jealousy was tearing him apart and interfering with our friendship and our work. I went to bed with him, thinking this would help. It didn't. It felt incestuous to him. We all imagined we could do anything we conceived of as correct, without having the psychological sophistication to carry it off. He moved downtown and withdrew from our work and largely from NACLA and would not speak to me for two months.

In the summer of 1968 Robert and I went to Cuba. After the first few weeks, I was free to come and go as I pleased, and I got to know Cubans of a variety of ages, backgrounds, politics, sexual preferences and religions. It was a complex and moving experience, but this is not the place to discuss it. We left the cats in their home this time with a couple from the SDS regional office staying in the apartment. When we got back three months later, there were twenty people living in the apartment and a million roaches. Cho-Cho had gotten plump and Arofa had gotten skinny. Both were desperately glad to see us. My editor—the one who had bought the novel *Going Down Fast* and given me guidelines for revising it—had been fired. The novel was now under the supervision of the equivalent of an office boy—just out of the army, young, inexperienced and powerless. Needless to say, the book came out with little notice and no publicity— but it got good reviews anyhow. I began another novel that fall—*Dance the Eagle to Sleep*. It went slowly because I was getting bronchitis on and off and because I was one of the two principals—with Goss—in starting a new organization specifically for off-campus organizing. It blossomed quickly. We had a teachers group, a group of social workers, of city planners, of people working in publishing. We had affinity groups and started a food co-op and a day care center. We had an affiliated theater group and put out a newsletter. Astonishingly, Wesleyan accepted my second book of poetry, *Hard Loving*. They had discouraged me from submitting it, saying it was too soon after the first. But I knew the poems were much stronger and that it was a powerful book. They agreed and planned to bring it out quickly, in less than a year.

Being a small woman, I was often injured in demonstrations. I used to get diarrhea beforehand, but then I would rev myself up. The movement had no place for cowardice or hesitation, and there is an electricity about a crowd in movement that carries you. Robert now went to demonstrations, but he was not in them. He went with his camera. He had a Nikon I had bought him. Michel had finally paid me back the money for the apartment. I needed it dreadfully when I was down-and-out, but now I just took it and bought Robert the camera of his dreams. He felt safe photographing. I understood that because of the fragility of his bones, he could not risk himself in a demonstration. So often in those years, my conscience made me do what I was most afraid of. That fall, I was dragged on a car for half a city block before my clothing ripped. My back was severely injured.

The spring of 1969, everything personal and political blew up. SDS was tearing itself apart in a spate of dogmatism and Marxist blather. I was essentially forced out of the off-campus organization I had helped create when my relationship with its cofounder collapsed. I found myself pregnant in spite of taking the pill—my life was so irregular I had missed days. I miscarried a child I had not known about. My health was rotten. My throat was bleeding and I was coughing blood. The movement doctor who treated me free said it was not worth his time. I had nearly destroyed my lungs through smoking and through being gassed, I had chronic bronchitis, and I would be dead in two to three years. I walked out of his office and stopped smoking that same hour. I did not mourn the pregnancy that had surprised me, but I was shocked by my own carelessness. Robert had a vasectomy, so I felt it was not fair to become pregnant, even if I did not plan to have the baby. The fear, the fuss, the nuisance were not right to inflict upon him. I began to think of being sterilized, but every doctor I approached said I was too young. Many of my friends had children, but that triggered no desire to procreate. When passed a friend's baby to hold and admire, I would stand awkwardly, acting out my discomfort—fearing if I relaxed for a moment, they might hand off the baby to me for good and I'd be stuck with it. I worked on this attitude and finally managed to fake an interest that, if never felt by the mother to be sufficient, was at least no longer insulting. I liked many of my friends' children as they grew older: I was a good aunt. But I never desired to possess them or have one of my own.

After I had been off cigarettes for a while, it became apparent my body's reaction to being poisoned with tobacco was to become allergic. At that time in history, it was like being allergic to air. Ninety percent of my friends smoked. All public places and meetings were full of tobacco smoke. I became extremely unpopular extremely fast. My allergy made me a pariah, seen as a puritan extremist, trying to force my antismoking bias on other people who were just having a good time.

Robert left his company and started a computer co-op in a ground-floor apartment two blocks from ours, on West End, begun with tremendous enthusiasm and idealism. They were to do socially beneficial work, making their technology available to those who needed it, and to take only as many innocuous paying jobs as they decided they needed to live on, minimally. "People in MIA will be making an explicit choice when they spend money, when they consume. To consume is to recognize that some time will have to be used to pay for that consumption and that time will not be available for those projects really worth doing." Unfortunately, although a couple of the people who worked for the co-op in a low-level way were used to scrabbling by on movement minimum pay, like Peter, the people who could actually do the computer programming and systems analysis were not about to live that way—certainly Robert wasn't. I enjoyed the comforts of the middle-class life, although when I was traveling for the antiwar or the women's movement, I could sleep on floors, under desks or tables, like everyone else.

That summer, the computer co-op rented a house in Truro for August. The experience was a revelation. I had fallen in love with the Cape when I was visiting with Goss just before Cuba, but a whole month there felt like paradise. Besides everyone in the house we had rented, we were also friends with a house of gay men. My smoking allergy annoyed everybody, but we were outside most of the time.

The house the computer co-op rented was made of whitewashed cinder block and sat on a hill among pitch pines, fragrant and runty. To this day, the cry of a seaside sparrow will call up to me the intense sensations of that August and the next. I had never been out of the city in the summer since those one-week vacations with my parents on little lakes in Michigan. The cats were taken on walks and even allowed outside when it became clear they would not wander. We were about half a mile from the ocean via a series of paths. The beach was a nude one—before the rich summer citizens of Truro put pressure on the National Park Service, one beach in Truro and one in Wellfleet had been nude since time out of memory. Things had been tense and factional in the city. It was bliss to get away. Every day we took long walks exploring sand roads. Every day I worked on my novel. I got more done that month than I had since I returned from Cuba. I finished the novel *Dance the Eagle to Sleep*.

Everyone else went back to the city, but Robert and I did not want to leave. We had to clear out of our house, but some people in the gay house had left, and we were invited to stay in an empty room upstairs for ten days. That week, a hurricane passed out to sea. Tall breakers crashed in. Everyone was stoned much of the time and basically treated the beach as a living room. We all went out on a sandbar to eat a picnic supper while watching the sunset over the bay. The surge of cold water from high winds that sprang up cut us off. I have never been much of a swimmer. I can barely stay afloat. The water rushed into the Pamet River and it quickly became deep. The current was swift and difficult to make way against. The water was numbingly cold. Well after the others had landed and strolled off, I finally managed to make it across, but I wrenched my back muscles badly. If I had drowned, no one would have noticed. My back injury from the old demonstration was exacerbated. Exhausted, I crawled into bed.

I woke in the middle of the night in such pain I thought I had a kidney stone, as Michel once had. It was agony to wait for the end of the week to return to New York. The men in the house turned on me. I was a prima donna, I was attempting to manipulate everyone, I was trying to drag Robert away. I became the villain, while I was immobilized with pain. I could not even straighten up.

Back in the city, I went to an orthopedic surgeon. He put me on complete bed rest and painkillers. For the next weeks, I lay in my bed and my muscles turned to water. Robert withdrew. Friends came once, tried to force or cajole or guilt-trip me out of bed, and then vanished, except for a couple of women friends. Ceci brought me my first television, a small black-and-white set we could rig so that I could see it without sitting up. I became addicted to *Star Trek,* then already in reruns, and to *Dark Shadows,* and to the news. After five weeks of this and no improvement, the orthopedic surgeon began to talk about operating on my spine. I got a friend from NACLA to bring me from the Columbia medical library anything she could find on back injuries. I looked at the statistics on improvement after operations and decided to quit my orthopedic surgeon.

I decided after further reading to try an osteopath. I called up one in Philadelphia who had written articles I liked, who sent me to his mentor.

He was one of the best doctors I have ever gone to, his wall covered with awards for the treatment of injuries and geriatric problems. He took me off the painkillers, gave me exercises and prescribed walking two miles a day. He had me change my shoes. I have rarely worn high heels since. When I need them for a reading or speaking at a podium, I carry them in my briefcase and put them on just before I mount the stage. I returned to life in pain but mobile.

During this period, we became close friends with Robin Morgan, the feminist who had been a child TV star and was now a good speaker, a theoretician of the movement, and a published poet. She was married to Kenneth Pitchford, who was predominantly gay and a published poet. I was crazy about Robin. She was short and pretty, with enormous brown eyes and a cutting wit and intense intelligence, a streak of dogmatism, a fury of seriousness. They had a "light machine." This was at the height of psychedelic mishegoss. With various friends we went regularly to the Fillmore East. We listened to rock then, religiously. That's the right term. We waited for new albums from the Beatles, the Stones, Dylan, as if being given The Word. We haggled over which of our favorites was the most politically correct, and we interpreted and reinterpreted lyrics. But we also danced ourselves limp and got stoned and heard revelations in the music. Anyhow, Robin and Kenneth had built a thing that projected moving shapes and lights on a screen. Robert was immediately enamored. We built one too, different but just as crazy. It used old lace tablecloths, a mirrored ball, prisms, a fan, a motor that turned, all sorts of hanging objects, all of this behind a screen. When I think of how many hours we spent in the next five years staring at this thing, it astonishes me. I cannot imagine just sitting and staring at anything today. I scarcely have time to see a movie unless I get it on video and fast-forward through the dull parts. Nobody I know sits around much. We're all rushed into exhaustion. I can't say I consider this acceleration an improvement, for I have to run twice as fast to stay in the same place economically. I work twice as hard and three times as rapidly for the same money.

In the newly sprung women's movement, I moved in a vortex of anger and joy, an intense sense of revelation. Writing an essay, "The Grand

Coolie Damn," was my break with the New Left, although I never turned on it the way some feminists did. I never thought we were all wrong, only that things did go sour. I became active in the new Women's Center downtown, and out of there I began organizing consciousness-raising groups. I stayed in one of them for the next year and a half. I was involved again in helping women get abortions and in the regular lobbying, busing to Albany to the legislature, although there was so much smoke in those offices, I was not very useful. I spoke at rallies and marched in demonstrations. I am an able rabble-rousing speaker, because I never talk about any subject I don't care about, passionately.

My new novel, *Dance the Eagle to Sleep,* went the round of publishers and amassed rapid rejections. It horrified most editors who read it, as violent, radical, too much like the kids demonstrating in the streets who frightened them. One said to me, "Why can't you write a nice love story set against a backdrop of war?" My agent did not like it either and was not truly behind it. He had preferred my unsold semiautobiographical novel. But after thirty fast rejections, the novel was bought on a lousy two-book contract by Doubleday and went immediately into production. I had two editors, one with power and one with charm. With the charming subeditor, I enjoyed many drunken luncheons. We both liked wine and food and exotic liqueurs. I used to walk home from the offices in the Thirties on the East Side to our apartment on Ninety-eighth and Broadway, because I was too drunk to take the subway and not about to waste money on a cab. I would sober up by the time I got home. None of our group would have appreciated my rolling in drunk.

I had long legs for my height and wore very short miniskirts. My hair went halfway down my back. I looked good, and so when *Dance* came out, I had a brief time as the flavor of the month in New York publishing, reviews all over the place, including a very enthusiastic one from John Simon in the *New York Times* and denunciations in right-wing and southern newspapers, my photo in *Time,* interviews, television. The works. I liked the attention the book was generating but I didn't like getting obscene phone calls (this was before the days of answering machines). I did not like the jealousy of other writers and friends. I did not like the feeling I had been turned into a commodity. Some idiot producer even wanted me to take a screen test. The fuss felt wrong. I did not know how to handle it. If a photographer asked me to sit on a table, I would do it. I had no idea how provocative some of those photos looked. I was too nervous to object until I saw them in print. Then I cringed and felt ridiculous. In truth, I was still a naive working-class girl without media smarts.

I was having brief meaningless affairs since the relationship with Goss, which had ended abruptly and left me burnt, so I stopped. Most of the men who came after me when Goss and I split were movement men trying to recruit me to not only their bed but also their projects. I was a good organizer and I felt like a riderless horse everyone was trying to saddle. Robert had not found me attractive since my back injury. I entered a long period of chastity. I was determined to change how I behaved, to be less passive, less reactive, less pliable, less masochistic, less apt to put everyone else first and myself last. I was determined to remake my sexuality and my way of being in the world. On the whole, I was successful and have been much less likable since. I had no desire to leave Robert, although I rather wished he were more interested in me, but mostly I wanted friendships and peace, a reflective quiet at the core.

I no longer went to fourteen meetings a week but only to four. I began contributing to the women's movement as much by writing articles, essays, pamphlets and poems as by organizing, although I was still doing that. The cats were happy. I was around a lot, writing and reading and thinking. I contemplated sex roles and women's position and my own. I was still involved in NACLA as well as the Women's Center, and was also active in *Leviathan,* an intellectual and political publication. The women's movement was electric and gave off sparks. I was seeing myself and the world and all my relationships, all the relationships of my life from my parents on, in a new way. I tried to communicate some of this to my mother. It was the first time I had tried in years to be close to her again. We had moments, but mostly she would not engage. But every day there was new women's theater, women's readings, women's zines, women's programs, women's demonstrations and guerrilla theater at bridal bazaars, the Miss America pageant, construction sites; everyday someone proposed a new way to look at some aspect of our lives that turned our perspectives upside down; every day I found something I had thought to be a personal problem was an issue shared by many, many women. I did not put myself forward as a leader, because I thought this was a chance for many women who had been silent to learn to speak out.

Robert was growing heavy with depression again. The movement in New York had splintered. I had always been a kind of liaison for him to the more political people, working out how he could relate to projects, how they could relate to him. The computer co-op was holding its own, but he was the only one able to find any contracts that could generate money, and he felt he was carrying the whole thing on his back. Infighting and factionalism isolated us. Groups that disagreed on minor points hated one another. An enemy was someone who differed from you about anything. The rhetoric had escalated and there was no longer a feeling of family, of community. Friends were beginning to peel off to Vermont and the West Coast.

The summer of 1970 the computer co-op rented the same house in Truro. I mainly wrote poetry. A lot of the time, we took long hikes, we went bird-watching, we read a great deal. Robert was talking constantly about getting out of New York. The movement, which had felt warm and nurturing, brothers and sisters together, now felt harsh and nasty, militant and crude. The rhetoric had turned into shouting and the infighting intensified. Everyone we knew in New York was in one or another faction, and I refused to align with any. I was one of the last people all sides could still relate to and try to recruit. I hated the factionalism, but I did not hate the people. I saw them as caught in a conflagration of guilt and despair. We had given our lives to the movement, and still the war escalated. In each of us, violent images imploded and we were tormented by our weakness—so our rhetoric turned more and more warlike and militant and dogmatic. We were recapitulating the faction fights of the 1930s we had found pitiful. We of the New Left were no longer talking to anyone except ourselves.

Except for the women's movement. We were expanding, we were

reaching out, we were taking in new women every day. We were in an intense rich period of discovery and the reinvention of every aspect of culture, biological destiny, gender, the family, the workplace—everything from birth till death and in between. I did not experience the dreadful tearing asunder of SDS in the same way as friends, because I was involved in something bursting with life and energy that was teaching me to remake myself stronger—mentally and socially. My health remained unstable. The doctor who had agreed to resume treating me, since I had stopped smoking, told me I would never recover but would proceed into emphysema if I stayed in New York City, because I was inhaling two and a half packs a day just by breathing the dirty city air.

Robert was keenly depressed. The computer co-op had not worked out as he had imagined. He was the only one bringing in income-producing work and he was responsible for a nest full of hungry birds. The movement he had intended to serve was ceasing to exist.

We began to look around Truro, but we could not find anything we could afford. Wellfleet was cheaper. We saw an acre at the end of a subdivision. Before we left the Cape, we bought it and we hired a builder who was recommended to us. I drew plans for a house that Robert vetoed because he thought it too expensive. We used the basic design but made it five feet smaller in all dimensions. I have regretted that choice daily. There was only one house in the subdivision, right next to ours; the builder intended to live here with his girlfriend, Penny, whom we met and liked. We were going to move to Cape Cod. We were once again abruptly changing our lives.

COMMUNITY

Loving feels lonely in a violent world,
irrelevant to people burning like last year's weeds
with bellies distended, with fish throats agape
and flesh melting down to glue.
We can no longer shut out the screaming
that leaks through the ventilation system,

the small bits of bone in the processed bread,
so we are trying to make a community
warm, loose as hair but shaped like a weapon.
Caring, we must use each other to death.
Love is arthritic. Mistrust swells like a prune.
Perhaps we gather so they may dig one big cheap grave.
From the roof of the Pentagon which is our Bastille
the generals armed like Martians watch through binoculars
the campfires of draftcards and barricades on the grass.
All summer helicopters whine over the ghetto.
Casting up jetsam of charred fingers and torn constitutions
the only world breaks on the door of morning.
We have to build our city, our camp
from used razorblades and bumpers and aspirin boxes
in the shadows of the nuclear plant that kills the fish
with Coke bottle lamps flickering
on the chemical night.

FOURTEEN

OPEN TO THE CAPE WINDS

When I first saw the land Robert and I bought in 1970, it was pine woods just beginning to go to climax oak, a hillside of sand and some clay overrun with lowbush blueberries, hawthorn, a few juniper. After the real estate man showed it to us, we returned alone. As we were looking it over, Robert pissed into the bushes, and a red-shouldered hawk rose up furious from where she had been feeding. Since I am enamored of hawks, I took this as a sign. We paid cash for the land, so we had only a $15,500 mortgage on the little house we built.

It was a thing of the times, the exodus from New York. The Cape was close enough to the computer industry in Boston and New York to sit well with Robert. He had pastoral dreams. He imagined cows and chickens and plowing the west forty. So we took Arofa and Cho-Cho and packed up into the unknown. There were only two other houses in the subdivision when we moved on a rainy February day with the help of friends, way at the end of a road. For the cats, it was the move of their dreams. As soon as they had settled in, we began to allow them outside in the daytime.

The new-built house was small, a box half buried in the sand, but the builder had chopped down too many trees, slashed a great furrow in the hill so that it was deeply rutted and washing out with every rain. I began to plant to stabilize the hillside. Today this land is lush and productive with sugar maples, birches, a weeping beech, thickets of roses, black and red currants, raspberry, blueberry and gooseberry, fruit trees, dogwoods, crabapples, wisteria bowers, rampant grapevines and intensive organic vegetable gardens. However, most of the land is pine forest well along into oak. For cats, it was, and is, paradise.

I fell into seed and nursery catalogs, discovering a new addiction I have never recovered from. Indeed, I feel quite virtuous when, reading a catalog with 150 old-fashioned and species roses in it, I order only fourteen. I am like a dieter who eats only one banana split instead of three, and thus feels you should admire her restraint, and is secretly convinced that with such evident self-denial, she will lose weight. Some things I planted that first year—the tiny rhododendrons, the three-inch-high seedlings of white fir, the raggedy forsythia—have flourished. Others like the ring of Austrian pines supposed to be a windbreak perished in the first month. Our soil was poor, but we were composting our garbage and mulching with thatch from the bay.

I took a month's residency at Kansas to pay off the electrician and the well driller. To spend as little as possible of my earnings, in Lawrence I lived in an autocratic ill-run commune with faculty and students. During those first years on the Cape, I was developing my reading style, learning to put poems across to an audience. I worked with musicians and other poets, trying ways of presenting. I performed with drums, chanting, a saxophone, a xylophone and other musicians who sometimes seemed determined to prove that words are superfluous in the presence of music. Finally I preferred just delivering the poems myself.

When I came back from Kansas, Robert was involved with a hapless waif he was already tired of. I remember Arofa taking me about to her favorite places on the land, showing me her discoveries, intensely excited and purring as she went. She became a fearsome hunter. Arofa killed cleanly, breaking the necks of her prey. She could run down rabbits. However, a sad thing occurred regularly during those days when baby rabbits left their nests. She would carry them home unharmed and soon unafraid, washing them and attempting to treat them as kittens. That made me feel guilty that we had not allowed her a litter before altering her. I would take them out and let them go.

Cho-Cho was far more the stereotypical cat, playing with her prey and mangling them before finally administering the coup de grâce. We could never afford to be sentimental about rodents, as the house attracted field and jumping mice. We were growing vegetables and fruit abundantly, bartering surplus for seafood from the fisherman who moved in next door and for supplies at the health food store. Our builder, after throwing our house together haphazardly, left his girlfriend and married someone else, so he never lived in the house he built beside ours.

For years, when something would go wrong, plumbers would examine our pipes and fittings and fall down laughing. The builder had saved money by doing it himself. This was before strict enforcement of building codes in town. Over the years, we learned many ways that corners had been cut—like installing a used and insufficient pump. Like leaving insulation out of the exterior walls of closets. The house has one interior door only twenty inches wide, so that it is hard to get any piece of furniture or even a large box through it. The wall oven leaked smoke and did not retain heat, as I discovered the first time I tried to bake bread.

During our early years, we had constant trouble with the well and the pump. The well repair man would arrive and wait for me to descend into the well pit before he would go down. I would catch our resident black rat snake in a paper bag and hold him until they finished the repairs. Then I would return him to his home in the wellhouse. I was notorious as the snake lady, because I have never been afraid of snakes. We had lots of rodents and appreciated the snake's services. I was very sorry when one day I descended into the well and found him desiccated, electrocuted. After the snake died, we could no longer use the well as a root cellar because mice would eat the cabbages and potatoes.

By New Year's Eve, I finished the first draft of the novel *Small Changes,* which I had been futilely trying to start in New York. I wrote eight hundred pages between returning from Kansas in April and

December 31. I celebrated by dancing all night in Provincetown. I was working in a far more disciplined and productive way than since our move from Brookline to Brooklyn.

The fisherman who lived next door was a complex man who had run radio communications for SNCC (Student Nonviolent Coordinating Committee) during voter registration. One of his many girlfriends had a horse and eventually two. I remember a bad thunderstorm when I heard a horrible clatter and her big old white horse Ajax was standing on my porch looking in mournfully. Then the neighbor's mother died, and he inherited her cat, a gorgeous black Persian named Daphne. Daphne did not like his household. Too many dogs, too much noise, too little attention. She moved in with us. Arofa and Cho-Cho hated her. She did not care for the company of other cats. Finally I put an ad in the paper and several takers fought over her. A local carpenter carried her off on a cushion like the regal queen she was.

Before we moved to the Cape, I had bought books on macramé, on dyeing with natural products, on collecting, eating and preserving wild food. I imagined taking up crafts to fill the long empty off-season months summer people like us believed the locals stoically endured. By the time we had been living in Wellfleet for six months, I had four meetings a week. We started Cape Cod Women's Liberation on a picket line outside an exhibit in Provincetown, billed as the top New England artists—sixty of them, including only two women and no Afro-American or Latino artists.

We came together in an informal group bridging several towns on the Outer Cape. We worked on rape and began to educate the police departments. Abortion was still illegal. There were no specific health facilities for women. Women usually held a variety of ill-paying and unorganized jobs—waitresses, chambermaids, house cleaners. Often they did not know even the few legal resources and recourses available. We held forums on domestic violence. The ex-girlfriend of our builder, Penny, became a close friend and a year later moved in with us. She lived in Robert's office, a flat-roofed building with a large cellar for wine storage located half a mile from the house. We worked the land, ate and did our political work together.

Penny was a cat person, and the cats adored her and crawled all over her—even Arofa. She had been a ballet dancer in New York until she was dropped by her partner during an opera—when a prop had been moved. She had a psychology degree, but when I met her, she was running a landscaping crew out of a truck wildly painted with peace and woman power symbols. She was a passionate feminist with a salty side, and like me, she had enjoyed many adventures, had traveled extensively, liked to dance, eat, drink and garden. We concentrated on fruit and vegetable production, but I was also enamored of roses, daylilies and interesting trees. I planted two weeping beeches, but one of them was struck by lightning—a terrifying moment. I had two women friends visiting. The lightning seemed to charge into the room, and the power went out. We found ourselves all three of us kneeling in the middle of the floor, clutching one another, deafened and shuddering.

Robert had built himself a large office on a stream, near a small pond. Since it was much bigger than he needed for his work, during these years usually somebody else was living there. Robert enjoyed the Cape, enjoyed the gardens, the landscape—he always was very open and attuned to natural beauty—oystering, clamming, little building projects. He played with the cats and gave them first-class attention. Robert and I talked a great deal, about politics, the world, what we were reading. We often had irritable fights—little spats that passed as quickly as clouds overhead. However, we also had fights that were far more serious every couple of months. They were terrible lacerating rending battles that felt every time like the end of the world, or at least the end of the marriage. They usually issued from his feeling stymied in his work or his life, unable to move forward. As in many marriages, the wife becomes the cause of the husband's frustration—who else is around to blame? It is hard to remember what the fights were about, or if they were about anything in particular and not just the result of an overwhelming malaise and a huge, often suppressed anger flooding out.

One way of being in the landscape we shared was wanting to know exactly what we were looking at. Knowing starts with naming, although it cannot end there. We collected guides not only to birds but to plants of the seashore, mollusks, butterflies and moths, reptiles and amphibians, trees, shrubs, wildflowers, rocks, animal tracks and scat (for winter identification). It used to annoy some visitors when we stopped cold to study a weed. We would go out for a walk with a knapsack of guides, although after a while, we could identify most of the animals and plants we met. Then we wanted to know their habits, what their presence said about the land, the ecology—how they lived, what they ate, their mating habits. We shared this approach and we had fun.

Joining the food co-op, we quickly became coordinators. At that time, there were far fewer year-round people on the Lower Cape and fewer stores and businesses open in the winter. Eight hundred people in three towns were members. Every Sunday afternoon we took orders at the Methodist church in the Head Start room. On Wednesday afternoon, bags of oatmeal and whole wheat flour, of carrots and potatoes were given out. We stayed active until the time we started going into Boston every week.

A peculiar local custom developed during the ban on swordfish, which was considered dangerous from supposedly high mercury levels. A local fisherman (also in an open relationship; they were common then) would catch a swordfish and bring it to the back room of the bookstore. A calling chain would notify everyone on the list and you would say how many pounds you wanted. A landscape painter would carve up the swordfish, and you would pay a price far below what the market had been when it was legal, and go home with your superfresh steaks. There's always a lot of barter on the Cape, as locals are often short of money but long on something else.

Robert was urging me to have outside relationships again. I had not been involved with anyone else in a year and a half, and we had not had sex in a year. I had been content with this arrangement for a long time, since I wanted to examine my habits in close encounters with the opposite sex and I wanted to change my behavior. But I found that chastity did not work for me in the long haul. I found myself writing less poetry and emotionally drying up.

But beginning to have sex with other men meant worries about pregnancy, and I was tired of constantly fearing it, month after month, the anxiety every time my period was late, the fuss with contraceptives. I was never handy with the diaphragm and more than once it ended up flipping out of my hands sticky with jelly and pasting itself to the bathroom ceiling. I had been in the original group after Puerto Rico on whom various dosages of the pill had been tried out, and I had had to be cauterized for excessive bleeding at one point. I looked for a doctor who would sterilize me. My friend Karen had undergone a new procedure, a laparoscopy (a new surgical procedure that was much simpler and safer than the older operation). It was called "Band-Aid sterilization" because it did not leave a scar. Since Karen and I are close in age, it seemed likely a doctor willing to listen to her would grant my request. And he did. I was scheduled for a laparoscopic in-hospital overnight procedure in a town north of Boston.

The problematic aspect for me was the anesthetic. Indeed, I awoke in the postop room covered with bruises, with various nurses and aides in a semicircle glaring down at me. Certain kinds of old-fashioned anesthetics have the effect of making me violent when I lose consciousness. Sore as I was—and I had far more aftereffects than I expected, including difficulty with my bladder for a month—there was no scar and I was free. I have never regretted taking charge of my body. I did not want children. I never felt I would be less of a woman, but I feared I would be less of a writer if I reproduced. I didn't feel anything special about my genetic composition warranted replicating it. When I came home from the hospital giddy on painkillers, I lay in my bed singing at the top of my lungs—with relief, with joy, with the sharp delicious taste of freedom. I could very well understand why other women wanted children, but it was not for me. I had the ability to put everything out of my mind except work, and I did not think that would lead to responsible and loving motherhood. I knew if I had a baby, I would feel trapped and resent my situation.

I began relationships with a poet, a park ranger and then with an academic who wrote mostly polemics. He was my link for a time to friends who were underground. I had known he was interested while we were both living in New York, but I was committed to chastity. Now I was willing. I found that having other relationships made me far less dependent on Robert, who went off to Germany frequently on software projects, leaving me alone in the country, and whose sexual interest in me was at best intermittent. Having other relationships kept me from being lonely or dependent on him. So did having other people live with us, something that characterized those years. Usually some friend was living in the house or in the office, usually a woman. I was not isolated in my marriage but living in a larger family. Maintaining the group was a priority for me, and a lot of my choices and difficulties arose from the necessity of keeping the group together. In the country that was critically important. I am not a jealous person, nor was Robert. I can live with one other person or with a group, so long as I feel cared for and my needs and boundaries are respected.

In many ways, being able to operate on my own made it smoother for me socially and politically. I could make friends more easily. When Robert and I had been a normal couple, we stopped seeing many friends of mine he did not like or approve of. He always had far stricter political standards for my friends than for his. His computer pals might work on defense contracts, because they could not avoid that. If friends of mine wrote for the movies or for *Playboy,* he wouldn't deal with them and would give me a hard time about seeing them.

I often had to explain and justify him, for he seemed strange to people we met. I liked going to parties without him—not because I wanted to pick someone up, for he was more apt to do that. I always wanted to check men out thoroughly before committing myself. But his presence cramped my interactions with friends and acquaintances. I had to worry about whether he had someone to talk to, whether he was having a good time. I preferred going to meetings with almost anyone else, because he would say things to provoke attention that got me into trouble politically or which I felt compelled to defend out of loyalty. I provided a reservoir of people with whom he could do things. But on the Cape, most of my friends were feminists for whom he was not a priority.

Although I had not chosen an open marriage and multiple relationships of my own volition, I easily justified it politically and I took advantage of it. I had a great many people in my life whom I could not have been close to otherwise. I could take chances on risky relationships and flee back into my stable one. I learned a lot that people with more conventional lives never have a shot at. I certainly had far more experience with men than 90 percent of the women I know, and it's been useful to me as a writer.

The relationship with the academic writer was bumpy. I was truthful with him, but he had another woman in New York who did not know about me and I didn't know about her. When I found out, I felt I had betrayed her unintentionally. The relationship blew up and he became hostile. For some years, he would review my novels acidly whenever he had a chance. However, while I was still seeing him—sometimes in New York and sometimes on the Cape—Robert became interested in me again. Our relationship heated up. I began to realize Robert was most sexual with me when somebody else wanted me.

I had many intense friendships with women in the feminist movement but ran into problems with some who resented my work habits, my discipline. From the time I arrived on the Cape, one of the things I chose explicitly was to put my writing first. Everything else in my life waxed and waned, but writing, I discovered during my restructuring, was my real core. Not any relationship. Not any love. Not any person. I had become more selfish and less accessible. I ceased to be the universal mommy of the tribe. I wanted to see people when I was done with my writing for the day, and not in the middle of my work time.

I was working on *Small Changes,* an immense task. Not only was it a long novel, but I felt I was struggling to invent a grammar of gender and sex roles in fiction. I remember many lunches in Cambridge with Nancy Henley, who was working on *She Said/He Said.* At those long lunches we discussed and debated observations about who laughed at whose jokes, how men and women occupied space, who got to touch whom and how, the use of first names, and dozens of daily interactions on the job and in social life.

I had various short relationships with men. Everyone who came and stayed with us was put to work on Robert's agricultural projects or my landscaping. We have the A. memorial brick walkway, the B. memorial steps carved into the hill with railroad ties, the C. retaining wall, the D. archway, the E. shed. I would never do that to visitors now, but it was the ethos of the time. You came, you stayed, you moved in if you wished, but you had to contribute labor. People who were not willing to work were considered bad guests and never invited again—or allowed to invite themselves. When you live on Cape Cod, you get used to fielding messages like this: "Hi, this is Jimmy Dildo. Remember, we met in a hallway in 1962? I'm here with my wife and six kiddies, and we can't find a motel room. Can we come and stay with you?" I became accomplished at responding, "Sure, come on over. We can't put you up, but I can give you lunch, and you can help us dig the stumps out of the new area we're clearing. Bring your work clothes." That got rid of most.

In the fall of 1972, I put in a two-week stint at the University of Michigan, my alma mater, in the Residential College. That was a new experiment, a small liberal arts college within the vast university. I enjoyed that residency far more than the one in Kansas. A number of the faculty were friendly, some knew my work, and the students were bright, open and interested. While there, I was the honored guest at tea in the Hopwood Room—I had won various Hopwoods at Michigan, including a major in poetry—when a young man appeared. He had read *Dance the Eagle to Sleep* and asked if I wanted to go dancing that night. This was so different from the usual fan reaction, I was delighted. While I was in Ann Arbor, I saw a lot of him, but I assumed it was over when I left. During these years, I always spent time with my old writing teacher and mentor Robert Haugh, with Professor Arnold Eastman, who taught Shakespeare and was one of the first "out" faculty I ever met. He had never been my professor, but we had become friends. He was politically savvy and a great wit. I also was extremely fond of Mary Cooley, who ran the Hopwood Room. Even after she retired, I kept in touch and saw her whenever I was near. She had never married but worked all her life, was an avid reader and gardener, extremely intelligent. I admired her as an independent woman of integrity, who lived alone and seemed to like it.

Not long after my return, the young man, Wayne, appeared at our door. I was flattered and alarmed, but Robert liked him and suggested he stay as long as he liked. The two of them worked well together, constantly carrying out projects like building a shed and putting up fences around the garden to keep rabbits out. Robert had become involved with a woman from my women's group. Dolores had moved from Provincetown to Cambridge because of a part-time teaching position. Around this time we began to go to Boston regularly. Robert was working with his old company and stayed over with Dolores in Cambridge, and she came out every weekend. Wayne got a job and we rented a two-room apartment together in Cambridge. All of us went back and forth regularly. Sometimes I would be four days on the Cape and three in Cambridge; sometimes five days on the Cape and two in Cambridge.

The relationships with Wayne and Dolores worked into our lifestyle and did not threaten the central relationship. In the long run, Robert and I preferred each other's company—in part because we did not have too much of it. Plus we all had fun together. Whatever you wanted to do, you had a ready-made group to do it, whether it was going dancing, taking a hike, playing with a Frisbee at the beach or cards at the dining room table, putting up a bird feeder or a picnic, arguing politics and talking, talking. Dolores wrote poetry and short prose pieces, so we exchanged and critiqued our work together. She was not easy to live with. She thought we were living high because we ate oysters a lot, not understanding that Wayne and Robert had commercial shellfish licenses and harvested them regularly. When she did the dishes, she let the water run for an hour until we had no hot water. My clothes were stored in the closet of the upstairs bedroom, and since she rose late, often I could not get dressed until I had been up for hours. It was all worth it, because I liked her warmth and intelligence. She was easy for me to understand, to communicate with, and I felt we were on the same side. We were intense about many of the same things. We both came from families without money and were unique in our families for having decided we wanted an education and having got one, regardless of difficulties. We identified with each other; indeed, we were of a similar body type, with long black hair, and sometimes were taken for blood sisters.

I got involved in Bread and Roses, a feminist group. I began to meet women in Cambridge. In addition to Cape Cod Women's Liberation, I also was in a consciousness-raising group including women from Wellfleet, Truro and Provincetown—a warmer group than the one I had joined in Manhattan. One night as I was leaving a meeting in Provincetown, I saw a kitten fighting with a seagull for a crust of bread. She was losing but had not yet been maimed. I brought her home—she climbed willingly into the car. I had no carrier, so bringing her home loose in the car was risky, but she was exhausted and starving.

She was a tricolored cat—in other words, a calico with the gene for white. She had enormous dark yellow eyes, so I named her Amber. I took her promptly to the vet, where she was wormed. It turned out she was pregnant, six months old and suffering from malnutrition. At that time, a pregnant woman could not get an abortion in Massachusetts—but a cat could. Her fetuses were undersized, and the vet did not think they could survive. She returned to us unpregnant and hungry, always hungry. She ate as much as the other cats combined.

At first, since she was tiny for six months, the other cats treated her as a kitten, played with her and tolerated her well. But as she grew into a sizable cat—bigger than both of them—they began to fight with her. They also ratted on her. She had learned to hunt while living on the streets of Provincetown, and I could not teach her to stop killing birds. Arofa would come crying to me whenever Amber caught a bird. I did not appreciate Amber's killing, but she was a nice, clean, friendly, affectionate cat who would eat just about anything. Fussy? No way. She ate cat food, she ate human food, she ate beetles and mice and birds. She never got fat, but she got hefty. Indeed, since she would finish anything the other cats left, they tended to eat hastily and thoroughly while Amber was here.

The fighting grew worse. I would be wakened at night by confrontations, yowls and hisses. I would rise to find a ball of varicolored fur churning in the living room. Cho-Cho was more apt to fight than Arofa, who just made hideous noises. Cho-Cho was seriously attacking. I had to find a home for Amber. A friend from my women's group, a sculptor, helped, and a home was found.

Around the same time as Amber was forced out, Robert decided that Dolores was too demanding and broke off. I was bitterly disappointed. Moreover, it put the quietus on Dolores's and my friendship, because all she wanted to do when I saw her was talk about how to get him back, and I knew that was hopeless. When he was finished, he was finished. Over the years, I had dealt with dozens of women who couldn't understand what had gone wrong and I was their only source of information and comfort.

I was somewhat secretive about my life when I met people, as I essentially had two husbands—not a situation widely recommended or apt to be viewed as a great idea in the women's movement. For me, it worked. They complemented each other. Robert was brighter but less sexual and less interested in me. He was closer to me politically and more mature. He was also far less accessible. Robert was skilled at getting his way with both of us. Wayne admired him, and Robert liked to be admired. Wayne's traveling with me made being on the road more comfortable. When he traveled with me, Robert was bored. But in any crowd, Wayne would find someone who knew someone he knew, or some connection. He managed to be at ease when he was the only man in a room full of women. He could keep his mouth shut and listen without feeling diminished, and he could talk intelligently. I never had to worry about him in groups. He floated, he enjoyed, and then he would be there afterward when I had talked my soul out and did not know who I was any longer. Not only didn't he feel abused, but he managed to have a good time, a constant wonder and delight to me. It certainly made it easier to do the kind of gigs required in those years: rooms full of intense political students seething with questions after a reading. Wayne was tall, good-looking, affable, with changeable sea-colored eyes. He had grown up in a working-class family in Flint, larger but similar to mine. He liked to cook, although some of his concoctions were more ambitious than delicious. He had been twenty-two when I met him at Michigan. I was thirty-six.

Wayne fell in love with a used white Thunderbird convertible with red seats. I hated that car. It was big with immense fins, hurt my back and burned gas at a staggering rate. It was a classic car and he cherished it, but he would never put more than a quarter of a tank in, because it was old and might die. Then he would be out the money he had spent on gas. This meant that we often ran empty and spent hours on the side of the road or hiked for miles to bring back a container. To Wayne that T-bird was the epitome of what a car should be, and he felt successful in it. I felt underwhelmed. I liked Volvos, for their comfort and dependability. Our tastes were often in opposition. We got on well most of the time, but I never felt we were deeply mated or suited. Still we understood a great deal about each other, because of where we both came from.

A woman Robert had been involved with in New York, now living in San Francisco, offered to join his company and move in. Estelle was a complication. I was not in favor of her coming, as I felt with her living in the office, the balance of my relationship with Robert would tip, and we would become less close. Robert was adamant, so I made the best of it and tried to befriend Estelle. I apparently succeeded, and she began to work with Cape Cod Women's Liberation. There was always tension between Wayne and Estelle, as if they were siblings fighting, but much of the time we all got along and had fun, whether hiking in the White Mountains, dancing in Provincetown, or discovering a forty-fifth way to cook oysters. I was very taken with her. We could do so many personal and political things together. This was especially important to me after Penny moved up to New Hampshire with a new lover, and since the loss of Dolores. Estelle and I were girlfriends. I loved that. We were a good family. Robert was happy, and our lives seemed full and rich with human connection.

Differences slowly appeared. Robert had withdrawn from me sexually and sometimes emotionally during short and long periods, but he never stopped telling me he loved me, writing occasional apologetic notes or poems to me, making it clear that I was at the center of his life. Gradually while Estelle lived in his office, this altered. I would notice that he often turned to her first with news, with ideas. She persuaded him to refrain from being affectionate with me when she was around. She objected to us acting as a couple in her presence, or indeed expressing any intimacy. The money I brought in was increasingly important to our group. Gradually I was becoming the major financial support. Wayne made a working-class wage laying cable while Robert was often between paying projects, and that meant Estelle was also at liberty. One difficulty was that Robert and Wayne hated reporters coming to interview me and resented any publicity, which cut way back on what I could do for my books.

Our land was not as beautiful as it is now, as Robert and Wayne liked to view it as a little farm. When something broke, they tossed it over the fence of the main garden till we had a dump there, including old TV antennas, broken glass doors and empty oil cans. But we've never grown as good fruit as we did then. Tree fruit requires fussing. Robert took a particular interest in growing peaches, apples and pears, and during that time, we had abundant tree fruit.

Cape Cod Women's Liberation was brought down by Rolling Rock beer. We held a fund-raising dance at town hall in Provincetown. One member of the committee offered to arrange for refreshments. She ordered many cases of Rolling Rock beer. Unfortunately for us, she greatly overestimated how much beer women would drink. Less than a quarter was consumed. We then discovered it was not returnable. We were broke and had to close our women's center and cancel a speaker. Recriminations made meetings unbearable. That beer sat in the basement of Robert's office rusting for a year until we finally sold it off cheap and under the table to a local bar. But the debt to the beer company bankrupted the group, and it folded. It was a fine dance, though. I used to throw dance parties at Robert's office, which had a big central room with hardwood floors. People danced a lot then. I miss that.

I paid Wayne's tuition at Cambridge-Goddard in political science, but that did not turn into anything that seized his attention. The relationship began to fray. He was twenty-five by now and discontent with my commitment to him. He felt that he was always second to Robert, which was true. He was young, my Judaism put him off, and we had little power struggles that were wearying.

Estelle was colder than Dolores but far more pragmatic. You could turn her loose in the kitchen or garden without inciting catastrophe. However, a lot went on under the surface, resentments I often missed until the consequences emerged. Still, we had fun. We took crazy excursions to see how a commercial dairy farm really operated (disgusting) and to a state fair. We went on hikes and picnics, to the beach and to conferences and meetings and meetings and meetings. We shared all household tasks, which rendered them far less boring and monotonous. Cleaning day was a game.

I had gotten to know Denise Levertov during this period and, much more intensely, Adrienne Rich. I knew many women in the arts in the Boston area and on the Cape. One great advantage of friendship with Denise and even more with Adrienne was the ability to talk about our writing in a real and intelligent way, without being accused of having a male attitude toward work. A problem with women friends on the Cape was their habit of dropping by. I had instituted a policy when I left New York of not letting people do this. I wanted them to call. This was before I had an answering machine, so I answered the phone. But I had no difficulty saying, this is not a good time. Not this morning. How about at three-thirty this afternoon? How about this evening? The other reason I did not let people drop in was because of my friends in the underground and our mutual fear that they would be discovered visiting me if people came idly by. Many of my friends had moved to the Cape to live an easier, more laid-back life and did not appreciate my writing schedule.

Thanksgiving 1974 brought trouble. We always had a crowd for Thanksgiving and I roasted a goose. That year, we had twelve, including two young boys. Wayne had given me for my birthday the year before a large aquarium and some tropical fish. I was not enamored of tropical fish. I'm no good with pets I can't have a relationship with. They died frequently. They ate their young, like Joyce's Ireland. I found them not so much soothing as depressing, but I learned to do the best I could to enjoy them, because when a lover gives you an expensive present, you have to like it. At Thanksgiving, the two boys were constantly asking Robert if they could feed the fish. They were nice kids, just excited about any animals—they were good with cats, dogs, turtles. Robert took out some frozen brine shrimp to feed the fish and used an electric knife to cut it. The knife slipped and almost severed the little finger of his left hand, his dominant hand.

I called the rescue squad, which is a miracle here. In the meantime, the oldest boy, who had learned first aid at school, did exactly the right thing with a tourniquet. Blood was spurting all over the place and Robert was going into shock. I wrapped him up and they took him to a local doctor, who looked at his hand and said quite honestly, "I can't do anything with this. Take him to the hospital." The hospital is in Hyannis—fifty minutes away. He went off in the ambulance and I followed in a car with Estelle. They could sew up the wound and roughly reattach the finger, but the nerve damage was extensive, so he could not write or manipulate objects with his dominant hand. It was months before Robert completed a series of operations with a doctor in Boston—called oddly enough Nailbuff—a specialist in digits. It was a long and frightening process. His hand was in various casts, various contraptions from operation to operation. By late May his wounds healed and he regained control. He could do everything he could do before, but he was bitter about the accident and the wasted time. It became my fault, because the boys were the children of a woman from my group.

In 1975, we entered a period of financial drought. Estelle and Robert had run out of paying contracts. He was scheduled to go to Germany (the ongoing project of many years with Tole and the German mathematician Petrie) in November, but nothing was bringing in money. Wayne was out of work too. Estelle also decided that I was in the way of her developing a meaningful relationship with Robert. I received an offer from Grand Valley College of the University of Michigan system to teach for the fall quarter there—a group of schools near Grand Rapids. Robert and Estelle urged me to take the offer, to make money and to give them the opportunity to resolve their underlying tensions, both work and emotional. At the same time, Wayne talked his family into sending him back to school for a Ph.D. at Michigan State University in East Lansing. He had decided he would never get anywhere without a Ph.D. and was tired of life as a semiskilled worker. I encouraged him. We parted amiably, and he continued to visit on vacations. I thought if Robert and Estelle worked things out, we could go on being a family without Wayne. I was aware Robert and I were happiest in a group situation, and I was less needy. I would do just about anything to hold what remained of our family together.

Through the last year, Estelle had been pressuring me to have a relationship with a woman. She kept trying to be a matchmaker. This was a time when many men were trying relationships with men and women were trying to love each other. A number of people I knew changed over permanently, but many tried it out and then switched back. A rare few found that they were bisexual. I have two friends who genuinely seem indifferent to the sex of lovers.

I was naive and blind about Estelle. I liked her and I assumed she liked me just as much, but I learned the next year that she had talked behind my back. Although exploring affairs with women, she was primarily interested in Robert, but not if he was still involved with me. I did not see any of this until later. I was passionately engaged in my writing, my political activity, and inclined to float along, assuming everybody was happy and doing just fine. I can be pretty stupid about things happening under the surface when I'm busy and fascinated by work.

I had many fantasies about teaching. This was, after all, part of the larger University of Michigan system. I had enjoyed my stint in the Residential College. I worked hard on the design of my courses, listed in both the English department and Women's Studies. I was teaching a poetry workshop, supposedly advanced; a mixed prose forms class, everything from journals to fiction; and a lit course—Towards the Evolution of Women's Culture. I rented an apartment in a house owned by one of the Women's Studies faculty, who found me a student roommate. Estelle drove me out and got me settled. I was living in Grand

Rapids and commuting about forty-five minutes to the campus in Grand Valley.

It was an unmitigated disaster. I was lonely, even though Wayne began coming to visit me when he could. I also saw another poet in a casual way and I made a friend of an anthropologist, a woman who had been born and brought up on the U.P.—the Upper Peninsula of Michigan. But I don't transplant well. I travel well enough, but when I am away from home for too long, I am miserable. This had not been true when I was younger, when I would pick up and go almost anywhere at almost any time for almost any reason and stay until whenever. I discovered to my shock that I had really put down roots on the Cape. I loved the land I lived on. I loved our crooked jerry-built tiny house, a box half buried in the sand of its hill. I missed Robert. I missed my garden, I missed my cats, I missed my office and my friends. My life was back there and I was in exile.

The apartment was flea ridden to the point where I would be kept awake at night by fleas biting me. My body was covered with small red welts that itched into torture. After several futile attempts to murder fleas, I flew home for Columbus Day weekend, demanding my landlady fumigate. She finally did.

I had not been back on campus more than a week when my lit class exploded. I was teaching a book a week: *Orlando* by Virginia Woolf, *Three Lives* by Gertrude Stein. I would lecture on Monday, have them discuss the work on Wednesday, and on Friday we would do something interesting like act out a play of Stein's. I was having a marvelous time. I loved the work I was teaching, I had something to say about every writer we took up, and I wanted the class to enjoy and want to read more. The class revolted. They accused me of being male identified because I was asking them to read and think and analyze what they read—to read critically. Confused, I asked them what they did in their other classes. "We discuss our feelings." "Then I'd expect you'd have plenty of opportunity to use up your feelings in other classes, and you can read and think about other people's work in this one." "You're oppressing us!"

I asked for the support of other women faculty, but they sided with the students. Feelings were what was important. Nowadays, women's studies is a rigorous academic discipline that still relates to the personal, but in that time and place, the split appearing between activists who wanted to change society and lifestyle women who wanted a pleasant enclave was emerging right on my head. I did not enjoy the class after that. I put in my time and covered things instead of illuminating them.

It was the height of New Age stuff, some of which I could relate to and some of which I found silly. My mother was a talented palm reader. It seemed to me what she read was really the person sitting there. I had learned about the tarot from my intense study of Yeats. The tarot came easily to me because many of the symbols felt like a rich storehouse of heretical Western European imagery. For a few years, I would do readings. I took barter. One painter would iron three items of clothing for a reading. An artist in glass and metalwork made me a beautiful lion of Judah on a chain superimposed on a Mogen David. Another young woman bartered fish her boyfriend caught.

But I could not get into astrology. I think people like either astronomy or astrology. When every day at Grand Valley I was asked what sign I was born under, I would say, under the sign of the flying red horse, meaning the corner Mobil station, or under the sign of Ford Motor Company, whose factories were nearby. At lunch in the faculty cafeteria, the school astrologer would pass from table to table. I did not fit in well. It seemed to me few of the women in feminist circles were political in any sense I could recognize. They lived in more or less stable lesbian couples and spent a lot of time on home improvement and interior decorating. My roommate was obsessed with her boyfriend and passed hours playing the same Joni Mitchell album over and over till I wished repeating phonographs had never been invented. I did not adore Grand Rapids. I could not get used to seeing a sign for a bookstore, walking in and discovering only Christian tracts. This was not my Michigan.

Estelle had propagandized for lesbian attachments, and indeed, this was a time in the women's movement when there was pressure to do just that. I went to bed with an old friend of mine who had come to see me, but I was learning that however easy sex was for me, women simply did not fall in love with me, even when I loved them. I think I was no longer a good lover for women, as I had been in adolescence. I had gotten lazy, used to heterosexual sex. I was used to some foreplay, then to it. Women required far more preparation than I was accustomed to. I realized that year that I was heterosexual and bound to stay that way. I did not feel guilty about it. I did not regret it. I simply accepted it and would not again be pressured, coerced or persuaded. I have always had close lesbian friends, but I was no longer tempted to try to make them into my lovers.

Every morning I woke with the sense I was in the wrong place, with the wrong people. I had grown a deep taproot, and away from my home, I withered emotionally. Robert never came out until it was time to fetch me home. In the meantime, Estelle and he quarreled. Far from finding liberation in my absence, they could not get along. Estelle returned to San Francisco, and Robert left for Germany, where he injured his leg. Every so often, he would exacerbate an old injury or incur a new one, usually in his knee. When he came out to Grand Rapids to fetch me in late December, he limped badly. I was deliriously happy to go home, but I sensed a coldness in him. I returned in a state of ecstasy, while he had created a life excluding me.

The cats looked terrible. Arofa's fur had turned grayish. I fed them and fussed them up and soon they were glossy and happy. Robert had been living on sausages and luncheon meats in Germany, leaving his digestive system a rutted road to the dump. I put us on a healthy diet and tried to get him to exercise.

It was a month before he told me he had seen a woman in early December he had fallen in love with. I had known Rosemarie years before on *Viet Report,* and when I was on NACLA. Again, Robert and I had been with her in Mexico on the way to Cuba. We had never been friends. I had found Rosemarie supercilious. I was not overjoyed, but there was nothing I could do except wait and see. After Wayne left, I had begun sharing Karen's little Somerville apartment, but I was imposing on her. With Robert bringing someone into our life with whom my encounters had been less than cordial, I needed a place in the city even more. My women friends were my only support, those on the Cape and in Boston. The coming year, 1976, I would need my friends in order to survive, I would need them badly.

IF THEY COME IN THE NIGHT

Long ago on a night of danger and vigil
a friend said, Why are you happy?
He explained (we lay together
on a hard cold floor) what prison
meant because he had done
time, and I talked of the death
of friends. Why are you happy
then, he asked, close to angry.

I said, I like my life. If I
have to give it back, if they
take it from me, let me only
not feel I wasted any, let me
not feel I forgot to love anyone
I meant to love, that I forgot
to give what I held in my hands,
that I forgot to do some little
piece of the work that wanted
to come through.

Sun and moonshine, starshine,
the muted grey light off the waters
of the bay at night, the white
light of the fog stealing in,
the first spears of the morning
touching a face
I love. We all lose

everything. We lose
ourselves. We are lost.

Only what we manage to do
lasts, what love sculpts from us;
but what I count, my rubies, my
children, are those moments
wide open when I know clearly
who I am, who you are, what we
do, a marigold, an oakleaf, a meteor,
with all my senses hungry and filled
at once like a pitcher with light.

FIFTEEN

THE LAND THAT OWNS ME

The summer from hell was almost upon me. That spring, I became ill. We were still short of money, and I had to take all the gigs that came in, no matter how much traveling was involved, so there was no time to recover. While I was in Cazenovia, New York, in early May at the women's writing center, I ran a fever and could not shake a bad cough. I was having trouble with my lungs for the first time since I had left New York, and it frightened me.

We were living alone, the two of us, although we had lots of visitors. I realized that we got on best when there were other people around. I was worried about our connection, worried about my health. Cape Cod Women's Liberation was dead. My consciousness-raising group had stopped meeting, as many of us had left the Cape. We have a lot of turnover. People come, people go, they can't make a living, they imagine they will make more money in the city or become better known. They lose their rental. They lose their jobs. They break up.

I saw Wayne while doing a couple of gigs in the Midwest in April, and our relationship felt decayed. He would not tell me what was wrong, but after a while, I got it out of him. He was seriously involved with a very young woman but did not want me to meet her. He said the magic had gone out of our love. That is the sort of statement bound to put me in a rage, since I don't believe in magic in relationships, only in goodwill and hard work. He insisted he wanted the connection to continue. I was willing to give it a try, because he had been one of my only sources of comfort in Grand Rapids.

A young man I had known since he was seventeen and joined the SDS Regional in New York was living in Cambridge. We had been through a lot politically and personally over the years. When he had come up from underground, I was the first person he called. Now he was working in a restaurant. He had a roommate he had told me about, but whom I had not met, Ira Wood, generally called Woody.

On Pesach, I was coming over to see my friend. It was a warm sunny day in mid-April, with the leaves just beginning to open and dogs in packs barking and happy, every car with its windows down and its tape deck booming in the music wars that come as the weather lets people outside. Woody remembers seeing me stride down the street dressed very butch, rail thin and wearing leather. I remember seeing a young man standing on the porch of my friend's tiny rickety wooden house, curly haired, of medium height with intense blue-green eyes. This being 1976, his dark brown hair was worn in a huge Afro. In preparation for a seder, he was ineffectually beating a bowl of egg whites. He introduced himself, and I took the bowl away from him. They were never going to whip up the way he was doing it. It made us both laugh. Somehow, he had known I would do that. I learned much, much later that he had invented this little scene as a way of meeting me. It worked. After that, I had dinner with him a couple of times and spent time both with him and my friend and him alone. I checked him out with mutual friends, but with no urgency. He had great charm and a gentle manner, but he was as young as Wayne. I was too depressed to be interested. Then I got sick on my travels and half forgot him.

The last week in May, Robert was in Germany and Wayne came while I was not yet well enough to manage by myself. The very first night, things reached such intense hostility that I locked myself in my bedroom, hiding there with the cats until the day he was due to go into the city to leave. He wanted me to sign over to him part of the land, so he could live there with his girlfriend, whom I had never met. He felt that since he had lived with Robert and me but owned none of the land, in the spirit of the times it was due him. From the point of view of my own survival, I could not see giving him the lot across the road that he wanted. I viewed that lot as a sort of savings account for an emergency. If I was dead broke, I could sell the land I bought over Robert's objections. Wayne was getting his Ph.D. and would have a steady job. I was having trouble making enough to hold the house together.

This era was a low point of my personal life. My effort to make a close relationship with Estelle had been a failure. Robert was distant from me and in love with a woman I had not liked. Wayne was out of my life. Penny was up in New Hampshire having economic, personal and health problems. Various other friends of mine were up shit creek: one in an abusive relationship, another having a breakdown, another in an automobile accident that left her crippled for months. I was wearing perilously thin emotionally and physically. I had dropped too much weight—not intentionally. I had lost my generally zesty appetite. I was alone a lot and did not bother to cook. The cats had suffered during the fall, while I was in exile, aging a couple of years in those months. They had recovered considerably, but like me, they were not as they had been.

When Wayne's week with me ended, he dropped me in Cambridge at my old friend's house shared with Woody, on a dead-end street near the Martin Luther King grade school and the local projects. I was extremely upset after the confrontations with Wayne. I am a giving person in close relationships, so that often it comes as a shock to lovers when I can't be pushed any further and simply dig in. They keep expecting me to crumble. I don't. I know the difference between someone treating me as a person and someone using me as a resource. The two-hour ride into Cambridge had verged on nightmare.

Woody, my old friend and I were a good combination, political and talkative and amazingly silly. We would smuggle a bottle of Kahlúa into a local ice cream store and eat makeshift sundaes. We gave dance parties and lavish suppers. We sat stoned through movies and afterward improvised better plots. Their companionship cheered me. Woody offered to come out and keep me company, quasi-taking care of me. Robert was due back in another ten days.

It was only the first week of June but the spring had been warm, sometimes hot. Many roses were in bloom, sour cherries ripe, the gardens overflowing with broccoli, snow peas, salad greens. Although the landscaping was not nearly as beautiful as it is now, it was paradise next to hot weather in Cambridge near the projects. We had always talked easily. Now we were a little awkward, neither of us sure what the other had in mind. All that Woody remembers of supper is the sour cherry soup, a cold soup I learned from my grandmother. We sat up very late in the living room until finally he made a move—I wasn't about to.

It took us both a long time to realize what we began that evening was a commitment that would grow and fill us. For one thing, I was used to thinking of Robert as the center of my emotional life. Like Wayne, Woody was much younger than me, and as Wayne had grown dissatisfied with what he judged an unequal situation, I rather expected the same from Woody. It took a while for me to perceive him clearly. It was a slow process over the next four years of growing together, of learning to take this at first fragile connection seriously. I did not want another relationship with someone much younger than me. I had been occasionally seeing an older writer who lived in New York, and I was consciously looking for someone nearer my own age.

I was probably less able to consider it important at first, because I felt I was protecting myself from my pain with Robert by hiding with Woody, by enjoying his nature, which was far more emotional and far warmer than Robert's temperament. I was living primarily in Wellfleet; he was living in Cambridge. We both worked where we lived. Woody did not think he could be that important to me, since I was married to Robert. It took both of us some time to understand what we could have together.

Finally Rosemarie arrived, chipper and hostile. I was, according to Rosemarie, the image of a suburban housewife, trudging about the house in slippers (which I wore only while getting breakfast for everyone), my hair braided. She saw me as overweight, although I was actually painfully thin, but my breasts were big—and hers were not. She wrote all this down and gave it to Robert, who took it all very seriously. A woman he was sexually obsessed with criticizing me made me far less valuable. I needed repair. I was inadequate, since I did not please her—or him, it would seem. This had happened before with male friends of his, whose disapproval would make him question my worth, but it had never happened with a woman. Usually I had a decent relationship with his girlfriends, if not a close one. This was the first time a much younger woman had looked at me as an older discardable woman. It was a shock.

She was melted wax with him, sexually masochistic. He saw her as far more feminine than I was, far more submissive. That excited him. He spent almost all his time with her, and when he bothered to come home, he brought her with him. I had to find a place in the city I could go to regularly, so I located a commune where I could have a room up on the third floor cheaply, a three-story wooden house between two hospitals, just a few houses from the Somerville line. I learned I could actually write there. It was a safe place.

I had trouble believing what was happening. I found Robert cruel; I found Rosemarie abusive. I was used to a certain rhetoric about sisterhood and to women trying to look out for one another, at least pretending to. I experienced her contempt whenever I was near her. She moved to the office after the first few days, so that they could have more privacy. I was pleased to have her out of the house. I wished I could have her out of my life. He would repeat what she said, vicious criticism, scathing remarks, as if half expecting me to agree with them. I was sloppy, I was obsessed with food, I was self-important about my writing, which wasn't politically correct or important. I took up all available space. I was demanding and possessive. I was really just a housewife with intellectual pretensions, self-centered and whiny, who did not treat Robert and his feelings with the respect they deserved. I was preventing him from growing. In spite of the multitude of other relationships Robert had enjoyed over the years, I always felt he was on my side, that he had my welfare in mind. Suddenly I found that to be an illusion. In previous configurations, we had fun together. We traveled, ate, worked and played as a family, no matter what tensions might exist. It had been an advantage to have a group. Now we were not a family. We were a civil war.

I wondered if I were going crazy. I had been writing *Woman on the Edge of Time,* with many scenes in a mental institution. It came out that spring. Now I wondered if I had lost my sanity, because I was confused by the reality of my life and relationships. I was having trouble believing what I was enduring. I was tearing apart inside. My pain made me feel broken, demented. I was like a dog that snaps at her wounds as she runs. It is hard for me to convey how strongly I had believed in my connection with Robert, how much I felt that relationship to be part of me. Now part of me was torn away. I was bleeding myself anemic. So much of my life had been built around his needs, his wishes, his experiments—for I had been more than grateful to be given the years it had taken me to start making a living as a writer—that the fact he might no longer wish to be with me was a big shock. I have trouble remembering details because I went around in a fog of pain.

Basically, my friends persuaded me I hadn't gone mad and that I should hold my ground. When I talked about moving into Cambridge, my friends calmed me and advised me to wait out what they thought was his momentary obsession. Almost everyone was convinced Robert would snap out of it. Rosemarie wasn't exactly popular. She acted superior and seemed cold, although she was neither with Robert. Of course, my friends were also loyal, so they disliked her. Robert denied he was doing anything unusual—didn't I want him to have real commitments instead of brief meaningless affairs—but he imitated her attitude and behavior toward me. He was besotted with her and largely ignored me. I felt like a chambermaid. I was the menial household servant providing meals and clean laundry—including her sheets—and I was sick of the role. I went on strike. I stopped cooking, cleaning, picking up and let the garden go.

I was running to the city regularly, staying in my commune, hanging out with my new lover, Woody, and my old friend, hanging out with women friends. Robert did not object to the amount of time I was spending in Boston. They took over the house while I was gone. I guessed it would please both of them if I simply disappeared. I returned to the Cape feeling as if I no longer belonged there. It was not only that Robert was in love with Rosemarie and sexually besotted with her: I had gone through that many times. It was that he was dismissive of me, contemptuous. If Rosemarie disliked me, it had to be my fault. There had to be something wrong with me. To me it was painfully obvious she wanted to be his only relationship. She was not interested in multiple relationships, no matter what rhetoric she might spout. She saw him, reasonably enough, as husband material. She was an academic from a well-off family, thin, blond and sure of herself. She had been married once before, and obviously, she wished to be so again. I realized that open relationships could not work unless every party to them was committed to the group.

When I returned from Boston, Robert was off with Rosemarie in his office. I walked around the land, the birch and maple and white firs I had planted, the gardens we had created, the rhododendrons and roses and daylilies, the raspberries and grapevines that had only begun to bear, and suddenly instead of feeling crazy or broken, I got angry. There were signs of her presence, her hegemony everyplace in the house. I packed her things into two boxes and put them on the porch. That evening, I had a fierce desire to burn down the house. It seemed a fitting gesture. I went so far as to collect Arofa and Cho-Cho and put them in the downstairs bedroom with their carrying case and food and water dishes, ready to be brought out to the car. I started to go through my things to decide what I would take.

Then I had my second moment of clarity in the midst of my private tornado of angst. I was looking out at the main garden, the late July light gilding the ripening tomatoes on their stakes and the lacy leaves of the honey locust outside my office, the first marigolds orange among the bush beans. This house was mine, not his. I had paid for most of it. I had bought the land adjacent to it and the land across the road over his objections and out of advances on various paperbacks. We now had close to four acres. I loved this land and this place, and I was not leaving it. Why destroy a house I had designed? Why make the cats live in a tiny hot apartment in the city? Why abandon what I loved to a man who did not care about me or our life together?

I am astonished when I review this important and miserable summer how little documentation there is—a couple of poems. I seem never to have written anyone about my situation: instead my long-distance bills were astronomical, for I was on the phone daily and nightly to friends in Boston and to Penny in New Hampshire. That night I spoke to Penny to clear my mind; then I called Robert at his office. I told him the situation was unendurable, that I resented the way he was treating me, and he could live at the office with Rosemarie or he could change how he was behaving with me. But I would not deal with Rosemarie any longer. Either he put some effort into our relationship, or it was terminated.

I had just hung up when Penny called him, I later learned. She told him he was behaving like an asshole, and if he wanted to move out, just to do so, and stop tormenting me. He should be honest about what he wanted. I think he was shocked to realize that other people were observing and judging him.

That night he asked Rosemarie to leave for a time, to return to Long Island while he worked on his relationship with me. She was furious and never forgave him. She had been so sure of him that this reversal shocked her. Their connection abraded, although each made attempts for the next few months. There was a large charred area in the middle of all of our feelings, our interactions. I did not understand why he had agreed to send her away, but I did not think it was because he could not stand to be without me. I suspected more practical considerations of property and finances were involved, but I could not get an answer from him. He only said he did it because I asked him to.

I would never after this point trust Robert the way I had. Until the summer of 1976, I was quite convinced that no matter what involvements he or I had, our connection was strong, was at the center of both of us and would survive. We had been living with multiple relationships since 1966, and I took our strange lifestyle for granted as suited to us. Now I no longer retained that conviction. I had been shunted aside and almost banished. I believed that if I had walked out and moved to Boston, he would have merrily installed Rosemarie in the house, and they would have lived there together. That might or might not have worked out. When I had acquiesced to Estelle's and his desire to be alone, they had quarreled and broken off both their personal and work relationship. But I was not interested in whether he would be happy alone with Rosemarie. I no longer felt sure of my connection with him. I was eager to strengthen and repair that relationship, but I no longer fully trusted it, or him. I had a growing persistent suspicion that he was looking to replace me with a wife more to his liking. His work situation remained problematic and sometimes impossible. I earned money and put that money into the household, but I did not bring in enough for a truly affluent lifestyle. He greatly enjoyed dining out at fancy restaurants and traveling for pleasure. My allergy to cigarette smoke made both of those problematic for me in the mid-1970s. I was not as yielding as I had been.

In truth, I had changed. I was stronger. I was stronger physically. Although I had been ill in May, my recovery was quick. By early June, I was healthy again. I was stronger in my conviction of my own worth. Even the limited success I had with my writing—and I never expected to write bestsellers—had bolstered my innate sense that I was supposed to write, and that my writing was something some or even many other people could relate to. I had changed agents the year before. My new agent, Lois Wallace, was getting foreign sales for me. *Woman on the Edge of Time* was being translated into several languages. Feminism had given me a spine. At some point in those weeks, Robert remarked that he had expected me to publish something eventually, probably poems, but that he never expected people to pay so much attention. I had always thought he supported my writing because he believed in it. I had been wrong.

My reputation was growing, and sometimes when Robert was with me, there would be a fuss he found disturbing. Woody was far less bothered, since he knew me as a writer before he knew me as a person. He took a certain amount of fame for granted. Robert never did. I had changed and did not want to change back. I still had peasant virtues. I could cook almost anything, gourmet or budget, and make it taste good. I was a talented gardener. I was cool in emergencies and capable of action. I enjoyed luxuries but could live on much less. I communicated well with animals. I relished pleasures of the mind and the flesh equally. I could make a dwelling comfortable and attractive on little money. I liked sex and I knew men's bodies and how to give and how to take pleasure. Sex came easily to me. But I wasn't the earth mother I had been. I watched my time carefully and put work first. I was no longer flattered by the attention of almost anybody. I was not nearly as willing to sacrifice myself to Robert or anyone else. When we grew short on money again that fall, I discarded offers that I go off to Idaho or Arkansas and teach for a semester. I wouldn't go into exile alone to support him. My assistant and the wastepaper basket were the only ones who knew of these letters. I knew if I mentioned them to Robert, he would expect me to go; but I had set limits to what I would sacrifice.

I also would no longer put anyone into my study to sleep. He had a large office; I had a small crowded one, although one I loved. I moved the bed out. I was demanding more respect for my writing and my writing time, not a popular move with Robert. He had four large rooms at his office, and two of them served well for guests. The office downstairs, used by my assistant, also had a bed in it. But my study—the room where I worked and kept my books and paper and files—was now off limits to everyone but me—and the cats.

We took a great many walks that fall. We explored sand roads on the Cape in areas where we had never gone and we revisited old discoveries. We were both trying. When I was given any grounds for hope, I succumbed. I had always imagined we would grow old together. I had thought that he would lose interest in affairs and we would settle into a calmer and deeper companionship. During this period, Woody came out frequently, and he and Robert got along, although never as well as Wayne and Robert had. Robert knew that Woody was on my side, totally, and there was little in that for him.

Robert was still seeing Rosemarie occasionally, but it was not satisfying. She did not want a part-time relationship. He felt I had caused the breach by my ultimatum, one that I did not regret. After that, whenever he was angry with me, he would bring up my interference in his intimacy with Rosemarie. I felt I had saved myself and perhaps our marriage. Of the latter I was hopeful, but not convinced. I knew I had chosen to preserve myself. He could accuse me, but he could inspire no guilt. I was not ashamed of having gotten her out of my life. If she had bothered to be polite to me, no doubt in the long run she could have done far more damage—but she was too sure of her hold on Robert and too contemptuous of me to make the effort at a friendly facade.

Robert talked of moving back to New York. I listened but did not chime in with my perennial willingness. I had put down roots on the Cape. Still, he was spending more time with me than he had since Estelle arrived. My primary emotional support was coming from Woody and close female friends, but I felt as if Robert and I had at least partly repaired our intimacy. It was a heavily damaged structure but one we could still inhabit, so for a time, we did.

TO HAVE WITHOUT HOLDING

Learning to love differently is hard,
love with the hands wide open, love
with the doors banging on their hinges,
the cupboard unlocked, the wind
roaring and whimpering in the rooms
rustling the sheets and snapping the blinds
that thwack like rubber bands
in an open palm.

It hurts to love wide open
stretching the muscles that feel
as if they are made of wet plaster,
then of blunt knives, then
of sharp knives.

It hurts to thwart the reflexes
of grab, of clutch; to love and let
go again and again. It pesters to remember
the lover who is not in the bed,

to hold back what is owed to the work
that gutters like a candle in a cave
without air, to love consciously,
conscientiously, concretely, constructively.

I can't do it, you say, it's killing
me; but you thrive, you glow
on the street like a neon raspberry.
You float and sail, a helium balloon
bright bachelor's button blue and bobbing
on the cold and hot winds of our breath,
as we make and unmake in passionate
diastole and systole the rhythm
of our unbounded bonding, to have
and not to hold, to love
with minimized malice, hunger
and anger moment by moment balanced.

SIXTEEN

INTERLUDE ON SLEEP AND GARDENING WITH CATS

Cats are athletes of sleep, champions. A cat's ability to drop off any time and almost anywhere never stops enchanting and amazing me. Sleep is mysterious to me. Sometimes I climb into bed exhausted and cannot imagine how I can ever move from this restless raw fatigue into unconsciousness. It appears to me to require some kind of divine intervention to sink from one state into the other. There are nights when I cannot cross over, doomed to look at the greenish light of the clock again and again, telling myself if I fall asleep now I'll still get four hours sleep, three and a half, three. Other times of course, I doze readily and then it's morning.

Some nights when I have trouble sleeping, Malkah comes into bed and purrs me to sleep. She seems to bring sleep with her, like a dark halo around her thick apricot and white fur. She presses her bulk into my side and sometimes gently kneads me. Sleep seems to emanate from her and I slide down into it.

I make an effort to train my cats to sleep at night and get their exercise during the day. Each has a preferred spot on the bed, fine unless they all get in a pile and leave no room for a mammal bigger than a squirrel. In the daytime, they nap where they choose. Dinah and Oboe like my monitor or the sunny bay window. Malkah and Max switch off the two

Marge Piercy on her land in Wellfleet, 1974. Photograph by Robert Shapiro

couches in the living room, only in cold weather sharing one. Usually at least one other cat is with each of them, but the pairing-off varies. Efi is most often curled with Malkah, the two grays together with or without Max, but every day is a new ball game. Any configuration can be found. This morning, it is Oboe, Efi and Malkah. I wonder what rules the pairings, why Efi and Oboe, the two cats who pair with anyone at their choice, one day prefer Max and the next Malkah or Dinah. Cat affinities are mysterious. You will almost never find Malkah and Dinah curled together.

Woody is the epitome of a restless sleeper, kicking his legs, turning over and over like a roast on a spit, mumbling in his sleep, dragging the covers off the bed's edge. He has his own bed in his room—an accident of how we began—but we had not been married long when he began to use it. Sometimes he goes to sleep in my room, then moves to his. In very cold weather or during storms, we sleep in my bed. During power outages, we sleep in his—with its independent stove. Sometimes I think the vigor and freshness of our sexual relationship has something to do with often sleeping separately. When we get a new kitten, that kitten sleeps in his room until ready to be integrated with the population. Then, every time, they move to my bed, which the presence of the other cats makes ultra desirable. Woody complains while he is the foster mother, but then he complains when they desert his bed. He likes to complain. It feels natural to him. He was unhappy a long time, and complaining makes him feel as if he is warding off greater evil.

The cats like it when we begin working outside in spring—all but Efi, who is a little alarmed and increasingly curious. Max in particular likes to oversee our activities and will often come and stick his face into mine while I am kneeling. He arrives with a curious high interrogative meow and then proceeds to insert himself into my work. He examines the plants, the tools, the hole. We have to cover with agricultural cloth all newly dug-up and seeded patches in the vegetable gardens. Otherwise Max thinks we have created great new litter boxes for him. Freshly ploughed earth is irresistible. Even Malkah sometimes succumbs. Once the seedlings are up and growing, the patch loses its appeal.

I took Efi out on a leash for the first time yesterday. She was terrified and stood and howled. Then she began to be curious and to sniff the air and the ground and the greenery. But in ten minutes she was more than ready to go back in. It was an acceptable beginning; I hope I can teach her to walk on a leash as Arofa did. None of the other cats will. Max was a master at slithering out. With Malkah I would not even try. It would terrify her, and she never ventures far. She is on a leash of her own making. The gray cats I tried very hard to teach to walk on leashes. They would simply collapse, civil disobedience style, and let themselves be dragged. Sometimes I would put them on a harness and attach a long clothesline to it while we were outside with them, so that they could run around and still be safe. They liked that but preferred an enclosure Woody built for them or the gazebo. The other cats were intrigued by Efi's first walk. We went along, accompanied by everybody except Malkah, who reacted with shock and anger. She hissed at me. She did not think Efi should be outside. Oboe and Max took a great interest in her stroll and accompanied her.

Lately Efi has been sleeping with me too. Until recently, she curled up with one or more of them but never pressed into my side. Now she has studied Malkah's pleasure and imitates it. She is slowly becoming more of a lap cat. Sometimes she will push one of the other cats out of my lap, as Oboe used to do when he was young and bumptious. Now she demands me and demands Woody. Mine, she says, mine! Oboe adores her. He finds her exquisite and spoils her with his attention, but she returns it fully. Except when Efi and Malkah go on the mouse safari, Efi tends to be sharply diurnal, like the Korats. She goes to bed when we do and gets up when we get up.

Oboe and Dinah visibly dream. My Colette, a Burmese, had nightmares, especially when she was young. She would whimper and moan and sometimes her fur would stand up. I would have to wake and soothe her. Both Max and Malkah sometimes have bad dreams and cry out, but not as often as the year we rescued them from the shelter. Efi seems to sleep with a smile on her face.

When I was much younger, I had elaborate dreams. Sometimes I would dream the same thing twice in a row, the second time revising and refining the story. There were characters, environments, denouements. As I have become more productive and write constantly for publication, I dream far less vividly. I produce simple anxiety dreams, nonsense fragments of my day focused on sex or anxiety. I rarely use my dreams in writing. I know poets who are obsessed with dreams and try to create poems from them, but I think people's dreams are mostly of interest to the individual who just woke up. One of the nuisances of communal living is having to listen to other people's dreams at breakfast.

Often when I am away I miss the cats in my bed. In spite of their occasional restlessness and mine, I sleep better with my cats than without. It is one of the times we are all mammals together, sharing the same experience as well as the same space. We take mutual comfort in one another's warm presence and soft breathing. Who sleeps with whom and where is of paramount importance to cats, just as it is to people. It is one of the ways they express their trust, their affection, their bonding. Of course, when Woody is gone, I sleep little and fitfully. I miss him most in the evenings, the night, the morning. During the day I work, but after work, I feel his absence like a vacuum I circle aimlessly. We need each other in a daily way, need to talk, to touch in order to feel complete. Perhaps we are overdependent, but we fill a need each has had lifelong.

SLEEPING WITH CATS

I am at once source
and sink of heat; giver
and taker. I am a vast

soft mountain of slow breathing.
The smells I exude soothe them:
the lingering odor of sex,
of soap, even of perfume,
its afteraroma sunk into skin
mingling with sweat and the traces
of food and drink.

They are curled into flowers
of fur, they are coiled
hot seashells of flesh
in my armpit, around my head
a dark sighing halo.
They are plastered to my side,
a poultice fixing sore muscles
better than a heating pad.
They snuggle up to my sex
purring. They embrace my feet.

Some cats I place like a pillow.
In the morning they rest where
I arranged them, still sleeping.
Some cats start at my head
and end between my legs
like a textbook lover. Some
slip out to prowl the living room
patrolling, restive, then
leap back to fight about
hegemony over my knees.

Every one of them cares
passionately where they sleep
and with whom.
Sleeping together is a euphemism

for people but tantamount
to marriage for cats.
Mammals together we snuggle
and snore through the cold nights
while the stars swing round
the pole and the great horned
owl hunts for flesh like ours.

SEVENTEEN

SOME THINGS WEAR OUT AND SOME THINGS DON'T

Ira and I worked on a play for community theater, because he'd been active as a playwright and an actor in several theater groups in Boston. He had driven a school bus during the antibusing violence and helped protect an Afro-American family whose safety was threatened in a predominantly white neighborhood. The play was begun in crude form when Woody was working with a theater group that broke up. Since there was a demand locally for a play about racial violence, we decided to start over and do a professional job. I had never written a play; a new genre excited me. I discovered that working with live actors with their own agendas was very different from working with characters existing only in my mind and on the page. You could write a character as a sleazy self-pitying lowlife, and the actor could play him as the young James Dean. Still, we liked writing together, and it brought us closer.

One warm day that fall, Woody and I went to a party at a dune shack—what such buildings on the National Seashore are called, although this was a rather elegant one. We knew few people at the party, but most of them knew who I was. One man began talking very loudly in front of me about idiot women's liberationists and what he wanted to do to them. I stood up and poured my drink in his lap. I told him to charge me for the dry cleaning and we walked out.

It was not the smartest thing I've ever done, but I was not sorry. However, we had been brought out to the party by Jeep and neither of us had a notion how to get back. We headed in what we considered the probable direction out of the dunes. Even in late October, there are days on the Cape, sunstruck and bronzed, with the heat of summer but with harder edges and stronger colors. We held hands and staggered up and down the dunes, golden with late afternoon, speckled with patches of reddened wild cranberries and stunted oaks. Happy in spite of being lost, we rested in the occasional patch of shade in the lee of a sand hill. We felt close, and I was grateful that he had backed me up and did not try to make me feel guilty for leaving the party and getting us lost.

Eventually, a couple of hours later, we staggered out onto Route 6 and went in search of our car. When we finally returned to the house, Robert had gone out to supper with a friend. We nibbled leftovers from the refrigerator. Then we made love far more passionately and sensuously than we ever had before. It was a different kind of joining. We both felt immensely moved. I wept. For the first time, we told each other "I love you" and we meant it. We were to have rocky and rough times, but what changed that day never changed back. Afterward, we had a bond that was rooted perhaps in sex but was emotional and mental as well. From that evening on, we were in some primal sense bonded.

I was starting *Vida,* about a woman who lived underground, a political fugitive. I was strongly engaged by my subject and writing a great deal of poetry. Starting with my fourth collection, *Living in the Open,* Knopf has published my poetry. I was giving many readings, workshops and occasional lectures. After *Woman on the Edge of Time,* I was sometimes asked to talk about women's utopian writing or futurist feminism and address science fiction conferences.

That spring, Woody became involved with Linda, a young unmarried mother with a preschool daughter. She came from Long Island, as Woody did, from a professional family, but she had been living as a hippie on the fringes of the movement. She entered the relationship knowing about me and Robert but never liked the situation. This did not make for a tranquil life. The social climate was gradually changing. Almost no one we knew was having multiple relationships. Serial monogamy had returned. We were constantly having to explain ourselves to people we met. Our habit was becoming a liability.

That summer, Woody drove across country with two friends to work with the San Francisco Mime Troupe. In the meantime, I joined the Feminist Writers Guild. In our Boston branch, I met Elise, who was Woody's age and remains one of my best friends. Of Italian background, she grew up in Cherry Hill, outside Philadelphia. She had the face of a Raphael Madonna and great stubbornness and loyalty. She was interested in journalism but later decided her real passion was art. She supports herself as a university fund-raiser.

In August, I flew to San Francisco to give readings and a benefit for the Feminist Writers Guild. When I got to the Bay Area, Woody was limping badly. He was dragging himself up the hills of San Francisco, insisting nothing was really wrong. It did not take me long to figure out his injury was serious. A doctor who had been playing basketball with the gang from the Mime Troupe put it down to a strained ligament. When we returned to Cambridge, I made Woody see a doctor. His injury was a ruptured Achilles tendon. He went into the hospital to have it repaired, then lugged around a heavy cast up to his hip for six weeks. He has never regretted that operation. To this day, when he sees someone limping badly, he will remark that it could have been him, if I hadn't insisted.

Robert met a man his own age who flew his own plane, had dabbled in movies, had a fair amount of money and a much more compliant wife than I ever was. The two of them decided to build a small computer— what would be called a p.c. Robert had a contract from his old company that required him to write software but specifically excluded a hardware component. He decided to ignore that and go ahead. The man loved gadgets and so did Robert. Soon the office was jammed with machines blinking lights and whirring tape, with half unpacked boxes of gear, with the cannibalized remains of failed machines.

The spring of 1978, I received a little shock. I was used to being complimented on the health of my cats when I brought them to the vet. This spring, he muttered and poked and said that Arofa was aging rapidly. She was losing weight. He did not, however, do the blood workup he should have. It occurred to me for the first time that I would not have her forever. I found the thought of losing her almost intolerable. We had become closer and closer. We went for short walks together. She sat beside my typewriter as I worked. She was a small cat and I could type with her tucked comfortably on my lap. She sat at the table with us while we ate. She slept in our bed. Except when I was on the road or in the city, she was always with me. She picked up my moods at once, the most empathic cat I ever had. I could tell her that something pleased or displeased me by placing a hand on her head. Cho-Cho had a more evolved life with cats. She had visitors, she had friends and enemies. Arofa was largely indifferent to other cats.

I encouraged Robert's involvement in the small computer project, because it had been a long time—before Estelle left—since he had been engaged by work. I wondered that year if Woody would not be happier with Linda than running between us and never seeming to satisfy anyone—but as I watched her, I doubted it. She used jealousy on him too coldly and calculatingly. If he spent much time with me, she would go to bed with someone, a worker from her child's day care center, a friend Woody had introduced her to. Woody was prone to jealousy, and he would become obsessed with her adventures—which, of course, increased with his response. She had no interest in his writing and did not encourage it.

Robert went into therapy, claiming his major problem was being unable to express anger. Since we had huge fights, I could not see this as a real problem. It seemed to me he had more trouble expressing positive emotions. I was assuming he still had them. He began to dislike Woody, suggesting I end the relationship. Woody did not take him as seriously as Robert was used to and did not treat him as the alpha male. Before 1976, I would have argued but complied, or at least seen Woody only in Cambridge. But Woody had become my main emotional and my main sexual connection.

For the first time since we had been together, Robert was having trouble meeting women who wanted to get involved with him. He was hanging out with a younger crowd, and the women were not interested in brief affairs with an older married man they did not consider buff or handsome. He was always pursuing someone he met through Woody's friends, whom he shot pool or hung out with, or someone he met in Science for the People, a group of socially conscious scientists and computer people he had joined. During this period, it was difficult for me to bring women friends to the Cape, because Robert would immediately start bird-dogging them. He blamed me for his lack of success. But the times and mores were changing. Our arrangement required a lot of explaining when I met new friends, and they were often mistrustful, thinking I would therefore go to bed with anyone, including their husbands or boyfriends. I began to find our lifestyle no longer a way into relationships and friendships but an obstacle.

Elise was an exception to the discomfort many women felt in my house. Often women blamed me or felt I was somehow offering them to Robert. I wasn't, but I didn't feel I could change him, for if I tried to steer him away or tell him to lighten up, he would turn on me. I was interfering again. I was coming between him and what he wanted. Elise saw the situation for what it was. She was friendly to him but cool. She liked Woody better but did not act in any way hostile to Robert—she was just untouchable.

One good change in my life during this entire period was that my mother reached out to me. I sent her "Crescent moon like a canoe," a poem about her and my relationship with her. I was afraid it might anger and offend her, and I preferred we deal with it at once. I always sent her my poetry books, and she always read them. She liked my poetry much better than my fiction. To my surprise, she was deeply moved. She said, "I never knew you saw what was happening between your father and me. I never knew you understood."

From that point on, we talked in a way we hadn't since I reached puberty.

In his last years at Westinghouse, my father was the supervisor in Detroit—supervising himself, since they had closed the office except for him. Still, it meant higher pay as well as a lot of paperwork, which he did not mind, for he found it clean work—not blue collar. He was the last person in Michigan who could fix certain old machinery in the paper mills, the steel mills that still stood along the Detroit River. My parents spent half the year in Florida and half in Michigan. They sold the Detroit house for exactly what they had paid for it—property values had not risen in the inner city—and moved to the cottage, still in a constant state of rebuilding.

My father did not like moving back and forth. My mother did. She had reluctantly relinquished her friends in Detroit and the income she got from renting out rooms. She did not want to leave Michigan and her many friends at the cottage. She did not like the heat. My father always won, visiting his decisions on her. Like many working-class men, his powerlessness on the job turned into absolute power at home. They moved to Florida and lived in a trailer in a vast treeless wasteland. There was no point going outside, for there was nothing to see but other trailers to the horizon and the broiling sun beating down on baked clay. Nonetheless, this was Florida, the golden land that marked success to an entire generation of the working class.

Finally they bought a small house, one of the tiny Florida ranch houses that lined the streets of a development in Tequesta, rows of similar houses about ten feet apart where seniors without much money retired. When they first moved, you could find unspoiled open land, scrub palmetto, pinewoods, beaches that stretched for miles. My mother could still walk then, and when Robert and I flew down, we all strolled the beach and went to watch bald eagles raising their young in a state park nearby, examined armadillos, identified the birds we were used to seeing up north and exotic ones. I gave my father a book about saltwater fish. During the next year, he went fishing, which had always been his passion.

Gradually they lost interest in their surroundings. My mother gave up trying to grow anything and let my father do as he pleased with the front and back yards. They did enjoy their orange and grapefruit trees, making juice from baskets of fruit that felt like free stuff from the supermarket. He stopped saltwater fishing. I think he found the all-day trips difficult.

His bladder was not under control. His glaucoma was intensifying. One trip I brought marijuana down and persuaded him to try it, and it did control his glaucoma while he smoked it. When he ran out, however, he was not about to try to find a drug connection, and I was nervous about having to buy it and carry it on planes. I had noticed in passing where the drug sales occurred locally, but I could not imagine my old father shambling into that parking lot to make a deal.

My mother's blood pressure was high. I sent her clippings from *Prevention* magazine, I sent her health foods, whole grain foods and food supplements. Vitamins, minerals, natural remedies to lower blood pressure. Books on controlling blood pressure mentally. She began to call me every Monday night while my father played bridge at the senior center. She would complain about her life, how much she hated Florida, how lonely she was. "He sits in a chair and tells me how to sweep the floor, as if I haven't been doing it for sixty years, as if he has ever in his life swept a floor." She had cataracts but dismissed the possibility of an operation. Of course, I sent her endless pamphlets, books, articles about cataracts. My father saw no reason why she should go to an eye doctor, since she didn't drive. She could still read. Her best friend was a much younger woman, the local librarian. She said the woman reminded her of me; maybe it was the connection with books. All the last years of her life, except when I was out of the country, we talked Monday nights. When I had meetings, I rushed back from them to get a chance to speak with her before my father came home. A few times when I called, she hissed into the phone, *he has a cold, he has a toothache, he isn't going out.*

I was happier than I can convey to have a warm connection with her after so many years of confrontation and coldness and suspicion. She had not been able to be physically affectionate with me since I was eleven and began to grow breasts, and probably if we were in the same room, she could not have touched me. Still, the warmth of her voice was wonderful. I wanted to help, I tried, but her typical reaction to any suggestion I would make was: She couldn't do that. It couldn't be done that way. It wasn't possible. She was too old.

What I could do was buy her things she wanted. She developed a

passion for shawls, thinking them glamorous. When I was in Florida, I took her to expensive stores she would never enter on her own and bought her the most beautiful shawls I could find. I bought her perfume. I wanted to buy her dresses, but that was too fraught. She was immensely fat, almost totally round, and had been so for years. Then in the late 1970s, she began to shed weight. It was startling. She wasn't trying. "I've just lost my appetite. Nothing tastes good to me." Every time I saw her, she was thinner. Finally she would let me buy her dresses. However, six months later, she would be a size smaller, and the dresses would hang on her.

I told her things were not going well with Robert. This did not displease her, as she had never liked him. I told her a little about Woody, that we had written a play put on in several theaters, but not that we were involved. I had never explained to her my complicated marriage with Robert. It was not the sort of arrangement she would have believed possible.

Mostly I listened and told her stories that would amuse her, talked about the cats and the garden. A cat, Virgil, lived near them, nominally belonging to a neighbor but spending his time mostly with her. He was a comfort. The next time I was in Florida, I tried to talk my father into having someone come in to clean. The house stank of urine—my father was incontinent—and she could not see well enough to manage. His response was, "What else does she have to do? That's her job." I said, "Okay, why can't she retire?" He said cleaning was her duty. He was openly contemptuous of her. He was down in Florida living the good life in retirement, just like a middle-class man, and she held him back. She didn't know how to behave. She didn't play bridge. She was useless.

When Robert and I visited them, we stayed in a hotel on the beach, as the house was difficult to endure. We went down regularly, because Robert's mother had moved to an expensive high-rise in North Miami Beach, just across the highway from the ocean. Her apartment was all white with some blue touches—blue imitation flowers, a blue flowered pillow. When we first visited, I went for a walk on the beach, where, without realizing it, I got tar on my bare feet and tracked it onto her white rug. She never forgave me. We slept in a daybed with little privacy.

Robert always got a backache, but he would not consider staying in a motel; she would be insulted. The view from her balcony was superb, facing an inland waterway wide as a lake. Pelicans flew by at balcony level.

One trip to Florida coincided on our return with the enormous snow-storm of the winter of 1978. We got to Boston just as Logan Airport closed. We circled and circled and then were directed away. We landed along with various other big jets in Bangor, Maine, which shortly closed too. There were Lufthansa jets, Air Canada, British Airways, all the American companies. Three feet of snow fell in Boston. People skied on the streets. Cars were abandoned on all major roads. The governor declared martial law and highways were closed. We were stuck in Bangor, Maine, with suitcases of summer clothes.

All the motels and hotels were full. We were sent out to a bleak motel on the edge of town full of potato jobbers and traveling salesmen. By the third day, there were only two items left on the menu. Robert was bored out of his mind, and I was worried sick about the cats. If there was that much snow, was anyone feeding them? I missed Woody desperately. Our ennui united us in resolve.

I found a couple who lived just the other side of the Cape Cod Canal, and I got on the phone. In Provincetown, where we had departed, the storm surge had cracked the runway—and washed over the vehicles there, including our car. But Hyannis was open. Only four inches of snow had fallen on the Cape. I found a local pilot who would fly us all into Hyannis. On the Cape, the governor's proclamation was being quietly ignored.

We had wind damage, boughs down and a couple of fallen trees, but little snow. The cats were frantic. We were tremendously glad to be back. The hardship and adventure brought us together, and we were pleasant to each other. We picked up our car, a Volvo, at Provincetown. It had no finish. All the paint had been sandblasted off down to the undercoat. However, it started. I drove it home, following Robert in our other car.

All through 1978, Robert was around little, working full-time and evenings at the office with his new partner, immersed in their project.

Then the next winter, the roof fell in. The company that had him under contract demanded the software he was supposed to be working on and discovered that contrary to his contract, he had been building hardware. The contract was terminated. They had not been successful with their project, although they built a prototype. He and his friend blamed each other. Robert sank into a terrible depression. He suggested I break off with Woody and we have no more relationships with other people.

I felt strongly committed to Woody. Nor did I trust Robert. I had no sense that this disgust with multiple relationships arose from anything more than that he had been having trouble finding women. He was talking about how boring his work was and how he might stop working altogether for a year or two. He was weary of trying to support interesting work from computer contracts. He wanted to play, he wanted to do only work that fascinated him.

I suggested we go to England together. A couple of my novels that had sold to the Women's Press were being brought out in spring of 1979. I thought it worthwhile to go over and do publicity, to make myself known in England. It was an investment, since they paid few of my expenses, although they did set up various gigs. Since they weren't paying for lodging, we stayed in a grungy bed-and-breakfast off Earl's Court. I hoped that taking Robert as my guest to England would cheer him up, break his depression, give us back some intimacy. I had book signings, TV and radio shows, newspaper interviews, readings—including the University of London, a women's conference, a couple in pubs, where I had to come and go quickly because of the smoke. Nobody in England understood being allergic to cigarette smoke, and they thought me full of myself, a fussy hypochondriac somewhat lower on the social scale than a sanctimonious vegan.

I kept remembering how well our marriage had worked for both of us in the good years, how he had supported me in my writing, how we had enjoyed keeping house, making love, sharing books and ideas, walking, learning about wine and identifying birds and plants. Surely we could recover our joy together. The past of our relationship seemed more vibrant, more real than the pallid present. Robert spent time at the

British Museum, went sightseeing, bought clothes and books. Finally I was done except for a reading on Sunday. That Thursday, we took the train to Exeter, rented a car and set off. Almost immediately, we got into an accident. Robert was not used to driving on the left side of the road. A great big log lorry came at us, and he drove into what he thought was a hedge. Hedgerows in Devon have rocks as their core. Back we went to the rental agency. It did not put Robert in a good mood. Much of the time in England, he was sulking. He disliked the food, the British, London, whatever.

Fortunately, once we got up on Dartmoor, we encountered wild ponies, hawks, curlews, blackface sheep, dun cattle and prehistoric ruins—stone circles, standing stones, hut circles. We walked and walked from one set of ruins to the next, from one copse to a bog to a clapper bridge over a stream, built of stone slabs. We climbed several tors and explored ruins to the horizon. I had gotten sick in London. Air pollution sickens me, and I had been exposed to an unavoidable amount of cigarette smoke. I was coughing from the bottom of my lungs. Dartmoor has pure clear air, and I felt better. Walking is my best exercise. I love Dartmoor. I have been back many times and written about it in *Gone to Soldiers* and various poems. Something in me resonates to its green vastness, its wildness, its antiquities scattered about without signs or protection. We were suddenly good companions again, exploring. This trip would work, I knew it.

The food in Devon was better than we had been able to afford in London: smoked trout, salmon, sole, saltwater lamb. Even the vegetables were good. We stayed at a fisherman's motel built over a rushing stream, the Exe, near an old stone bridge and a seventeenth-century coaching inn where we ate. Then we drove on to Cornwall. We spent the night in St. Mawes in a house where Byron had stayed. The owner was an Eastern European woman who set out an elegant breakfast. I had booked the best room in the house, Byron's room. That night, I managed to seduce Robert, convinced that the spirit of Lord Byron was helping. With this breakthrough, I was sure things would improve. Noisy rooks (I call them noisy, but I confess I like the cries of crows and ravens and rooks) roosted in the trees outside the white Regency house. It had a circular stairway that was perfect, a frozen song in space.

The next night we arrived at what I shall call Dead Bird Manor. It sounded wonderful in the guidebook, with a cordon bleu chef. It was near Clovelly, set in a valley among wooded hills—a fine Victorian house with a stuffy Victorian spirit. They offered us tea, cookies and a paper when we arrived. We immediately offended them by asking for the wrong paper. "We don't carry that left rag." It was downhill from there. The parlor was decorated with glass cases of dead and dowdy birds. Upstairs the room was tiny, mattress well used and sagging, plumbing noisy, radiators dripping and gurgling. We could not pass each other getting around the bed.

Supper came. The guests anticipated the meal in silence. They did not speak to each other. Perhaps they were all telepaths, or perhaps they were people at the end of their marriages with nothing more to say—a state I was beginning to fully comprehend. The meal was pretentious: overcooked broccoli with an orange glue they called hollandaise sauce. Tough meat they called veal. Everyone was scraping at it with their knives and no one was talking. I began to giggle. Robert glared at me, but I couldn't stop. It was all silly and inflated and pompous. I giggled my way through the dreadful meal. When we went upstairs, I discovered that Robert had withdrawn again. There were to be no more breakthroughs on the trip.

When we got back to London, it was over ninety degrees. London when it's hot is much like hell. I did the pub reading with several other poets and left, which they thought rude, but I was starting to cough again. We took a train to Leeds. We were due to be picked up by someone in the British equivalent of Science for the People, a family who lived on a farm. We had all our luggage with us. I had done a great deal of media, including TV, and given numerous readings, so I had a lot of clothes in a big suitcase, and my portable typewriter because I was doing revisions on *Vida,* which had just sold. I had all the books I was using in my readings. I was wearing a flowered summer dress in the heat.

The woman supposed to collect us was an hour and fifteen minutes late. We kept calling her house. Finally she turned up. "Oh, I saw you earlier, but I didn't think it could *possibly* be you. I didn't expect you to be dressed *that way,* and you had so much luggage." She managed to feel superior about my wearing a pretty summer dress. I had been through the puritanical drab butch dressing nonsense in the women's movement in the States, going without a brassiere for two years because that was politically correct—until I realized I was stooping, just as I had before my mother let me wear one. I bought six the next week. I decided a dress code for feminists was ridiculous. Liberation for me is choice.

As a means of bringing us closer, the trip had been a failure. I was reminded of Greece, when I had the impression I was carrying him around on my back, begging him to like something. There is a point in relationships when the way someone chews her breakfast cereal is a clear sign of moral decay. Certainly I'm making myself sound stronger and more single-minded than I was. Sometimes I looked at Robert with a cold eye and considered my options. Sometimes he went at me and reduced me to tears, especially when people were around, as several friends noted. Sometimes he was affectionate and we worked together in the garden or took long walks. There would always be times in any week when we were talking about something interesting, political, natural, and we would communicate well and feel close. That summer we stopped having sex—not that it had been so frequent an occurrence the past year. We still shared a bed, but I found it increasingly hard to sleep with some-one who was not interested in me sexually. I had not abandoned hope, but it was abandoning me, gradually, drop by agonizing drop. In the best of times I am not an easy woman to get along with, but when someone is estranged from me, I can be annoying indeed. Everything about me seems too much, too fast, too sure, too loud.

That summer my Norwegian and Danish publishers asked me to come over in September to do publicity. They would pay for a companion. Weekends, we would be responsible for ourselves. Robert was going to Germany shortly after that. His connection with Petrie and Tole was heating up again. Petrie got him funding. When I thought about taking him along, I felt ill. I knew he would sulk. He would not gladly endure the media fuss. I asked Woody if he wanted to accompany me.

Oslo is a business center, not the world's most glamorous or historically interesting city, but it was new to us, and my publishers were friendly and welcoming. On the weekend, we took a train over the high mountains to Bergen and stopped at a fjord. There were twenty waterfalls visible from our little pension. We made the mistake of asking for a drink when we arrived. The innkeeper nodded solemnly and admitted that sherry was possible. We were taken down to a basement, through a bolted door, to a locked cabinet where exactly one jigger was measured out to each of us, with a stern look. It was as if we had requested a local pretty boy to play with. We drank our bit of sherry and did not ask again. We loved Bergen, running around as tourists. I visited local feminists, who told me drunken domestic abuse was their leading problem. We had a flash of insight into the pension keeper's attitude toward alcohol.

Then we headed for Denmark, where we ate and drank ourselves silly. I was on the Danish equivalent of *60 Minutes*. The producer had the bright idea that since I was doing publicity for *Woman on the Edge of Time,* the shoot should be in a large mental institution. Neither the burly interviewer nor I was permitted to wear a coat, although the temperature was about forty. As soon as the television crew started filming, the inmates pushed in front of the camera, swarming. "You American?" One grinning partially toothless lad kept asking, "You rich?" It was a mad scene, indeed.

While we were in Europe, Linda took up with a fellow student, and Woody came home to find their relationship over. Robert had become involved with a poet from the Fine Arts Work Center. He found her sexually exciting and fascinating, so he dropped his idea about resuming monogamy. He also was interested in a woman he met at Science for the People in Boston. He was choosing between two affairs and feeling just fine.

At the same time, *Vida* sold to the movies. Although the film was never made, I got a chunk of money I decided to put in the house. First I wanted larger windows in the master bedroom, different from the little inexpensive awning windows the builder had used all over the house. I also decided, since we had no basement, attic or garage, we needed storage space. I designed a hall to go where part of the bedroom had been, and then the bedroom itself would stick out on the east side for more light and air. There would be a large storage room and then an extra bedroom, designed for Woody. He was romantic about ecology at the time and insisted that rather than connecting to the oil burner heating the rest of the house, this new wing should be heated by a woodstove. He was to regret that nostalgia many times in winters to come as he cut down and then chopped up trees with his trusty hand ax, as he went out to split logs at six in the morning, as he hauled in wood (and spiders and mice and wood roaches), digging logs out of three-foot drifts, as he lived in a room either roaring hot or icy. One frigid March, tired of sodden pine boughs, I found him smashing up an old desk.

I asked Robert, if he no longer wanted a sexual relationship with me, to move into the downstairs bedroom that had been Wayne's. I installed my assistant's office in what had been our bedroom. He took Arofa in with him every night and made an immense fuss over her. She had never been so happy. At one point, he entered the bedroom, now mine except for my assistant's desk and files. The new larger windows were in place and light poured in. He sat on the bare floor and began to weep. "It's so pretty," he said. "And I'll never sleep here."

"But it's *your* choice," I said.

He began to hint that he wanted to move into the new room. It had its own door to the outside, and he could come and go without dealing with me. I said I had designed and built it for Woody, and he had an entire huge office at the end of a road overlooking a stream and a pond. I was not going to set him up so that he could live in the house without relating to me while moving in his new lover.

He began doing all the things he had done in the summer of 1976 and being surprised I did not break down or run off to the city. There was an underground struggle going on about who was going to leave. I became cold and stubborn, nasty. If he wanted to get free of me, he was going to have to leave. This was my house and I was staying. He could always make me cry, but he could no longer sway me. I was a bitch. I would not let go of my home. I was wasting away physically, losing weight by the day, a regime I called the Marge Piercy Total Weight Loss through Total Relationship Loss Diet, but I was all teeth and stubborn resolve.

I did not like myself during this period, although I had plenty of support from friends. Our relationship was by this point so bizarre in the mores of the time that everyone expected it to explode. Almost all our friends who'd had multiple relationships had settled into monogamy again, except for a few gay friends who continued until AIDS scared them. We were the lone weird stragglers from the experiments of the 1960s. Also, we had been having a rocky ride since the summer of 1976, and everyone was bored with hearing what he said and did and what I said and did and felt. It was an old sad story that needed to come to an end. My love for Robert had undergone a slow starvation and there was little left; but the ruins made me grieve for what had been lost. I wanted it over, but at the same time, every step out of the marriage pained me. If he did not like me, I did not much like myself those months.

It was a strange December. Robert did not observe Jewish holidays, as I did before him and do now, but he made a fuss about Christmas. He always wanted lots of presents and gave me extravagant gifts, but never more than that year. Not that I didn't enjoy the fuss: I thought it sumptuous fun. I love being given things and I like shopping for other people, when I can afford it. But that year, there were piles and piles of gifts. Then the day after Christmas, he left. He said he was going off backpacking and did not provide any more information. By the third day, his poet girlfriend was calling me on the hour, demanding to know where he was. It did not take much detective work to learn he had gone off to Negril in Jamaica with his girlfriend from Science for the People, a wealthy young woman who had been unhappily married, had accumulated several advanced degrees but had never found anything she wanted to do.

Robert's poet girlfriend almost drove me mad, calling every few hours. I told her what I knew, making her furious. Well into January, Robert returned. He came to the house at five and waited for me to make supper. I charred the chicken livers and potatoes, everything but the salad. He announced he was leaving to lead a simpler life. He saw me as entangling him with material objects, with the garden he suddenly hated, with the house he despised now. He was going to simplify everything and get rid of what he didn't need. No, he didn't want a divorce. But he wanted to wander around, to do what he wished. He wanted to be free. He was dying in the relationship, he said, dying. He complained about everything from not having fun in Greece after his father's death to various problems with various girlfriends scattered over the years. I had heard all this endless times, the litany of my sins. I was "an unacceptable compromise" he had negotiated with himself. He had entered the relationship with ambivalence and he was stuck in that commitment. It was, he said, killing him emotionally. His voice broke as he declared his unhappiness. He said I was always arguing him into continuing, but he was done now. I did not argue. I too thought we were done.

I wondered whether if I had sacrificed Woody to him, we could have made it. I did not believe that. He had accumulated a baggage of deep dark fuming anger that nothing but separation could dispel. Some of his resentments went back to our first year, around that accident in the Porsche, and more resentments had piled up every year since. I could recite them with him, for I had heard them all many times. The very first anger was still inside him smoldering.

Over the next couple of months, he would give in to fleeting second thoughts, leaving notes and messages and once chocolates, insisting it was not over. I knew it was. It was as dead as a relationship could be.

THE WEIGHT

1.
I lived in the winter drought of his anger,
cold and dry and bright. I could not breathe.
My sinuses bled. Whatever innocent object
I touched, door knob or light switch,

sparks leapt to my hand in shock.
Simply crossing a room generated static.
Any contact could give sudden sharp pain.

2.
All too long I have been carrying a weight
balanced on my head as I climb the stairs
up from the subway in rush hour jostle,
up from the garden wading in mud.
It is a large iron pot supposed to hold
something. Only now when I have finally
been forced to put it down, do I find
it empty except for a gritty stain
on the bottom. You have told me
this exercise was good for my posture.
Why then did my back always ache?

3.
All too often I have wakened at night
with that weight crouched on my chest,
an attack dog pinning me down. I would
open my eyes and see its eyes glowing
like the grates of twin coal furnaces
in red and hot menacing regard.
A low growl sang in its chest, vibrating
into my chest and belly its warning.

4.
If it rained for three weeks in August,
you knew I had caused it by weeping.
If your paper was not accepted, I had
corrupted the judges or led you astray
into beaches, dinner parties and cleaning

the house when you could have been working
an eighteen-hour day. If a woman would not
return the importunate pressure of your hand
on her shoulder, it was because I was watching
or because you believed she thought I
was watching. My watching and my looking away
equally displeased.
> *Whatever I gave you*
was wrong. It did not cost enough;
it cost too much. It was too fancy, for
that week you were a revolutionary
trekking on dry bread salted with sweat
and rhetoric. It was too plain; that week
you were the superb connoisseur whose palate
could be struck like a tuning fork only
by the perfect, to sing its true note.

5.
Wife was a box you kept pushing me down
into like a trunk crammed to overflowing
with off-season clothes, whose lid
you must push on to shut. You sat
on my head. You sat on my belly.
I kept leaking out like laughing
gas and you held your nose
lest I infect you with outrageous joy.

Gradually you lowered all the tents
of our pleasures and stowed them away.
We could not walk together in dunes or
marsh. No talk or travel. You would only fuck
in one position on alternate Thursdays
if the moon was in the right ascendancy.

Oh, Cancer, Cancer, you scuttle and snap.
Go and do with others all the things
you told me we could not afford.

Your anger was a climate I inhabited
like a desert in dry frigid weather
of high thin air and ivory sun,
sand dunes the wind lifted into stinging
clouds that blinded and choked me,
where the only ice was in the blood.

EIGHTEEN

DEATH AND
DISINTEGRATION

I *had been nervous about* the amount of attention Robert was paying to Arofa. Indeed, after he moved out, he made no move to see her or Cho-Cho. Arofa was inconsolable. She looked for him upstairs, downstairs, every day, every night. For three months, she had received more attention from him than she ever had, and now, none. She lost weight. Cho-Cho, a born survivor, adapted. She could tell I was upset and began to sleep curled around my head at night, a purring halo of fur. Arofa went on a hunger strike, shrinking ghost-thin.

It was the dead of winter and the heating in the remodeled bedroom did not work correctly: it was cold. I lay awake frightened in the night. A roaring feminist, I had never conquered my ignorance of finances. Robert discouraged my interest, and his accountant had been outright hostile. When the movie money came in, I tried to talk to the accountant about how to deal with it, but he simply dismissed me. He always addressed me as Mrs. Shapiro, although as our accountant, or Robert's anyhow, he knew my legal name was Piercy.

I wanted a clean break and a legal divorce. I wanted the house, the land, one of the cars. I wanted the cats. I needn't have worried about that. I was happy to give him whatever else he wanted, determined to avoid a court battle. I needed a dignified end. I was content he should keep his building and land, the corporation. We fought about bills, of course. He expected me to sell the house, but I refused. I intended to stay on, which seemed to shock him.

Woody had been involved in the Massachusetts artist-in-the-schools program for years. Now he was also working at an upscale restaurant on Beacon Hill. We had taken an apartment together at the corner of Pearl and Putnam, not a fancy neighborhood and a long dangerous trek from the subway on Mass. Avenue, but big, light and cheap. I spent three days a week in the city and four days in the country; he did the opposite. I brought the cats with me. Arofa enjoyed riding in the car. Cho-Cho would produce a deep moaning and bellowing—a sound that always sounded like ERROR! ERROR!—until we passed the exit for the vet. Then she would calm down.

By the end of March, Arofa began to enjoy life. It was early spring, things were coming alive. She began to sun herself and go for walks. She would allow Woody to pet her, would purr for him and even climb in his lap. Her interest in play returned, and she began to boss us around and oversee the household in her old way. Still, she was too thin. They seemed to like the apartment in the city, racing down the long central corridor, sliding on the smooth wood floors like kids on ice. Going back and forth brought Arofa out of her depression, but she was showing her age. She had little appetite and had to be coaxed with delicacies.

In April, Woody and I sat down and decided we would have a monogamous relationship. First, the social climate that encouraged open marriages no longer existed. Second, Woody had a tendency toward jealousy I had no desire to exploit. Third, it was simpler. I considered that we loved strongly enough to satisfy each other emotionally and sexually. In many ways, having an open marriage had worked for me. I had enjoyed other serious and trivial relationships, most of which I have not mentioned. I got to satisfy my curiosity about sex and about people with a wide variety of partners. I had little curiosity left, and a great desire to be loved and calm and finally together with someone who really wanted to be together with me. I wanted to concentrate on writing and on having a pleasant and warm central relationship. If you want fidelity, a retired roué may be your best bet. I've never been tempted to cheat on Ira. It has no appeal.

While Robert was in Germany, I began to investigate divorce. I interviewed three lawyers. Having to explain to very straight lawyers what our relationship had been was excruciating. I wrote him that I thought he should be doing this, but he did not have any desire to. Divorce was a priority for me from the night he moved out, but not for him. Then I found a lawyer with a movement background in a law collective who would do the divorce for a reasonable price. She did not seem to think we were sex fiends.

Finally he returned and we could settle down to negotiating. Robert did not want a divorce until he went home with his girlfriend and met her parents and fully understood her situation. He returned from that visit not only agreeing to a divorce, but willing to fly down to the Dominican Republic the next week for a quick one. He wanted the stock, his land and corporation and the liquid assets. He and his accountant insisted I pay the previous year's taxes as the price of divorce. It cleaned me out, but I had the house and a car and the land.

When you are in a couple, each settles on jobs they find appealing or the least repugnant, and ignores other tasks. I made a lot of mistakes that first year: financial mistakes, mistakes in running the house, mistakes with the car. I was slowly learning, and so was Woody. Arofa was visibly declining. I had to go to Denmark and Norway that fall, and Woody wanted to come. Penny took off from work, which she could ill afford, to take care of the cats. While we were gone, Arofa began to fail. The vet wanted to euthanize her, but Penny refused.

Penny kept her alive by playing tapes of me reading poetry. When I got home, I could see she was dying. She was painfully thin, just bones and her beautiful coat, but she was affectionate, still passionately alive and alert. Essentially she stopped eating. I could get a tiny bit of baby food into her, but that was it. I tried to give her fluids, but she threw up. She could not urinate. The vet said she had uremic poisoning and would die within twenty-four hours. She did not sleep the night of her crisis but all night kept nudging me to pet her.

I could not let her die at the vet's. She was too bright. She always knew what was up. Her sight went first. Then she could not stand. She needed my touch to know she was not alone. I had coerced friends into giving me some barbiturates, and I fed them to her pounded into water in a mortar and pestle. The vet said one would put her in a coma, she was so fragile. She took the one and never faltered. She was clinging to consciousness. She would not go down. She would not die. She wanted so passionately to live, it made me weep. Then her hearing began to go. I was terrified I would not be able to comfort her if she could not hear me. She was beginning to cry hoarsely, insistently, as if she knew she was dying and was fighting it. She sounded afraid. I made up a witch's brew of barbiturates and tranquilizers. She took it gladly, I don't know why. She died very slowly, purring all the while and holding on to me. Woody was working at the restaurant that night and could not get off. Two friends sat with me. Finally she went into a coma and they left. I carried her to bed with me.

All night long I held her and so did Cho-Cho, washing her. In the morning she was still in the coma. I was terrified she would manage to wake, blind and deaf. I laid my face against her flank, put a pillow over her and smothered her. For forty-eight hours, I had been crying almost constantly. Then I buried her with her leash, name tags, toys. I wrapped her in red velvet for a shroud and put a piece of Chinese embroidery over her. In the spring, I planted a wisteria vine over her. It is huge and vigorous, clambering over its arbor, with fragrant, long drooping blossoms hanging down abundantly in May. It often reblooms.

Cho-Cho kept calling for her, looking for her, although I had shown her the body and she had sniffed it. She could not accept that her lifelong companion was gone. I decided that week I would never have just two cats again. It is much too difficult for the survivor when their whole cat family is just one other. Cho-Cho stopped eating, very uncharacteristic. She would not use her litter box. I fell into Woody when he arrived, and wept until I choked.

I decided I would get another cat but not a Siamese. Woody and I pursued an ad in the *Boston Globe*. There we found heaps of Burmese at the breeder's, a woman who seemed bored by her cats. It was a big cluttered house with the shades drawn, the dimness punctuated by sets of great yellow eyes staring. All the cats were in piles of rich dark brown fur cuddling one another, except for two exiles: two big sable cats she said were three months old, but I could tell they were six or eight at least. She would not give us papers. From the little she said, years later I pieced together the story after I had been a breeder briefly. A male at stud had escaped from his cage and impregnated his daughter. She did not of course tell us this but only that it had been an accidental breeding.

We went for a walk to decide. Woody had fallen in love with them at once. I knew something was fishy, but they needed us. The other cats were excluding them, including their mother. They clutched each other. The breeder said she intended to have the female put to sleep, as she was not a proper Burmese. Her legs were too long, revealing her Siamese ancestry.

We brought them to the apartment on Pearl Street. Woody named the male Jim Beam, and I named the female Colette. I have always loved Colette's writing. Jim Beam was immediately interested and friendly, but Colette hid under a chair. I remembered reading that you should never take the runt of a litter, the terrified one, but in size she was no runt. I captured her, held her and licked her like a mother cat. She was astonished and began to purr. From then on, except when she was angry with me, she was my cat. She fell in love that night. It was hardly sanitary, but it conveyed affection and trust in a language she understood.

We brought them back to the Cape the next day. I thought Cho-Cho might be interested, since she had been so lonely. I lacked experience introducing cats to one another, so we just brought in the carrier and let them out. Cho-Cho took one look, one sniff, and howled. She was hostile, she was furious, and she never did warm up. They were friendly enough. Colette in particular tried to seduce Cho-Cho, who was perhaps too old to endure new housemates. Of course, looking back, she had never liked other cats coming in. Not Daphne, not Amber.

However, as soon as the Burmese arrived, she started eating and gained back the weight she had lost. Cho-Cho never became fat, but she recovered her appetite and began using the litter box again. She might not be happy. She might not view the Burmese as an adequate replacement for her lost friend, but they distracted her. They whet her interest in living. She had to know what they were doing every moment. She had to keep an eye on them, she had to boss them around, she had to train them correctly.

It was not that I did not miss Arofa. To this day, I dream about her. I kept seeing her ghost. But I have always believed that if you love a pet, when they die, you find a pet who needs a home, and that is how you show your love. To me, giving love to new cats commemorated her in the only way that mattered.

The next January, my mother asked us to drive down to Florida, as she had things she wanted to give me. "We'll fly," I said. "No," she insisted. "You'll have too much to carry back." We drove leisurely, stopping at Assateague and Chincoteague, at Cape Hatteras, at Charleston, at the Georgia Sea Islands. When we got to Tequesta, my mother worried me. She looked handsome but was extremely thin. Her hair had been done. She was wearing a pretty new dress (her only new dress, as I learned), but she seemed troubled. She wanted to talk with us, she wanted desperately to communicate. Woody remembers her bringing out clippings from newspapers to ask us what we thought about this politician, that piece of legislation, events in foreign or domestic policy, a murder case. She could not talk politics with my father, for he had become a Nixon, then a Reagan, Republican. She needed to talk with a hunger that would not be denied.

She gave us some silver plate cutlery, which we still use. She gave us dishes from my childhood. She gave back books of mine I had sent her and photographs. Then one night my father went out, and in great excitement, she called us into her bedroom. She began to pull out of various hiding places, one-dollar, two-dollar, five-dollar bills from umbrellas, from under the rug, from behind drawers, from pockets of clothes put away, from inside picture frames.

"Mother, what is this?"

"It's for you. I saved it. *He* doesn't watch at the checkout counter. I can hide a little most times. It's all for you!"

Late that night we sat in the hotel room counting the money. It was just over $1,200 in nothing larger than a five. I have a poem about that night called "The Annuity." It looked as if we had robbed a candy store, the piles of worn, faded, crumpled dollar bills.

Woody was a little appalled by my mother's extravagant behavior, her sulking, her tantrums, her passionate insistence on talking, but he also saw her as thwarted, almost a child deprived. She liked him. He was the only man in my life she had ever met that she genuinely liked. "Marry him," she kept telling me, staring up into my face with that intense insistence, although her eyes because of the cataracts were no longer dark and piercing but a milky brown.

"I just got divorced," I said. "Enough is enough."

"Marry him!" she insisted.

"I'll see," I said. "There's no hurry."

"I want to see you married to him."

What a change from her previous attitude toward my marriages, but I was aghast that I had been married twice already and discouraged about how things with Robert had ended up. We were not even friends. I was friends with various ex-lovers, but not with him. We had no connection.

She also gave me a box of Christmas ornaments, although I protested I never had a Christmas tree. She said I should have one for her. I planned to put the box in the new hall closet and give it to some friend who observed Christmas. Robert had insisted on presents, but we never put up a tree or sent cards. My mother had grown up feeling deprived of what Christian children around her enjoyed. Not having Christmas was part of being poor to her. She loved anything festive, cheerful, colorful, gaudy. She never felt dressed up if she didn't wear bright colors and perhaps some sequins. It was their lights and color she liked about Christmas trees. "They're trees dressed up," she said.

We drove home much more quickly, still not sure what my mother had wanted to give us that was so important we had to drive down for it. I decided she had just wanted to see Woody, and that the $1,200 had cost her such effort to put together, it felt like something that would need a truck to carry back north.

The cats had been at Elise's Cambridge apartment, where Jim had revealed some of his willful and wicked character by terrorizing her cat Zoe. Elise had shut Jim Beam into a spare bedroom. We were annoyed, protective of our darling. She just didn't understand him, we thought, but she had seen the bully in him long before we recognized it. Both Burmese were growing into large sleek dark brown muscular cats. A friend once saw Jim slipping through the undergrowth and shouted, "What's that!" He said the first thing he thought of was a panther.

We had not intended to let them outside, but they chose otherwise. Jim knocked out the screen and led the way. We tried putting them on leashes. He would simply wriggle free in ninety seconds. Colette was not much slower. They wanted to be indoor/outdoor cats, and so they were.

Slowly we decided to let go of the apartment in the city. One summer we sublet it and became instant landlords. We tried sharing it: another disaster. Our young roommate looked on us as parents who should take care of him. He could not imagine that a woman had anything to do but cater to him. Also, rents in Cambridge were skyrocketing. Woody moved out here, and we rented a room from Elise for our time in the city. She had an apartment on a pleasant tree-lined street near Central Square in Cambridge.

Colette went into heat. She was fierce. She backed Woody into a corner and would not let him out. We got her altered at once, but we were too sentimental about Jim. Some idiot assistant at the vet's said he was so beautiful, we shouldn't have him altered until he was full grown. Well, he soon discovered sex. He pushed out the screen and went gallivanting. He was seen two miles away on the other side of Route 6. We tried to keep him in. When we left a friend here while we were doing readings, she was so terrorized by him, she hid in Woody's study with the door locked.

He began his lifelong campaign of marking territory. While we had him, half our house smelled of piss. We couldn't leave a shirt on the floor. We finally got him altered, but too late to abrade his macho personality, now fully formed. The vet bills he ran up fighting with other cats ran into the thousands over the years. He had his moments. He always met us at the foot of the drive. He was strongly affectionate with Woody, especially. He was Woody's cat. They played games together of dominance and submission that Jim Beam craved. He needed Woody to dominate him, just as he needed to dominate every cat for miles. Perhaps he should have had therapy, but frankly I doubt there was a cat therapist closer than Manhattan. He was a magnificent hunter, but his sister was better. Jim Beam was so strong, he did not feel soft when you picked him up. He was all steel muscles. I could not hold him when he did not want to be confined.

Among cats, he was a Genghis Khan. His energy was electric and his will, absolute. He never wavered from what he wanted. He simply would not change his mind and would not give up: the image of a tyrant in the form of a gorgeous sleek cat. When you have a pet who is by all objective standards bad, it is like any other love relationship with someone who is half crazy. You cling to the good times and make excuses; you understand and understand. Jim was wildly affectionate and absolutely ours.

Then Jim Beam fell in love. It was a male tabby (Jim was definitely gay in spite of his fathering kittens all over Wellfleet before we had the brains to get him fixed) who had been dumped by some irresponsible summer person. He had lived through the winter in a tree. Jim Beam brought him home like a prize, a large brown tabby with heavy jowls and a chewed ear, a pugilistic air but a fighter who had been beaten. He had everything wrong with him: fleas, worms, ear mites. We had him altered and cleaned up and named him Boris.

Boris could not stay in the house at night unless it was bitter cold. His time as a feral cat had formed him. If we did not let him out when he wanted, he would piss on the door. Otherwise, he was gentle, sweet, friendly. He had a sexual relationship with my nightgowns. He would grab them by what he considered the scruff of their neck and drag them about between his legs, purring madly. He would eat anything. You only have to live with fussy house cats to know how you can love a cat who eats everything—the cheap stuff in the big cans, dried-up food the others refused, leftovers from supper. I had seen him before, because two years ago he had come calling on Cho-Cho regularly. Cho-Cho must have retained a female scent, because toms were always waiting hopefully for the day she would surely come into heat. She had liked Boris as a suitor, but once he came in the house, she spat at him. It was not right that he should be inside. She would not permit him near her.

Jim Beam and Boris would hang out together inside and outside. Jim, who had adored his sister when he was younger, now rejected her. He did not want her palling with the two of them. Colette often sat on Arofa's grave, and she began to act more like Arofa. She stayed with me while I wrote and became my special lap cat. Still, there was a wild streak in her. I went to teach in Nashville for a writers' conference, where Reagan's firing of the air controllers stranded me. Colette was so furious that I was gone for nine days, she ran away from home and would not return until I did. Woody would call her and catch a glimpse of her on the hill across the road, but she would not come. When he walked toward her, she ran into the brambles.

Every so often she would go off in the summer and stay out all night. I could not sleep, afraid she would be eaten by a great horned owl or the coyotes that had begun to flourish on the Cape. She would sometimes get a bladder infection after one of those excursions. Otherwise, she was a healthy strong cat. I found her beautiful, although the vet would say she had a face only a mother could love, for it was a pushed-in pug face. She was my brown Amazon. I adored her. Colette could open doors. She would stand on her hind legs and turn the doorknob, throwing her weight forward. When I shut the cats into the back of the house, they would line up and wait for Colette to open the door and let them out.

My mother was increasingly upset. On her birthday in late November she called me, crying. My father was determined to move them into a high-rise complex, total life care. You bought into it, paid a hefty fee every month, and were to be provided with an instant and elegant social life. She did not want to move from the neighborhood where gradually she had made friends and she had Virgil for company. There were no pets allowed in the high-rise. She looked at the people there, and they were not her kind. The women looked shellacked. The men had far more money than my father. My father had been playing the stock market since he moved to Florida. Not in affluent terms, but in terms of the kind of money he had never seen, he was doing well through his stockbroker and loved to talk about it. He felt like a success. I asked Mother if, since he was moving them into a facility, she would rather be in one up north near us. She said she would much prefer that, but he wouldn't consider it. She could not imagine doing it in spite of him. His glaucoma was much worse, and he had been driving on a sidewalk when the police stopped him and he lost his license. As for the new facility, she had a clearer sense of social class than my father and knew they would not fit in.

It was Chanukah, and we had been planning a little party with latkes and dreydls and friends. Friday I had a splitting headache, unusual for me, all afternoon and evening. That evening my father called. "It's your mother," he said. "She had a stroke this afternoon. She's in the hospital."

It was hard to pry information out of him. I could not figure out how serious it was until the next morning when I spoke with her doctor. My mother had been cleaning up after lunch. My father was napping. She had a stroke and fell. As she went down, she broke a fluorescent light. My father picked up every tiny piece of glass before he called the rescue squad. She was conscious for a while and then she lost consciousness, never to regain it. He chose that she should not be on any machines except a respirator, so the doctor gave her no chance. In fact, he thought she had been brain-dead before the rescue squad arrived.

Chanukah was close to Christmas that year, and we could not get a flight. It was Sunday before we could fly to Florida, on the same plane but in separated seats, since we were on standby. She died while we were in the air. I felt it. I knew she was dead before we landed. They had a burial plot in Detroit, but he had stopped paying for it. All the arrangements for her death were made by my father, none of them complying with Jewish law or tradition. As usual, he simply pretended she was not Jewish. I saw my brother approach the coffin, open according to Christian practice. He knelt and crossed himself. I knew then what my mother had speculated to me was true: that he had converted to Catholicism. I was surprised but said nothing. My father had her cremated and was going to have the undertaker dispose of the ashes. I insisted on taking them.

My father was in a strangely jovial mood, as I said before. He would be moving into the high-rise in a few months, when his apartment was ready. He said, "I'll be baching it," with a twinkle in his eye. I think he was remembering the bachelor life he led in his twenties and early thirties, before he met my mother. I arranged for a cleaning service, since I could imagine what the house would be like in a week. After I left, the woman came in twice, then wouldn't return. She said she could not work for him.

He asked Grant and me to get rid of her things. Grant's wife, Lilly, and I went through them, bundling most of it for Goodwill. I let Lilly take almost everything she desired. I wanted my mother's jade necklace, the one she had always told me was my father's engagement present to her. When I asked him, he had no idea what I was talking about. He did not remember giving it to her. I also took the wedding ring that had been cut from her hand. I took the cameo brooch my grandfather Morris had bought for my grandmother Hannah in Naples, when they were waiting for a boat to take them to the States, after they had escaped from Russia. I took her box of buttons, some from dresses she had worn in my early childhood, a bowl I had given her for her birthday years before, a tile trivet I had bought her in Florence. I found all the shawls I bought her wrapped in plastic, never worn, some with the tags still on them, and those I brought home. She hoped for so much, and she got so little. I was weeping constantly, and my family kept looking at me as if I were crazy. Almost every present I had ever given her was wrapped up and stowed away, presumably for some future time when it would be right to use them, when she would feel loved. I could not tell if my brother mourned her. I could not read him. We were as opaque to each other as a cat and a bull.

The librarian who had become her friend mourned her. I was sure Virgil would miss her. I did not know if anyone else cared. She had enjoyed many friends, but most were dead, the others scattered in the North. I found clippings on stroke in her dresser drawer. She had known she was at risk but said nothing. Grant had already endured a stroke. I tried to speak with Grant and Lilly, but we couldn't talk with any honesty. They were closer and more sympathetic to my father than I was. I had never been able to communicate with my father, and my own sense of my mother was totally at odds with his opinion. I have always seen her as someone with immense energy and potential, thwarted, starved, stunted, able to be sublimely happy when given a chance, but seldom given that opening, that little space of attention and respect.

I found all the books and pamphlets, the health foods, the whole grain foods, the supplements, the biofeedback gadgets stuffed way up on the top shelf of the kitchen cabinets, where she could have put them only by standing on a step stool, but where she would never have to look at them. She did not throw them out, but she never touched them except to stow them out of sight. I went around that dirty dreary house weeping, already missing her. I had grown used to our communication.

We took a red-eye flight back Christmas Eve, rough and bumpy, but we could sit together. I held my mother's ashes in my lap. It was mild when we got home in the dawn. That day I dug her ashes into my garden alongside Arofa. I would plant a rosebush over her, next to the wisteria I had planted the year before over Arofa. We went into the woods and chopped down a small pitch pine and put the ornaments on it. Although we don't otherwise observe Christmas, I have had a tree since, because she asked me to. It's a small remembrance, just as I light the yahrtzeit candle for her the first night of Chanukah. My one consolation was that we had become close the last years of her life. Now there would be no more Monday-night conversations. I realized Grant would not say kaddish for her, so I did, for the next year. As I was reciting the words, which were nonsense to me, day after day, just rhythmic syllables, I began to realize I needed to learn Hebrew. It was maddening and embarrassing that I had no idea at all what I was saying every day, facing east and thinking of my mother whose face I would never see again except in dreams—in dreams again and again.

PUTTING THE GOOD THINGS AWAY

In the drawer were folded fine
batiste slips embroidered with scrolls

and posies, edged with handmade
lace too good for her to wear.

Daily she put on shmatehs
fit only to wash the car
or the windows, rags
that had never been pretty

even when new: somewhere
such dresses are sold only
to women without money to waste
on themselves, on pleasure,

to women who hate their bodies,
to women whose lives close on them.
Such dresses come bleached by tears,
packed in salt like herring.

Yet she put the good things away
for the good day that must surely
come, when promises would open
like tulips their satin cups

for her to drink the sweet
sacramental wine of fulfillment.
The story shone in her as through
tinted glass, how the mother

gave up and did without
and was in the end crowned
with what? scallions? crowned
queen of the dead place

in the heart where old dreams
whistle on bone flutes,
where run-over pets are forgotten,
where lost stockings go?

In the coffin she was beautiful
not because of the undertaker's
garish cosmetics but because
that face at eighty was still

her face at eighteen peering
over the drab long dress
of poverty, clutching a book.
Where did you read your dreams, Mother?

Because her expression softened
from the pucker of disappointment,
the grimace of swallowed rage,
she looked a white-haired girl.

The anger turned inward, the anger
turned inward, where
could it go except to make pain?
It flowed into me with her milk.

Her anger annealed me.
I was dipped into the cauldron
of boiling rage and rose
a warrior and a witch

but still vulnerable
there where she held me.
She could always wound me
for she knew the secret places.

She could always touch me
for she knew the pressure
points of pleasure and pain.
Our minds were woven together.

I gave her presents and she hid
them away, wrapped in plastic.
Too good, she said, too good.
I'm saving them. So after her death

I sort them, the ugly things
that were sufficient for every
day and the pretty things for which
no day of hers was ever good enough.

NINETEEN

INTERLUDE: OLD CATS

Dinah and Oboe are old now. I have had old cats before. Cho-Cho lived to be twenty-one. An old cat is a wonderful companion. They know the routines of the house. Things that sent them under the bed like the vacuum cleaner only rate a yawn. They know how to please you and how to ask for what they want, sometimes, like Dinah, at full volume and stridently. But mostly they are mellower and calmer than they were in their youth.

They are also a constant reminder of time, of aging, of their own mortality and yours. Whenever I touch Oboe, I feel his spine. Each knob is discrete. His fur is no longer the plush stuff that gave him his nickname, the Velvet Prince. His silver gray fur has a rusty cast in the sun. Wild leaps and tree climbing are beyond him. He scrambled up on the shed roof last week but could not get down. He still enjoys climbing the high fence around the Ram Garden and sauntering along the fence top, crying to me to come and pet him. Many cats enjoy making you reach up to them. It equalizes.

I massage him often these days, as it seems to help him and he likes the attention. I have never become completely accustomed—resigned or accepting—of his aged body. I touch him with affection and with pity. I do not mind being forced to think of dying. It's a good idea to be aware of one's own mortality and the rapid gallop of time, its stone-clad hoof-beats striking on my skull. He cowers when he knows I am about to give him his medicine, which makes me sad, but afterward, he is cheerful again. He understands it makes him feel better.

Dinah still feels soft and her bones do not jut. Rather, age has affected her performance, roughened her voice to a sandpapery screech, made her a little forgetful. She will start to do something and then stop cold, puzzled. She knows she had something in mind, but she cannot remember what. She eats and then forgets she has eaten and badgers Woody for food, then seems astonished she does not really want it—of course, since she finished a meal half an hour before. She sleeps a great deal and very soundly, which worries me when she goes to sleep outside.

Dinah was the kitten who would not grow up, who hated motherhood, who turned her favorite offspring into her playmate. She still plays, with Efi usually. But in the middle of playing she will stop with that same puzzled look and gaze around her, trying to remember what she was up to. She stares at Woody or at me fixedly with her round green eyes. I think it is partly that her vision is poor in old age, but also she seems to be asking a question. These are not unimportant questions: what is happening to me? What will become of me? She is peremptory, as if aware she has only so much time left to run into the summer garden among the flowers, to roll on her back on the warm bricks, to chase feathers on a string, to play tag or king of the mountain with Efi, to eat her favorite foods, to demand to sleep on my pillow, to be petted, to be picked up and carried about as she was when a kitten.

Amazingly, yesterday the cat next door, who picks on Max and, when he can catch up to her, on Malkah, attacked Dinah while she was sleeping on the patio by the gazebo. I heard her crying out and his hostile bellowing. I ran out just in time to see her claw his nose and that cat, a great big longhaired and middle-aged orange tabby, take off with tiny Dinah on his tail pursuing him. She drove him off the land and then came back, not a hair out of place. I checked her over and she had not a scratch.

Oboe is more patient, unless it is a matter of being on the wrong side of a door, whether to go out, to come in, or to enter a room where we are and he isn't. But then he has always insisted on his right to have doors opened that separated him from us. He is still top cat, even with his reduced strength. When Max steps out of line, Oboe cuffs him and Max lies down to receive discipline. Oboe still views Malkah and Efi and Dinah as his to protect and possess.

There is a sadness to living with old cats; also a comfort and pleasure, for you know each other thoroughly and the trust is almost absolute. The gray cats always sleep with me, but they also are with me when I read and when I meditate. It is a peaceful and intimate connection. The knowledge of how much I will miss them is always with me, but so is the sense of my own time flowing out, my life passing and the necessity to value it as I value them. Old cats are precious. I pity people who only like kittens.

A vet told me a story of a woman who came into his office with an old cat she wanted to put down. After examining the cat, the vet said he could not find anything wrong with it. It was healthy and he would not euthanize it. The woman insisted. As an argument the woman kept saying, "But he's old. He can't jump anymore. I want a kitten. It depresses me to look at him." Perhaps the woman couldn't live with herself.

I see my future aging in the elderly cats too, but I do not have the worship of youth that characterizes our time. I cherish my old cats. Oboe sleeps through the night these days, pressed against my side under the covers. Of all the cats, he is my most intimate. We are beings who love and trust one another. That knowledge, that trust cannot be replaced. We have been part of each other.

DIGNITY

Near the end of your life you regard
me with a gaze clear and lucid
saying simply, I am, I will not be.

How foolish to imagine animals
don't comprehend death. Old
cats study it like a recalcitrant mouse.

You seek out warmth for your bones
close now to the sleek coat
that barely wraps them,

little knobs of spine, the jut
of hip bones, the skull
my fingers lightly caress.

Sometimes in the night you cry:
a deep piteous banner of gone
desire and current sorrow,

the fear that the night is long
and hungry and you pace
among its teeth feeling time

slipping through you cold and
slick. If I rise and fetch you back
to bed, you curl against me purring

able to grasp pleasure by the nape
even inside pain. Your austere
dying opens its rose of ash.

TWENTY

LA VITA NUOVA

Woody offered me a kind of support through my mother's death I really had not expected of any man I was with. It moved me. He did not take to my father, and my father mostly pretended Woody did not exist. In a few months, my father sold the house and moved into a high-rise in the long-term-care retirement community. His glaucoma was getting steadily worse, without my mother to remind him four times a day to put in his eyedrops.

Boris had been living with us for a year and a half. I talked to the vet about him, saying he seemed to be gaining weight but wasn't eating that much. The vet made a joke about snacking and did no further examination (Boris was the last cat tended by that vet). When we returned from the city April 1, the day after my birthday, he was dragging his belly, frighteningly distended. We brought him in and he was diagnosed with incurable feline infectious peritonitis. He died on the operating table. We brought him home to bury him.

Jim Beam went crazy. For a month at night he insisted we open every cabinet door, every closet door. He searched for Boris, and he wailed, disconsolate. We did not have Boris long, but he was a lovable reprobate, grateful for a home, grateful for food, for attention, for kindness. We felt his loss and decided to get another cat. We attended cat shows to see what we wanted.

The shows were a world of their own. Unlike dog shows, there are no professional trainers, owners show their animals, and we are not talking big bucks or often any money. While presenting their perfect cats, combed and catered to, the owners are not cowed by contemporary standards of thin beauty. They are often large people who eat gourmet takeout in front of their cages and are mostly interested in cats and one another, arranging matings and gossiping about other breeders and judges.

Woody fell in love with a Korat—cats from southeastern Asia, usually from Thailand, an ancient breed believed to have been developed by Buddhist monks hundreds of years ago. Unlike Siamese, they are cobby: not lean and long but stocky little cats, silver gray with intense green eyes, take-charge dispositions and infinite affection, the ultimate lap cats. They relate strongly to other cats but most passionately to people. The breeder told us they were a traditional wedding present. Intending to breed Korats, we selected a female kitten who took to us at once. We would come back for her when she was old enough to leave her mother.

We decided to marry. We fixed on June 2, 1982, because then our anniversary would be the same day as the anniversary of our first love-making, the night we had begun together. We were married by Rabbi Debra Hachen in the apartment in Cambridge we shared with Elise. We wrote part of our ceremony and were married under a chuppah made of a shawl I had given my mother. While we were being married, the turkey we had roasted was waiting in the kitchen. Afterward, when Woody went in to carve it, a gray tail was sticking out. Elise's kitten Gretta, daughter of a famous Russian Blue bar cat in Provincetown, had eaten her way into the turkey's cavity and collapsed, her little belly totally full. Imagine being inside the most sumptuous meal you can envision. We removed her, kept our mouths shut and served the turkey. It was a warm day, and we sat on the back porch with twenty guests, drinking champagne.

On June 19, we held a second ceremony on our land in Wellfleet. About eighty people came, from the Midwest, from New York or Boston, from the Cape. We had a local couple opening shellfish on the front terrace. We had roasted another turkey (minus cat this time). Friends brought entrées, salads and desserts. We provided wine and beer. Elise baked a double challah in the shape of a naked embracing couple. The day began beautifully. We held the ceremony below in a clearing. Local artists Gloria Narden and Peter Watts lent us huge flags sewn with moons and cats and ships. It looked like a medieval fair, people everywhere among the gardens, children under the rhododendrons in full flower, pink, lavender, white, yellow and red, children playing house under the overarching weeping beech. After the ceremony, we had planned on dancing.

About three-thirty, it began to rain, so everybody crowded into the house. Strange pairings resulted. Our guests included novelists, poets, nature writers, my agent, academics; and local people, the bookstore owner, the librarian, painters and writers, fishermen, carpenters, an insurance salesman, paramedics. The dancing ended because eighty people were in a small house eating, drinking and trying to hear one another over the music. To move across the room took twenty minutes. It was the third time I had married, but the first time it had been done with ceremony and carried out in beauty and joy. We were making a commitment we meant and still mean.

That evening, we left Penny and Elise in charge and departed on our honeymoon to an unannounced destination. We had reservations at a motel four towns away, on a Sound beach where we walked for hours. In the morning, we came quietly home. I had told my father about the wedding, but he did not respond. He never learned Woody's name or acknowledged that we were married, although over the next few years, I had occasion to remind him frequently.

The next day we drove to Worcester and picked up our Korat kitten, Dinah. She ran to us, climbed into my arms and purred her way home. We were so excited, Woody was speeding when we were stopped by a state trooper. As he was taking the license and registration, Dinah climbed on the back of Woody's seat and rubbed against the trooper's hand. He did not give us a ticket. She was tiny but fearless—as she is to this day.

She was our wedding present to ourselves. At first both the brown cats arched their backs and hissed. They seemed insulted. She stood her ground. Probably because she was so tiny, Cho-Cho was not as hostile as she had been to the Burmese. But Dinah made little progress with Jim Beam or Colette, until Jim got into a fight. We could always tell from his posture when he returned home whether he had won or lost, in his opinion. This time, he had won. However, he had a bitten paw that abscessed, blown up to the size of a tennis ball. He was grounded and bored: a perfect opportunity for seduction. Dinah did not stop until she had him curled up with her.

Jim Beam fell in love with her. He groomed her. Whenever Jim entered the house, Dinah would run to him, fussing over him as a conquering hero. If she didn't appear, he would search for her. Her favorite way to sleep was in the center of a ring created by Jim's long brown body. He could completely surround her, for even when she was full grown, he was twice her size, twice her weight. However, do not imagine that he dominated her. She would take no guff from him. If he got smart with her, was rough or pushy, she would throw him across the room. He never fought back. When she was angry with him, he caved. Their love affair lasted the rest of his life.

Cho-Cho suffered a gradual decline in health. Her vision was going. She had cataracts. She went outside less, and I did not encourage it, as I felt she would have trouble defending herself. I arranged chairs so that she could get on the dining room table and onto my desk. She was diagnosed that year with an inoperable tumor, but it was not causing her pain. Colette and Jim Beam mostly ignored her. Dinah would curl up with her when neither of the brown cats was available. Colette had slowly accepted Dinah, but when she wanted to sit on my lap, she would simply dump Dinah on the floor. If she felt like sharing me, she would graciously do so; but if that didn't please her, she exercised her rights. She was a proud cat, very conscious of her prerogatives. She had a number of interesting habits. If we went away for longer than a week, Colette would punish us: when we came home, she would pluck a bird out of the air and kill it in front of us. She knew she was not supposed to kill birds, and normally did not. But on those occasions, she not only killed but did it as spectacularly and visibly as possible. Then she would run off and stay out the rest of the day.

She loved scents. She would walk along the herb garden, on a flagstone path between the main garden and the upper garden (named the Rosa Luxemburg but usually referred to as the Rosa) toward the wisteria and a stand of rosebushes. Herbs grow on both sides of the walk. She had her favorite scents—mint, lemon balm, thyme—but when she came to the hyssop she made a face and once or twice I heard her hiss at it. She

Ira Wood and Marge Piercy on their wedding day, Wellfleet, June 1982.

loved roses. Unlike Arofa, who would sniff a rose and then take a bite, she would simply bury her nose in the flower. She also liked daisies, which do not to me have a sweet scent. She is the only cat I ever had who liked perfume. She would pick her way with incredible care among my perfume bottles and gently rub against them. Sometimes when I would pick her up, she smelled of Chanel No. 5 or Femme.

She could be a complete klutz and knock things sideways and spill her food on the floor and push over the water dish. She could be graceful as a ballet dancer and pick her way through a maze of tiny bottles without upsetting any. I was always conscious of her walking on her toes on her long long legs, which Burmese are not supposed to have. Both Burmese had strong powerful tails. You could grip them by the tail without bothering them. It was a way to get Jim's attention. If they hit you with their tail, you felt it. Whomp! Colette would use her tail as an instrument of punishment on Dinah, when she was too obstreperous. When Dinah was little, I carried her around in my blouse, buttoned into it. From the beginning, Dinah was possessive of Woody. It is that way to this day.

Woody and I had a bumpy time at the beginning of our marriage. Working off Cape meant a lot of commuting. He had never had a garden, and the first year, everything went to weeds and rot. However, he missed the wonderful fresh tomatoes. That inspired him to pay attention to growing vegetables. He also wanted to be able to use the outside as space for summer entertaining. Everything outside the house tended to occur in the woods behind it—where we held our ceremony. The house was set into the hill, at the crown. We had made a clearing in a flat place about halfway down to the marsh, where there was a natural circle of pines. As an outdoor room, it had two disadvantages. It was within auditory range of the next house. It was too near the marsh, so on mosquitoey years, that clearing swarmed with them. We began to move recreational space to the south side of the house. Just removing the accumulated junk took a week. Then we began to make plans, developing the gardens gradually over the next ten years. The last addition was a screened-in octagonal gazebo, the brick terrace in front of it, and the cut flower gardens between it and the ram garden.

Two writers living together is considered difficult, but we have both found it better than being with people who don't understand. I have been intimate with people who resented my writing, were jealous of it, were offended by it, tried to ignore it. Woody is a harsh critic of my work, and sometimes when he is particularly cutting, it creates considerable tension. But in the long run I find his criticism invaluable. He understands what I need. One of the first things he did after our wedding was to redo my office, building a large sturdy new desk ten feet long, insisting I pick out a very good chair, and encouraging me to invest in personal computers.

It isn't always easy living together. In fact, often it is damned hard. We are both volatile, both strong willed. Sometimes we each see the other as imposing his or her will. We are both sensitive and used to rejection and may perceive it where it doesn't exist. But we remain truly committed. We are lovers now as much as we were in 1976 when we began. We still find each other interesting companions. Woody, raised in the suburban middle class, is more socially skilled and polite and respecting of social glue. I am more abrasive, more political. The opinions of others mean far more to him than they ever can to me. I don't worry much socially. If there's a silence at a dinner party, it doesn't bother me. Someone will speak up eventually, I'm sure; he isn't. He finds me more arrogant than he likes; I find him moodier. But we are a pair. I never have to watch my back when he's in the room. He's on my side with the same conviction and loyalty as I am on his. I never take that for granted. Nor do I take for granted being loved or being desired: I tried too long for a good central relationship.

THE CHUPPAH

The chuppah stands on four poles.
The home has its four corners.
The chuppah stands on four poles.
The marriage stands on four legs.
Four points loose the winds
that blow on the walls of the house,
the south wind that brings the warm rain,
the east wind that brings the cold rain,
the north wind that brings the cold sun
and the snow, the long west wind
bringing the weather off the far plains.

Here we live open to the seasons.
Here the winds caress and cuff us
contrary and fierce as bears.
Here the winds are caught and snarling
in the pines, a cat in a net clawing
breaking twigs to fight loose.
Here the winds brush your face
soft in the morning as feathers
that float down from a dove's breast.

Here the moon sails up out of the ocean
dripping like a just washed apple.

Here the sun wakes us like a baby.
Therefore the chuppah has no sides.

It is not a box.
It is not a coffin.
It is not a dead end.
Therefore the chuppah has no walls.
We have made a home together
open to the weather of our time.
We are mills that turn in the winds of struggle
converting fierce energy into bread.

The canopy is the cloth of our table
where we share fruit and vegetables
of our labor, where our care for the earth
comes back and we take its body in ours.

The canopy is the cover of our bed
where our bodies open their portals wide,
where we eat and drink the blood
of our love, where the skin shines red
as a swallowed sunrise and we burn
in one furnace of joy molten as steel
and the dream is flesh and flower.

O my love O my love we dance
under the chuppah standing over us
like an animal on its four legs,
like a table on which we set our love
as a feast, like a tent
under which we work
not safe but no longer solitary
in the searing heat of our time.

TWENTY-ONE

ALL RIVERS WIND AT LAST
TO THE SEA

Cho-Cho insisted on going out one summer day, and I thought there was no harm in her enjoying the sun. She disappeared. We called her, we searched far into the marsh, all over the surrounding land, but that night she did not come back, not the next day, not the next night. I wrote a poem about her walking into the marsh to die. Then on the third day, we heard a hoarse cry in the distance. When we went to investigate, we found Cho-Cho, dehydrated and exhausted. She never went outside again.

She began to find climbing stairs too difficult. She lived, essentially, on a chair in the dining room and had to be taken to her litter box several times a day. Accidents happened. She ate, slept, purred and seemed still to enjoy, but she had no mobility. She was blind. She could no longer keep herself clean and had to endure being bathed. In early summer the next year, it became clear that she was in pain. The cancer had metastasized. She was the first cat I ever had killed by a vet, and it was a difficult decision. In truth, I waited too long, for her and for us. Her quality of life toward the end was not much better than that of a turnip. I was sentimental and reluctant—and foolish.

My father had been living in the retirement community for a year and a half when phone calls started from their business office. The first had to do with his account there being overdrawn. He had told them his Social Security checks would be automatically deposited, but they were not arriving. That was the first cavalry charge down to Florida. I had practice pushing Social Security around on behalf of my mother when she had lacked a birth certificate. I was reasonably good at threading bureaucracies. We ran down my father's check, deposited in a bank in West Palm Beach. He turned out to have small bank accounts in different banks miles apart—a hangover from the Depression, so that if one bank failed, another might survive.

The next crisis was his income taxes. I had to go down and straighten that out with an accountant. He had forgotten all about taxes, and his records were a mess. By now my father was not managing. His clothes were dirty, since when he threw them on the floor, they did not wash, iron or fold themselves any longer. He was drinking too much and not eating enough. Meals were provided in the dining room, but he had to know what time it was and get himself down there. The local bank where he established a living trust hired a caretaker four hours every day, a southern woman who made sly cracks about Jews and treated him like a wayward child. In some ways, that's exactly what he was.

The next time I was called, my father's pension check was the problem. No one knew where the pension checks he had listed as half his income were going. He was confused, his mind kiting back to 1937 and 1942 with reasonable acuity, but out of sync with the present. He had no idea who I was by now. He called me "Bert," my mother's name, and tried to order me around. He laughed dryly and often at jokes comprehensible only to himself. He moved in an awkward shuffle.

We loaded him into the back of a rented car and drove to every bank in three counties. It took two days. Woody managed to persuade Westinghouse to tell us where the check was being deposited, but that bank no longer existed. Finally we found the bank that had eaten the earlier bank, where we located an account where his pension checks were going. I had to get a power of attorney to move everything over. Then I stuck the document in a drawer.

His surviving younger brother came down with his wife to take care of him, but that only lasted three weeks. They wanted me to move in. He thought, during the rare moments when he knew me, that I should keep house for him. His sister Grace offered to stay, but he refused. I argued with him, since I thought she would be good for him. She had given up a chance to marry fifty years before to care for her aged father, who was reputed to be just as cranky and hard to get along with as my father. "No," he said vehemently. "She's no fun. She doesn't even drink."

I had never been close to my father, and I was not about to move to Florida. Woody was an artist in residence in the Barnstable school system; I had sold my next novel subject to satisfactory revisions and set up readings and workshops every other week. My father could not get out of the contract with the retirement community, so there was no question of moving him north. He hated the facility by now. He had a few cronies he played poker with, but otherwise, he did not fit in. Having an account with Merrill Lynch did not turn him into an acceptable middle-class retiree. He was loud, dirty and opinionated. He was a working-class man who had labored at hard dangerous jobs around machinery all his life. He was used to drinking, playing cards and hanging out with guys like himself, but men in the retirement community had been accountants, middle-level management, teachers. He never understood social class, although my mother had grasped it very well. She knew she would not be acceptable in the retirement community, but my father never imagined a problem. The office frequently harassed me about him. He did not dress well, his apartment was filthy, his behavior was inappropriate. I can be difficult for bureaucrats to deal with.

The next call came after he had gone outside at 2 A.M. without putting on his pants, wandering in the parking lot looking for lunch. They stuck him in the psychiatric ward of a local hospital. I called my friend Ruth Ann Robson, fiction writer and poet, who was working as a lawyer in Belle Glade. Ever since she had been a student of mine at Nashville, we have kept in touch. She did the paperwork to get him out. However, the facility insisted he go into their equivalent of a nursing home, a building in the center of the complex where they kept people who could no longer care for themselves. I demanded that they preserve his apartment for him, that this be viewed as temporary. In the meantime, there he was with people much worse off than he was, babbling, drooling, parked medicated in the dreary rooms and drearier corridors waiting to die.

By this time, the office people knew I was trouble and that I had a crack lawyer. I had to activate the power of attorney. I took over his checkbooks, straightened out his taxes, paid his bills and tried to rationalize everything. For the next months, I did his paperwork. We got him out of the nursing home and back into his apartment. He said he would die if he stayed in that place, and I believed him.

Then began a period in which not the facility but my father was calling up, often well after midnight. His glaucoma had progressed to the frightening point where he could not tell day from night. I got him a clock with very big numbers. I bought him a tape recorder so he could communicate with me by tapes, back and forth. He seemed to like that. However, that did not stop him from calling at 3 A.M. to our Cape Cod house, waking both of us, to shout, "You stole my pencils!" "You took money from the drawer!" After a month of this, we got our first answering machine.

The basic problem was that he felt he had lost control. He was a man for whom the feeling of being in control, even if he was powerless in much of his life, was very important. Feeling superior to his wife was part of his basic identity. He truly never noticed all the work she did until she was missing and no one did it. Then he had this puzzled air, as to why the food didn't appear on the table the way he liked it, why he didn't remember to take his medication no matter how many large timers I sent him, why the dishes stayed dirty in the sink, the floor was sticky and his clothes were no longer clean or pressed.

My mother had ironed everything. She ironed dishtowels and bath towels, sheets and pillowcases, his handkerchiefs and his underwear. Now nothing was right. He was angry but no one quailed. If he yelled at me, I backed away and let him seethe. He kept the TV on from dawn until midnight for company, because he could no longer make friends. He had depended on a certain context. In Detroit, on the job, he was a big man. He was important in his union. He was the only worker who could fix the old machinery nobody else could figure out. He was the guy who made jokes at the poker table and knew the good fishing spots. He had left his importance and his social network behind in Detroit and at the lake. In Florida, he was just an old geezer. My mother had been right about not moving to Florida, and she had been right about the retirement community complex. He was angry and kept saying, "This was supposed to be fun."

He wanted his checkbook back, and I gave it to him. I knew it would get screwed up, but I didn't think that mattered as much as his retaining some sense of control. From a distance, I oversaw what was happening and made sure the money stretched. The bank, which had control of his living trust, insisted on adding another person to cover four more hours of caring for him. It was a man who abused my father, so we fired him. It was strange to be spending so much time and money making sure my father survived, because we did not become closer. Communication never improved. Unlike my mother, he never read anything I wrote. He still couldn't remember who Woody was—or pretended not to. We could not tell how much of a fog he was in. Sometimes I could make him laugh. If we took him to a restaurant for steaks and drinks, he would tell us stories about the 1930s and 1940s and 1950s. But we could never make any further contact with him in a personal way.

We grew to hate Florida during those years. Woody's family was living in Columbia, South Carolina. His father worked as a manager in the textile business, running around all over the South. Sometimes we were able to arrange to see them. Other people we knew loved to go south in the winter; we dreaded it. I was not much of a daughter. I dealt with crises, I got my father out of trouble and I managed his finances and tried to find solutions to his problems, but without love. There was duty on my side and anger on his. I would taste guilt that I felt so little for him, but I could not fake it. I still missed my mother, and I had a core of resentment about how he had behaved to her, especially around her stroke. In the retirement community facility, they imagined I adored my father, because I fought them to accede to his wishes. Nonsense. I wasn't going to put up with him, so they were going to have to. An old organizer, I organized his situation. I found myself cold, but I was truthful with Woody: I could not pretend to feel what I didn't. My father was no hypocrite, never expressing affection toward me either.

In the fall of 1985, we received a phone call from the facility. My father had been eliminating on the floor, and when they took him to the nursing facility, they found a bad sore on his leg. He was rushed to the hospital, where he was diagnosed with a staph infection. I was still trying to get information when the hospital told me he had died. I think he simply decided to, dreading the nursing home again. In the hospital, he turned his face to the wall and died.

I brought his ashes north and threw them in the sea, which he had loved. I recognized he had strengthened me in my childhood with his disregard, made me more competitive, forced me to do whatever I feared, climbing ladders, scrambling over rocks. I could not please him, but trying made me brighter, more persistent. He taught me a respect for logic. He probably gave me my sense of humor. Where other girls grew soft to please, he hardened me with his temper.

Through all this time, I was writing fiction and poetry, giving thirty to forty readings a year, workshops, occasional speeches and lectures. Some years before we married and for a couple of years afterward, I served as a Governor Dukakis appointee to the Massachusetts Endowment for the Humanities. After my second term expired, he appointed me to the Cultural Council. I liked that work better than dealing with academics and academic issues. I saw my role as fighting for money for literature, always the stepchild of funding. Music, film, video, drama, the graphic arts get the lion's share. I also saw myself as representing women, minorities, and the smaller art groups that did not have the clout of the Boston Symphony or the Museum of Fine Arts. I did a lot of committee work and I think I was effective, certainly I was the only writer on the council board. I became close to Ann Hawley, the director during those years. I was vitally involved until 1991, when the incoming Weld administration appointee got rid of me. I was in the middle of a series of painful eye operations and unable to attend meetings. They insisted I appear or resign.

During these years, several of us started a local chapter of NOW.

Through the 1980s, that was my important local political work. We had a program on the public radio station and I ran a legislative update network. We worked on campaigns that were important to women, like Gerry Studds's reelection to the House of Representatives. We brought in speakers for public meetings.

In 1984, Dinah began to go into heat regularly. In the misguided notion that it was going to be a cinch, we decided to breed Korats. On April 1, Woody drove her to Worcester, to get laid. Woody left Dinah with the stud, spent the night in Cambridge at Elise's, and the next day picked her up. Dinah's pregnancy went smoothly enough, although she was small and disliked lugging a belly around. Much nonsense is written about how cats are great natural mothers: some are, some aren't. Dinah hated motherhood. Giving birth terrified her. With the first kitten half born, she started racing around the house, panicked. I put on plastic gloves and delivered the kitten, after turning it. It was a breach birth. I had to deliver the second kitten also. The third, the only female, and the fourth came out normally.

For the first twenty-four hours after the traumatic birth scene, Dinah was an ideal mother. She nursed her little blobs of life. By the second day, she was bored. It was not possible for any cat or person to lie down to read or sleep or sit still without Dinah sneaking up and leaving the kittens with them and racing away pell-mell. We had fierce confrontations about nursing. She didn't like it. I insisted on it, remaining with her while she nursed, although I began fairly early to supplement her milk with kitten milk replacement formula.

Two of the kittens flourished, but two began to fail. I kept them alive by feeding them kitten formula every two hours. However, I had to go off to a conference. While I was gone, two kittens died. Woody tried, but he frankly had no aptitude for nursing. We had not named the kittens but identified them, as Dinah's breeder suggested, with nail polish. Purple foot and red foot died. Female and orange foot flourished. When they reached seven weeks, we named the female Morgan. The male was named for his reedy insistent voice, Oboe.

I had intended to sell Oboe and keep Morgan, but the kittens made it clear they felt differently. Morgan did not want to be in a house with so many other cats. Oboe was his mother's favorite and already bonded to me. When Morgan was twelve weeks old, the son of a local contractor came to the house to meet her, and there was instant attraction. We bartered her for having the driveway graveled. Oboe stayed. When Dinah came into heat again, we took her to the vet and had her altered. She purred all the way there and all the way back, as if she understood. Now, whenever she begins to gain weight, she puts herself on a diet. She seems to believe if she gains too much weight, she will have kittens again. However, she managed to give birth to her lifelong playmate, platonic lover, best friend. They are still inseparable.

At Christmastime, the power went out in the house. When we got an electrician, he found that the power lines to the house had been damaged by the builders when Woody's room was added. The line needed replacing. Now, the electrician knew about Korats. He wanted one. He presented us with a bill, said it had to be paid for the work to proceed and power (and heat and water) to be restored, but he would take Oboe as full payment. We found the money. It was a tight time, but not that tight.

Colette was angry at me for letting Dinah have kittens. She remained aloof for the rest of the year, from June through December. She stayed out several nights during the summer, no longer my shadow. She did not forgive me until January, when we had to leave the Cape.

I am not sure when I actually began to write *Gone to Soldiers*. However, it was such a long novel that we ran out of money while I was still working on third draft. Then I was offered the Elliston Chair as poet in residence at the University of Cincinnati, where over the years I had given readings several times. The teaching duties ran from the beginning of January to the beginning of April. I accepted with the condition that the housing provided accommodate Woody and the four cats, whose pictures I sent along. I wasn't going to leave the cats alone for months as I had Arofa and Cho-Cho. The university agreed. We were given a loft in a predominantly Afro-American partially gentrified area called Over the Rhine.

The cats yowled their way across country, two to a carrying case. Once in the loft, Jim Beam fell into a state of despair. We had been afraid he would spray everything and try to get out. He didn't want to go outside in Cincinnati, and he had no desire whatsoever to mark this space as his territory. He loved his land passionately and wanted to be nowhere else. The other cats were far more adaptable. Colette was pleased to be with us. Immediately she began to forgive me and reclaimed my lap. Colette, Dinah and Oboe loved the big space of the loft, where they played constantly. We were around a great deal, giving them more attention than they got at home. After all, there was little to do beside work. We had no garden to tend, no house to take care of, few friends to see. For all the cats except Jim, it was a delightful time. This was not a neighborhood you would stroll around in. The block across from us had been torn down in urban renewal never renewed. The one house standing had a chain-link fence around it and a German shepherd kept outside in wintry weather, who barked all night. BARKED ALL NIGHT. That winter Woody and I discovered earplugs.

We were bored. Every morning, Jim Beam sang a baritone solo, entitled "How Beautiful Is Wellfleet with Its Marshes, Pines and Delicious Saltwater Grass-Fed Mice." Woody counted the days to departure, usually wrong. For two weeks, there were twenty-seven days left. At home our hours were fifty minutes long and each day held only twenty-two of them. Here the days were twenty-eight hours long and every week had at least eight.

Sometimes it felt like a time warp, and we were caught in 1955. The city administration was busy banning things and censoring art. The abortion clinic was bombed. Even the academics told Kentucky jokes, saying to me, *They are our Polacks,* and *The best thing that ever came out of Kentucky was an empty bus.* Yet the nicest people I met were from Kentucky, and it surely was prettier across the bridges over the Ohio. We lived near downtown where after 5 P.M., boulevards wide as the deck of aircraft carriers were witness to three cars in the distance. We could have picnicked in the middle of any of them. The river itself was impressive, muttering as it carried along hillsides it had torn off. We watched the Ohio in flood carrying whole trees, bits of roofing, boats and buildings it nibbled on. The river was coppery with mud and slashed along.

We made a few friends, but mostly we went to malls for amusement—and Woody sees malls as a preview of hell. We walked to the farmers' market in the middle of the ghetto every week to buy fruits and vegetables, observing that they certainly knew 147 ways to use a pig. Finally I completed a fourth draft of *Gone to Soldiers* and submitted it to my agent. It was a very long novel, and I did not have any idea if she could sell it. When spring came, we returned to Wellfleet, gratefully. In spite of the date, we hit a bad snowstorm on the Pennsylvania Turnpike. It was terrifying, huge trucks all around us and the road slippery, the visibility nil, the cats howling. We were pulling a trailer, which slewed us crookedly from left to right. If Woody were a less good driver, we would have died, but we arrived home alive and happy, two humans and four cats. Jim Beam charged out of the car and ran in circles, tail straight up like a flag. I was grateful too that I was with a man who was just as glad to be home as I was. Our confluences still thrill me.

BURIAL BY SALT

The day after Thanksgiving I took you to the sea.
The sky was low and scudding. The wind was stiff.
The sea broke over itself in seething froth
like whipped up eggwhites, blowing to settle
in slowly popping masses at my feet.

I ran, boots on, into the bucking surf
taking you in handfuls, tossing you
into wind, into water, into the elements:
go back, give back. Time is all spent,
the flesh is spent to ashes.

Mother's were colored like a mosaic,
vivid hues of the inside of conch shells,

pastels, pearls, green, salmon as feathers
of tropical birds. They fit in my cupped hands.
I put her in the rose garden and said kaddish.

Your ashes are old movies, black into grey.
Heavy as iron filings, they sag the box
sides. They fill it to overflowing.
Handful after handful I give to the waves
which seize and churn you over and under.

I am silent as I give you to the cold
winter ocean grey as a ship of war,
the color of your eyes, grey with green
and blue washed in, that so seldom met
my gaze, that looked right through me.

What is to be said? Did you have a religion?
If so, you never spoke of it to me.
I remember you saying No, *saying it often*
and loud, I remember your saying, Never,
I remember, I won't have that in my house.

I grew up under the threat of your anger
as peasants occupy the slopes of a volcano
sniffing the wind, repeating old adages,
reading birdflight and always waiting, even
in sleep for the ground to quake and open.

My injustices, my pains, my resentments;
they are numerous, precious as the marbles
I kept in a jar, not so much for playing
as simply rolling in my hands to see
the colors trap the light and swell.

Tossing your ashes in my hands as the waves
drag the sand from under me, trying to topple
me into the turning eddy of far storms,
I want to cast that anger from me, finally
to say, you begot me and although my body

my hair my eyes are my mother's so that at your
funeral, your brother called me by her name,
I will agree that in the long bones of my legs,
in my knees, in my Welsh mouth that sits oddly
in my Jewish Tartar face, you are imprinted.

I was born the wrong sex to a woman
in her mid-forties who had tried to get pregnant
for five years. A hard birth,
I was her miracle and your disappointment.
Everything followed from that, downhill.

I search now through the ashes of my old pain
to find something to praise, and I find that
withholding love, you made me strive to be worthy,
reaching, always reaching, thinking that when I leaped
high enough you would be watching. You weren't.

That did not cancel the leaping or the fruit
at last grasped in the hand and gnawed to the pit.
You were the stone on which I built my strength.
Your indifference honed me. Your coldness
toughened my flesh. Your anger stropped me.

I was reading maps for family trips at age
five, navigating from the back seat. Till
I was twenty, I did not know other children

did not direct all turns and plot route numbers.
When Mother feigned helplessness, I was factotum.

Nurse, houseboy, carpenter's helper, maid,
whatever chinks appeared I filled, responsible
and rebellious with equal passion, equal time,
and thus quite primed to charge like a rocket
out the door trailing sparks at seventeen.

We were illsuited as fox and bull. Once
I stopped following baseball, we could not talk.
I'd ask you how some process was done—open
hearth steel, how generators worked.
Your answers had a clarity I savored.

I did with mother as I had promised her,
I took her from you and brought her home to me,
I buried her as a Jew and mourn her still.
To you I made no promises. You asked none.
Forty-nine years we spoke of nothing real.

For decades I thought someday we would talk
at last. In California I came to you in the mountains
at the dam carrying that fantasy like a picnic
lunch beautifully cooked and packed, but never
to be eaten. Not by you and me.

When I think of the rare good times
I am ten or eleven and we are working together
on some task in silence. In silence I faded into
the cartoon son. Hand me the chisel. I handed.
Bevel the edge smooth. I always got bored.

I'd start asking questions, I'd start asking
why and wherefore and how come and who said so.
I was lonely on the icefield, I was lonely
in the ice caves of your sometime favor.
I kept trying to start a fire or conversation.

Time burns down and the dark rushes in in waves.
I can't lie. What was between us was history,
not love. I have striven to be just to you,
stranger, first cause, old man, my father,
and now I give you over to salt and silence.

TWENTY-TWO

DIGGING IN FOR THE LONG HAUL

Gone to Soldiers did the best of any of my novels up to then, so that for a time we felt quite affluent. We managed to save some of the money and some we used to put a room on the house—a dining room with skylights and windows on three sides, a pleasant airy room surrounded by garden and trees. We also had the house shingled and added a bay window to the living room, great for starting plants too tender for the hotbed—peppers, eggplants, basil. The cats resent that use. They think the bay window is theirs to loll in, overseeing the gardens.

Oboe was developing into a cat of grave dignity. Unlike his mother, who never wanted to grow up, Oboe couldn't wait. He became portly, gentlemanly, gentle—except for a tendency to be jealous of Colette, because of her preeminent position as my lap cat. She slept beside me in bed with her head on my pillow. Woody called it a ridiculous sight, but except in the hottest weather, that was her position—her long lean body stretched out against me, her head on my pillow. She liked our working in the garden, whereas Jim Beam usually pretended he did not know us outside—except that he would come when called. Often he was way into the marsh in the evening. Woody or I would call or whistle for him and far far off we would hear him bellowing an answer. He would come crying as he ambled along, although it might take him ten minutes to arrive.

The Burmese were social cats. They greeted company and explored them. We would shut Jim Beam out of the downstairs room that is my assistant's office but occasionally serves as a guest room. He found a way through the vents and ducts, and would suddenly appear in that room in the middle of the night. He was not hostile but interested. He seemed to expect praise for his exploits and was visibly disappointed when a guest threw him out.

There were many things about training cats that we did not know when we got the Burmese. Jim developed the habit of crying in the night, around 3 A.M. It always woke me, but not Woody. I would chase Jim and throw him in the bathroom. It wasn't until years later I understood that far from discouraging him by chasing, yelling and throwing him in the bathroom, I was inventing a game he played sedulously. When Max cries too early in the morning, I am careful to do nothing exciting or amusing. I ignore him if I can, or hold him under the covers with me. Therefore he seldom wakes me before the alarm goes off. Most mornings he waits to see if I am really getting up before he moves. For Jim Beam, punishment was attention, and he vastly preferred being punished to being ignored. One of his worst habits was picking on Colette when he was bored. The higher the temperature, the more restless and wicked he was. I used to say, we should put Jim Beam in the freezer for an hour. Certainly in the winter, he was a better behaved cat, cuddling with the others, affection-ate. In the summer, he was a heller. Some summers, he got into a fight every three weeks. He would no sooner recover from his abscess and antibiotics and being kept in, than he would go out and get into another fight, often with the same damned cat.

Partly it was the invasion of the summer people. Jim maintained a large territory, much larger than any cat I have known since Brutus. Unfortunately, in the summer, it included the houses of people who brought their dogs or cats with them. He never mellowed out and never became less combative while he could swagger around. He was a gorgeous cat. Whenever we took him to the vet's, other cats would stare at him and preen themselves. He had a circle of male friends as well as enemies. He was always being called on by other cats. When we finally began to let Oboe and Dinah go out, Jim gained a little respect for Oboe, but not much. Oboe was not about to trot off with him into the marsh or hang out with seven other male cats under the full moon on a hillock near the creek, Dunn's Run. Oboe remained a homebody.

We let go of our pied-à-terre in Cambridge, but still travel to Boston regularly. Those were years when we went frequently to Europe, usually for a combination of publicity for a book publication and research for a novel I was writing. Woody had two novels published, wrote a couple of screenplays under contract and one on spec, began to teach workshops at writers' conferences. We travel well together. I vastly prefer traveling with him, for he takes the edge off and eases the bleakness and the loneliness of being on the road.

In the late 1980s, twelve of us locals started a havurah—a term for a lay Jewish group that operates without a rabbi for most purposes, sort of do-it-yourself Judaism. We were a motley group in our thirties, forties and fifties, all living on the Cape year-round and trying to find a meaningful way to relate to Judaism. The nearest synagogue in Hyannis was traditional and impossible for a number of us to deal with. We began meeting every other Friday for a potluck and discussions, for holidays. The group grew quickly to fifteen. Several people joined because they wanted some kind of Jewish education for their children and a way for their children to get bar or bat mitzvahed.

Our first public event was a Purim party for children and their adult friends. We expected thirty people and over a hundred showed up. We began doing lay Friday night services once a month in the Chapel in the Pines, a place where folksingers performed. Services varied wildly, because we intentionally did not have a ritual committee. People might not like the services other people put on, but it was the right of every member to produce the kind of service they wanted. Some worked, some didn't, but it was loose and free and warm. We were a friendly group. It was a group with strong women running it, and it reflected that. It was nonhierarchical. In actuality, it was an anarchist havurah, casual in the extreme and open to all kinds, especially including gays and lesbians and those married to non-Jews. Our many potlucks brought people in who wanted the social occasion, wanted services, but also wanted to feed their kids.

The smaller core group of fifteen met every other Friday night. Soon the larger havurah spawned a discussion group, bar and bat mitzvah preparation tutoring, Hebrew classes that met weekly. I was one of the participants and continued studying Hebrew until our teacher, one of the most important women in the havurah, moved to Maine with her husband, a biologist with the park service. We had reached the intermediate level. I would have gone on forever studying with her; I loved our group and the lessons.

Sometimes rabbis would volunteer to do a service for us, if we would put them up on the Cape. We were a rather special group then. We also began, during the third year of the havurah, bringing in last-year students from the Hebrew Union College to conduct High Holiday services. After having a male student one year, we always requested women thereafter, a special pleasure for a lot of the women who had grown up when only men were rabbis. We called the havurah Am ha-Yam—people of the sea. Several of the people in the havurah made their living from the sea, including a woman who farmed shellfish and a man who lobstered, and our president Helaine, who with her husband ran a seafood-processing and wholesale plant on the pier in Provincetown. We sometimes had services in Provincetown, led by a serious young gay man who had studied for the rabbinate years before.

It was a lot of work. Our potlucks grew popular and began to attract hundreds of Jews from all over the Cape, including summer people who extended their vacations for our High Holiday services. We had a real community and a willingness to improvise and create some kind of spiritual connection. I led rituals myself. There are scenes I will always remember, like a young dyke from Provincetown carrying the Torah and weeping, because she had always felt excluded. On the other end of the pleasure spectrum, I remember when Helaine decided we of the core group should make gefilte fish for two hundred at Pesach instead of buying it. I was enthusiastic, because I had fond memories of my grandmother making it. Well, we each got a pail of smelly ground-up carp shipped from a Hassidic supplier in New York. The process took all day and our kitchen stank and so did we. I could not eat the resulting slop and did without gefilte fish that Passover. The Perels brought Sephardic traditions into the havurah to mix with the Ashkenazi expectations of most members, broadening but annoying to people comfortable only with their expected rituals. It was a time I felt tremendously and joyfully involved in Judaism.

Jim Beam on a pile of salt hay, Wellfleet, 1994. Photograph by Marge Piercy

I was diagnosed around this time with glaucoma and cataracts. Heredity wins a round: cataracts from my mother and grandmother; glaucoma from my father. I went to a doctor with all the best credentials and affiliations, who essentially played with my eyes for the next three years, telling me nothing could be done for me except to take various eyedrops, always in increasing amounts and with vastly increasing discomfort. I tried many New Age remedies on the side, an osteopath who said the pressure was caused by the misalignment of bones in the skull, herbs, poultices, daily periods of visualization. My pressure kept rising and my sight diminishing. I was going perceptibly blind, and it terrified me. Finally my gynecologist, one of my heroes (he is on those anti-choice hit lists), insisted I go to his ophthalmologist, who recommended an immediate operation, sending me to a glaucoma surgeon.

I will always remember that summer of pain and near blindness, when every normal activity was almost impossible. Without meditation, I don't know how I would have survived. I remember trying to walk by following the white of Woody's socks before me, stumbling through the woods, tripping over branches and roots and smacking into boughs still attached. I remember falling innumerable times. I must have been covered with bruises, but I could not see them. There was a laser "procedure" in both eyes that left me in agonizing pain. Eye doctors do not tend to prescribe painkillers. Mostly it is a field that attracts doctors who would dearly like to remove your eyes, take them away and work on them in private, and not have to deal with the rest of you at all. Then I had a major eye operation on my left eye. During eye operations, you are conscious. You are drugged and everything is blurry, but your eyes are open and you are quite, quite conscious. You can talk. I usually do so, at least occasionally.

Then came the period of office "procedures"—minor operations. The doctor would inject various drugs into my eye with a long needle and sometimes use a laser. It was painful. It was very painful afterward. It was painful in between these three-times-a-week procedures. Mondays the procedure was done in Hyannis, and my friend Ann would drive me. Wednesdays, Woody took me to Boston, and my friend Denya did it Fridays. Much of my life was used up going back and forth to be tortured, then lying on the couch in between using eyedrops and whimpering. I stepped on the cats constantly, because I could not see them. The drugs blurred the vision in my good eye. But I still managed to write. We bought a great big monitor, though I could barely see the keyboard. Fortunately, I am a touch typist. All summer into the fall, I was not to bend over, to lift anything, to lie other than flat on my back with my head propped up. I shocked my surgeon by asking whether Woody and I could have sex. He said no one had ever asked that before, but it had to be missionary position and I was not to be "overactive."

I had never been stung by a bee or a wasp before that summer, but during those months, I was stung five times. Going into the garden to pick herbs or vegetables, I would inadvertently close my hand on one of the social insects. I can't imagine how I cooked—slowly and with little imagination I suppose.

I woke one morning—it was the first day of my period—and I was numb from the chin down. I had no sensation in my body. Woody thought exercise would help, so we went for a walk, but things got worse. My heart was pounding furiously. I could not eat. I could barely swallow. I could only tell I had to urinate when liquid came out of me. I tried calling my surgeon, but he denied what was happening to me had any relation to what he was doing to me or any medication I was taking. Woody called a friend of his who worked in an emergency room, and he said it definitely sounded like a drug reaction to him. Finally I went to see my own doctor, Janet Whelan, in Provincetown.

One wonderful thing about Janet is that she doesn't fake it. She will tell you honestly when she has no idea what's wrong. She also talked to the glaucoma surgeon, who insisted that the eye was a self-enclosed system. Then she had me make a list of everything I was putting into my body and correlated it with the information from him about what he was injecting me with. Finally she worked it out. I had atropine poisoning. By this time, my heart rate and my blood pressure were almost off the scale and I could not feel my body at all.

She started me on fluids and drinking as much water as I could get down. I was to go off atropine immediately and stay off. Slowly, slowly through the next eight hours, my heart rate lessened, my blood pressure dropped and feeling returned from the chin down. It was extremely gradual, but I was no longer terrified. Woody freaked out that day and ran off to the ocean, unable to endure what appeared to be my total disintegration. He had little experience dealing with illness or incapacity, and my near disaster frightened him.

It was humiliating to be seen in public during these weeks, but a certain amount of business traveling was unavoidable. One eye was shrouded in a metal cage and bandages and my face was swollen and distorted. I am not vain. I had always taken my appearance pretty much for granted, but I found it embarrassing to walk into a public rest room and have teenage girls look at me and go, *Yetch!* Which happened.

About a week after my episode of atropine poisoning, Hurricane Bob hit the Cape with devastating winds and associated tornadoes. A swath was cut through the center of town, taking century-old maples and oaks and breaking them off or uprooting them and bashing in houses. Tangles of live wires swarmed buzzing and sparking over the streets and roads. We were on the side of the hurricane with tremendously high roaring winds but little rain. We cowered in the house with the cats. Occasionally I would go to the window, crisscrossed with masking tape, and hold Colette up to see. Even I could watch the wind blowing the trees side-ward like inside-out umbrellas, watch the branches going past like javelins. The wind bombarded us, shaking the house and deafening us. Human helplessness is what you most experience. We were not hit badly, except that we were without power for six days and lost trees, including our best apple tree and one of the sugar maples. Without power, we had no water. I had filled many containers, but we ran out by the third day. We have a gas stove, so we were able to cook—which meant we cooked all we could the first couple of days, since the freezer went, of course.

Friends in the National Seashore had power. We were able to store some of our frozen vegetables and meat in their freezer. We also took a bath there one day. We could not work. We took walks, but even that was hard, with so many trees and power lines down. It was hot and dry and itchy. Because it was mid-August, the town was eerily full of tourists still on vacation in a place without electricity, toilets, running water or stores. At night, there were no lights, no sounds other than natural ones. Foxes, coyotes, raccoons took back the Cape. There were huge fights at night in our compost pile, where we had thrown the rotting food we had to dis-card. Our garden had survived reasonably well. After the first two days, we were vegetarians living on what we grew.

One night I was wakened by Jim Beam growling, making fierce and frightened noises from a crouch on my dresser, fur raised. I went to the window to see what he was looking at. A huge coyote was standing on the porch not four feet away, visible in the moonlight. My impulse was to be perfectly still and simply watch, but I remembered what our biologist friend had said: you must make a lot of noise and scare coyotes away, or they will be fearless and return often. And kill and eat your cats. I made so much noise, Ira leapt from bed, anticipating a fire or worse.

It was hot after the hurricane and parched. The trees on the outer Cape were denuded. Everything from waist height down was green, but above that, it was barren November in August. Time slowed to a trickle. During this period of office operations three times a week, I wasn't supposed to bend over, lift anything. But Hurricane Bob had knocked down a huge pine tree across the path. Trees were down, and until someone could come with a power saw, the only way to leave or enter the house was to crawl under them. The only way to get water was to go to the dump with two buckets and stand in line with three thousand residents and ten thousand summer people to get both buckets filled from the water truck.

We were filthy. Going to the bathroom meant going into the woods with a trowel, and there was little water in which to wash your hands then or any other time. We ate off paper plates and drank from paper cups, but we had to cook in pans, and they must be washed. I have written about this period in the afterword to *City of Darkness, City of Light*, explaining how being in a world without power enabled me to enter the eighteenth century. It made people's lives vividly real, how difficult were minor things we take for granted. We lost a good friend. During the eye of Bob, he went outside and saw that the house of another friend in the havurah had been half leveled. The huge sign of the motel across the street had chopped into the house, smashing it. When Arne saw that, his heart stopped. He died instantly. The irony was that the friend was not injured. He happened to have gone into the kitchen and was standing at the far wall when the roof flew across the street. That fall, we put in a generator that cost as much as a used car. Now when the power goes, we have electricity at least for a couple of days, longer if we use it only certain hours for running the most essential things.

Most of the birds were gone. It was a couple of years before we saw goldfinches again. The crows survived and visited us frequently. The few locust trees left rebloomed, the long flowing grapelike white fragrant panicles that announce June hanging on the trees in October, along with lilacs blooming over the scarlet Virginia creeper in its fall foliage. We had an efflorescence of mice. Deer were always at hand. Those of us who live here found a new friendliness. Usually we locals never see one another during the summer, but now the Cape people operated as a society apart—or within—ignoring the summer people and helping one another in extraordinary ways.

After the last of the glaucoma procedures, I had to wait a month for a cataract operation. When *He, She and It* came out, I could not tour and could give only readings from my poetry—because I have memorized many of my poems and could perform them, but I could not see to read from the novel. I was cautious about discussing the extent of my problem, because I needed money, and I could do poetry readings just fine. Finally, the cataract operation was performed. I had hoped for good vision in my left eye, after all that pain and difficulty. However, the optical nerve had been injured and I am blind in the center of my left eye. I put off surgery on the eye I see with, my right eye, for four years, as long as I could.

For those four years, I had to wear a very strong bifocal contact lens in my right eye, but because of the size and thickness of it, I could only keep it in for six hours. Then I would put on glasses with the left lens opaque. Not only did they look weird, but it hurt to wear them. I had no depth vision and constantly stumbled. A headache kicked in as soon as I put the glasses on. Basically it worked out much better if between the first six hours and the second, I lay down in a darkened room. I was still using a lot of medication in both eyes and that was one of the convenient times to put it in. But if you have ever traveled on business when you must lie down for an hour to an hour and a half in the middle of the day, you may have some notion of the problem I faced. Nobody ever understood. They thought I was a prima donna, a secret drunk. "Oh, you have to take a nap?"

I kept writing on my large monitor. The cats formed a tight bunch, a solid cat family, staying as close to me as they could. Oboe would sometimes try to herd me, like a sheepdog with a recalcitrant sheep. Not one night passed during this period that I did not lie awake in the darkness and contemplate blindness, total and unforgiving. I thought constantly of the operations ahead of me, and I quailed. So much to go through, pain and disability, and last time the results had been disappointing. I knew that with any eye operation, I could lose my sight entirely, so I put off doing anything about the right eye as long as I could manage. The world was brown with cataract. Almost nobody besides Woody and my eye doctors knew how bad my vision was. I faked it. I bluffed. I had to make a living, which means doing gigs—readings, lectures, workshops—but toward the end, I could not travel alone. I got on the wrong plane because I could not read the gate numbers. Woody had to travel with me the last months. Fortunately, computers can print out poems in sixteen-point type.

My own ophthalmologist, Dr. Gorn, had taught a student who recently developed a different and far superior operation that did glaucoma and cataracts at once and got good results. Finally I had that done on my right eye. When the bandages came off from that single operation Dr. Shingleton performed, it was a miracle. I have decent vision so far in that eye. There is no cure for glaucoma, and I still face the likelihood of eventual blindness. But I am less afraid. I have been given some time with adequate sight.

I will always remember too my joy when the bandage came off my right eye, and I could see colors clearly, could see Woody's face again, could see my cats. The poor bastards had been stepped on and tripped over and barely played with. Yet they were loyal all through my trials. Friends who had been close dropped away, while others were immensely caring and helpful. Even Woody was not always there for me. But the cats were. My cats are not a substitute for lovers or children or friends, as people sometimes say, but precious for exactly what they are, a real and ongoing emotional connection that was sometimes all I had besides my work.

Now, the world seemed to me utterly peeled and shining, beautiful beyond expressing it. I could again find out what people and landscapes, the garden, the ocean looked like. I felt I would never have enough of gaping at an oak tree or a sunflower or a cardinal or my love. I do not take sight for granted. I rejoice in it. I am grateful for it. I love seeing. To have vision is a blessing I will cherish as long as I can. I am forever staring at things and drinking them in, a white speckled lily I have grown, an orange tomato, a swallowtail butterfly, Efi's eyes, which are the clearest darkest blue, bladder wrack on the ribbed sand beach, the different colors of the sky in winter and spring and summer and fall.

Our involvement in the havurah began to diminish. The death of the fishing industry on the Cape meant that Helaine and her husband, Mike, could no longer make a living. They moved to Hawaii, near their daughter. Several people in the core group left the Cape. Retired men who were more affluent and who came from reform synagogues in suburbs took over the havurah, ran it far more efficiently and "correctly" than we ever had. We go to occasional services but find that it does not feed us spiritually. It is run by men and much like the Judaism I rebelled against. There is no interest in less sexist god language or new forms of prayer. It's rather dry.

We began letting the Korats, Dinah and Oboe, go out in their harnesses on long ropes when we were outside. That enabled them to explore without danger. Colette, who had a well-developed sense of humor, thought it a great joke to sit on one of their ropes and hold on. She had many little jokes she would play on them, and sometimes on us. Occasionally she would take a pen and hide it and then sit watching me look for it.

I believe the cats read this manuscript at night when I am sleeping. I wrote that paragraph about Colette yesterday. This morning as a break, I took Efi out to walk around on her leash. Oboe appeared and grabbed the leash. Then he sat on it, just as Colette used to. But his intention did not seem to be to tease her. He was not pleased I had dropped her leash to pull bindweed off the phlox, and decided to take matters into his own paws. He is often concerned when she is on her leash and attempts to instruct her where to go and not to go. He herds her, in other words.

Then Max appeared out of the underbrush and watched, then pounced. He enjoyed sitting on the leash for a while, then he improved on the prank. He *pulled* the leash, using his teeth and claws. Efi came up to him and he began licking her. Then he let the leash go. Then he brought her to him again. Efi viewed this all as a game. She is fond of her leash and will sometimes yank it out of the drawer and try to slip into it so that perhaps she can magically go outside.

I have been watching Oboe's herding behavior, which I believe to be unusual in a cat. This morning, a gorgeous clear August morning with a wind from the north bringing a little energy, we took a four-mile walk in Truro along old railroad tracks to the bay and back, returning to a strawberry pancake breakfast. As I was clearing, I heard Oboe outside. I went to see what was wrong. I found him yelling at Malkah, who had walked, he thought, too close to a neighbor's house. He was circling her, bellowing. Finally he herded her back to the porch. Her docility with him is amusing. He led her then to the terrace by the gazebo, which he considers safe, and they stayed there together until they both came in for a late breakfast.

I imagine him observing Jim Beam through all his years as top cat and thinking, "I could do it better." Indeed, Oboe is the most courteous, gentle, responsible top cat I have ever observed. He does do it better. He has come into his own, and shines with inner strength, even now, when he is supposed to be dying, even now in his bony old age.

DIGGING IN

This fall you will taste carrots
you planted, you thinned, you mulched,
you weeded and watered. You don't
know yet they will taste like yours,
not others, not mine.
This earth is yours as you love it.

We drink the water of this hill
and give our garbage to its soil.
We haul thatch for it and seaweed.
Out of it rise supper and roses
for the bedroom and herbs
for your next cold.

Your flesh grows out of this hill
like the maple trees. Its sweetness
is baked by this sun. Your eyes

have taken in sea and the light leaves
of the locust and the dark bristles
of the pine.

When we work in the garden you say
that now it feels sexual, the plants
pushing through us, the shivering
of the leaves. As we make love
later the oaks bend over us,
the hill listens.

The cats come and sit on the foot
of the bed to watch us.
Afterwards they purr.
The tomatoes grow faster and the beans.
You are learning to live in circles
as well as straight lines.

TWENTY-THREE

THE WAY THINGS STAND
(AND SIT AND LIE)

Ten years ago, the grounds reached the farthest extent of cultivation. We cannot manage more. Much of our land is just as it was years ago, pinewoods giving way to oak, but an acre is devoted to gardens. Now we keep up what we have created and tweak it a bit, put in bushes to increase the screen, take down a tree shading vegetables, add lilies or daylilies, let something spread freely or cut it back, replace a storm-broken arbor. We are always deciding what is worth growing. We luxuriate in red, blue, yellow and white potatoes, wax, purple, green and striped beans and seven kinds of lettuce. For years, I was convinced that eggplants weren't worth the bother. With the new hybrids, we again grow gorgeous eggplants. What we do not grow is corn. Robert and Wayne fought a protracted war with raccoons, erecting an enormous cage for corn. They played radios at night. They set have-a-heart traps. Always the night before we were to harvest, the raccoons raided the patch. Nothing entered the traps except a skunk.

The raccoons piss me off sometimes—as when they picked the ripe grapes last year before I could. By and large, I like having them around. They're feisty creatures. We take in the bird feeders most nights in the winter so they don't eat all the sunflower seeds. Sometimes they throw a fit on the front porch and break the pots stored under the table to show their resentment. I don't mind their digging in the compost pile—no matter how deeply we bury lobster shells, they find them—any more than I mind deer nibbling on the shrubbery in hard springs. They were here before us, and they have rights. I enjoy a good relationship with the crows. When they're hungry, they put on raucous air shows outside my window till I give them cracked corn. One of my first acts upon moving in was to sacrifice to them the remains of a leg of lamb and to protect them from a couple of guys who liked to shoot at them. They teach their young to fly on our land, always a noisy day of shiny black choreography and a great deal of shrieking. They do not touch our crops.

Last winter I had a relationship with a particular crow, a sentinel. She—who can sex crows?—came every morning to check out the compost pile to see if there was anything worth summoning her band. Then she would watch me exercise on the treadmill. I think it amused her. She would perch right outside the window of my office. Once in spring I heard her sing. Several times I have heard the crows sing, and it moves me. Once or twice I have sunk on my knees to listen without realizing it. They are operatic. They remind me of Cho-Cho, with her little daily mew and her immense contralto when she was singing with another cat at night, through the screen door. "Caw" is hardly their only cry.

One night I had just returned from a series of readings in California and was suffering jet lag. It was the full moon of November, a mild night so I had opened two windows. Unable to sleep, I lay trying to relax when I heard the great horned owl, deep and resonant from very close. Right outside my bedroom is a good-sized Japanese dogwood, where she was clearly visible in silhouette. I became aware of an echo. Strange. You might get an echo sometimes at the front of the house, because there is a hill across the road, but on this side, the woods slope down to a freshwater marsh around Dunn's Run that feeds into the Herring River. What could cause an echo? She went on calling, mournfully, monotonously, commandingly: *Who, who* pause *who who who*. The echo persisted, higher pitched. I stood by the window. The higher-pitched answer continued, and then he arrived, her prospective mate—among the raptors, the male is smaller and has a higher-pitched voice. He alighted on the bough a few feet from her. They stared at each other and shuffled around. This went on till I went back to bed. Then I saw him fly off. So much for bird-watching at midnight. I was dozing when he returned. I got up again, nosy as ever. He had something in his beak, mouse or mole or vole. Again he alighted on the bough and did a shuffle dance before her. Finally he offered her the rodent. She accepted it. She ate it and then silently they flew off together to consummate their relationship.

Living here, I am seldom bored. There is so much to observe, to interact with, to understand—or attempt to. In different seasons we take different walks, on the beach, in the dunes, in the woods, by the ponds, near the saltwater or freshwater marshes. I want to live out my life here; I want to die here and become part of this fragile land. Our water supply is hull shaped, able to be contaminated by commercial carelessness, as one of the well fields in North Truro was poisoned by leaking gasoline. Drought this year has taken a toll. How will the alewives swim downstream to the sea, since the little rivulets and streams between the ponds have run dry? A hurricane stronger than Bob could take out our house.

I look at the marsh in the deep lush green of June, the tawny lion color of late summer, the deeper bronze of fall. I stare at the sand, washed black-red in ripples, as if a shadow fell across it, tiny grains of garnet. I watch the clouds pass overhead, much lower than on the mainland. The wind riffles the trees, surges around the house and we suddenly remember we are far out to sea on our narrow sand spit. I observe the rough heavily ribbed leaves of the beech, the slender elegant ladies' nail leaves of the peach, the feathery delicate intricately cut leaves of the locust, the broad happy leaves of the maple beginning to be splashed with orange. How I enjoy having sight, who know it is on loan. Living here after growing up in the center of cities, I have learned to attune myself to the seasons and the weather. I am trying to learn how to age, something our society seems to know little about. My body has changed, spread out, as my mind has grown more focused. I do not want to fight aging, but to find in it value and a different kind of strength and endurance—something I think particularly vital for a woman, since older women are so devalued and denigrated in our society.

Ira Wood, Wellfleet, 1997. Photograph by Marge Piercy

For the last ten years, I have demanded to have late Mondays to myself. Monday I work with my assistant, taking care of letters, bills, interviews—interface with the world—while doing the laundry. I make up a grocery list, and in the afternoon, Woody drives to Orleans, two towns over, to do the week's primary shopping. He brings groceries home at six. I do not cook supper nor eat with him. He is responsible for his own supper, either microwaving something at his office, eating out with a friend, or picking up takeout. Monday from seven to ten is my quiet time. I will not go to a meeting or see anyone; I turn off the phone. I shut off my computer. I think long and hard about my week past and the week coming and my life. Then I meditate—not the casual meditation of the week, ten minutes here and there, but a long deep meditation that feels holy and healing. This practice is part of how I stay sane and productive and open to others. For the first couple of years, Woody was surly about Monday evenings. He felt he was being kicked out of the house. Now he enjoys the time. Sometimes he will see friends or go to a movie, sometimes surf the

Web or learn a new program at his office. When an emergency or a gig that includes a Monday keeps me from my precious quiet time, I miss it in my nerves, my body, my sense of coherence. Deep meditation reweaves my psyche. Once when Woody was in therapy, his therapist asked him if he didn't think I was having an affair Monday night. I thought that amusing, since the whole purpose is not to speak with anyone.

One year, Woody decided to run for selectman. At first, it was a lark, playing at talking up the issues in the post office parking lot, creating bulk mailings. But when he was actually attacked by opponents, he threw himself into the campaign with ardor and won by a huge margin. He became the first Jewish selectman in Wellfleet history. He enjoyed town government for two years. Then in the third year, the town went to war with itself over someone hired as town manager. People who used to be close friends were ready to kill one another. At the same time, he began to feel that he had gone too great a distance from literature. He had imagined starting a small publishing company; now he talked about it seriously. I listened for ten months, and then I began to push him to do it instead of talk about it.

I had never expected to spend half my life in a small town, nor had Ira. But we are rooted here. By this time, he knows far more people in town than I do, since my only public activity here is the grassroots organization we began after the Brookline clinic murders, ROC—for Roots of Choice. We work on issues of choice, of domestic violence, issues that impact women's and children's health and safety. Alice Hoffman and I do a reading every other year to support the work. In village life, people barter and help one another. They also gossip and hold grudges for a generation. Local issues of land use, water, the dump, putting up a cell phone tower, paving a sand road all inspire great passion and rancor. It is livelier than you might expect and more engaging.

That year, Jim Beam was diagnosed with incurable kidney disease. That spring, I also noticed that Colette was beginning to slow down. She would miss a leap that had been easy for her. They were only fourteen— much too young for what was happening to them. I remembered their dubious genetic heritage and wondered what had kicked in suddenly.

We went abroad that summer, doing publicity and readings in England, then research for my novel *City of Darkness, City of Light* in France. We were gone three and a half weeks. When we got home, the deterioration in Jim's condition was appalling. While we were gone, he had lost a great deal of weight. The person in charge basically left food and disappeared. The cats were abandoned. I had cut down on his time outside to preserve his strength and to make sure he ate what he was supposed to. It was difficult to put him on a low-protein diet. He would turn up his nose at the prescribed food and go hunting.

The disease had gone into a more rampant stage. He needed, and hated, twice daily injections of liquid, administered from an IV bag and needle. He became a house cat, far more affectionate, especially toward Woody. The last three months of his life, he spent as much time as possible with Woody, as close as he could get. He was visibly failing, but we were able to keep him alive until mid-September, when he jumped off the bed to use his litter box and could not move his hind legs. He went into a coma on the way to the vet's and died a week before Rosh Hashona. We buried him at the edge of the wild lawn area, and planted a rhododendron on his grave. We both grieved for him. He had been the most difficult animal I ever lived with. He kept us awake nights, cost time and money with his fights, made it weird for guests, but he had been a strong presence in our lives, a beautiful cat and the first cat who was really Woody's. Then Colette was diagnosed with the same kidney disease that had killed Jim.

We went to a cat show in Framingham, really just to look around, for we had to be back well before sundown. It was Erev Rosh Hashona, the Jewish New Year, and we were going to services two towns over. At the show, we considered a Maine coon kitten who looked like a movie star, longhaired, ruddy, absolutely gorgeous. However, he paid little attention to us, and I think cats must want you before you have the right to take them home. Then it was time to head back to grab a quick supper before services.

As we were walking out, we noticed that a local shelter had set up cages in the hallway. I asked Ira to wait while I used the toilet. I have a rule when away from home: never pass a toilet—because who knows when you will see another? He was standing by a cage crowded with motley kittens when a little orange one grabbed him by the arm and came on to him. As I got back, he was talking to the kitten. "What a brave little boy, what a wise soul," he was saying, admiring the gumption and confidence of the tiny clump of fur clinging to him. The woman representing the shelter had taken the kitten out of the cage and put him in Ira's arms, where he began to purr at once and tell Ira how wonderful he was. We were both hooked. As soon as we had signed the papers, he then began to cry piteously and to reach out toward another orange kitten, cowering in the cage. That was his sister. I was not surprised, since the night before I had dreamt about two orange kittens. In the end we took her also. We had no idea how truly besieged they were with almost every sign of neglect and malnutrition. We tried to keep them in Woody's study, away from the other cats, but Colette opened the door and let the male cat, Max, out. The female was afraid to leave. Having liberated Max, Colette took to him. She seemed to adopt him. She cuddled with him and washed him. However, it turned out that Max had a respiratory infection. The vet was not impressed with the kittens, almost reluctant to handle them. They had tapeworms, they had roundworms, they were sniveling, they had fleas and they were skin and bones.

Colette caught Max's respiratory infection. The vet had diagnosed her already as having advanced kidney failure and did not give her long to live. Now he said with the respiratory infection, we should leave her there overnight while he ran tests on her. In the morning, she was dead. I was furious. I would never have left her to die alone if he had told me how weak she was. Jim Beam had gradually failed. Colette had been a little less than her usual Amazon self, but until the last week, she did not act sick. I felt I had failed her, letting her die alone in a cage, and I have been determined that should never happen again. We buried her beside her brother under another rhododendron, at the edge of the grassy area near the roses. She outlived him by only a month.

Her death was hardest on me, as Jim Beam's had the most impact on Woody. Jim Beam had weakened so, we had gotten our minds around his death. Colette I had expected to outlive him by years. She was more stoical than Jim, and I'm sure concealed her weakness. If something was wrong with him—he had been bitten, he had an abscess—he complained vocally. If something was wrong with her, we had to find out ourselves.

I will always remember Max with his respiratory infection outstretched on my bed, his long Sherlockian nose pointed into the steam from a humidifier we set up, seeming to understand exactly what he needed to do. Max was a wise and confident kitten, sure he had saved his sister and himself. After she had spent a week under the bed, I named her Malkah, queen, hoping that would influence her to come out. We called her the Apricot Shadow. I had to work hard to seduce her, but she is the most affectionate and responsive cat we have.

The cats are hardly the only animals we see. Deer come on our land sometimes. I have said we exercise in the mornings. I use free weights, a bicycle and a treadmill, although I confess I find all except the weights boring. Ira uses a NordicTrack. But some mornings we walk instead on local sand roads. Nine times we have seen coyotes. The first time I saw one, something in me said *WOLF* and the hair stood up on my arms. They are handsome but unmistakably feral. When I encountered one in late afternoon in the subdivision where I live, it simply yawned and trotted away, but usually they vanish into smoke. In the blink of an eye, they disappear, leaving you wondering if you actually saw an animal. Occasionally foxes visit, but since the area between us and Pole Dike Road was built up, we no longer have them on our land. I have watched fox kits playing, I have watched adults catching alewives in the streams, I have watched them eating wild grapes. When I was younger and had more leisure time, I would sit in the woods and observe marvelous things by remaining quiet. Perhaps as I age, I will have that time again. I trained myself to be utterly still. Meditation helps. I am not by nature a still person. Every year I do *tashlich*—at the Jewish New Year, it is customary to toss bread into outflowing waters on their way to the sea to cast with it your sins—which I interpret to be those aspects of my behavior, my thinking, my actions I need to change. Every year I try to throw away impatience. I have not yet succeeded. Like Efi, I want everything now. If

I am no longer ruled by sexual passion, it is only because I am satisfied with my lover, not because I became any less needy or any wiser. I have great discipline in my work, but in my life, I have often made a mess and overflowed onto the scenery, attempted too much, thrashed around and bumped into everyone in sight.

After the death of Jim Beam, Oboe became top cat. Suddenly he began to treat the orange kittens with paternal kindness. Dinah was still hostile, but Oboe had his ideas about how he would rule his newly acquired domain. He is perfectly able to chase off intruders without getting into a fight. He makes hideous noises and blows himself up, but basically, it's just strength of character. He took a particular interest in Malkah. She began to sidle out from hiding and curl up with him. Max and Malkah grew rapidly, from tiny fist-sized creatures to big beautiful cats. I believe they had an orange tabby mother. In Max you can see the Siamese, his long lean body, his long legs and tail, his aquamarine eyes. Malkah has a round face, huge round amber eyes, longer fur. He is darker orange and his belly and the tip of his tail are creamy. Her belly is snow white, and her stripes are a paler, milkier apricot. A starving kitten grew into a cat who does not like to see anybody's good food go to waste. If you give her a gourmet treat, she purrs as she nibbles.

At the cattery where we acquired Efi, we did not meet her mother, never a good sign. Efi went into heat for the first time when she was four months old. Three weeks later, she went into heat again. She was in agony, driving the other cats insane. Max hated to come in the house, as she had selected him as her sex object and flung herself on him, bowling him over in spite of her tiny size. I called the vet and tried to get them to alter her, but they said she was too young. After she had been in heat for eight days, I called again and insisted. My brief time as a breeder gave me the understanding that something was wrong. Indeed, she had an infected womb. She was burning up with fever and almost died. When we got her back, she was so weak she could not stand. Getting baby food into her was a major task. Malkah wrapped herself around Efi, keeping her warm. Within a week, she recovered. Efi is a being of immense energy. She is forever flying through the house about six inches off surfaces, skimming like a hovercraft. Crash. There goes Efi. There went Efi. Clatter, bang.

A couple of years ago, we began our press. It is mostly Woody's—he does 80 percent of the work. The press has an office in town, for he needs a place to meet with people, and the press needs more office equipment than we have room for. I like having the house to myself on the days my assistant does not come in, to be free of conversation and interruptions and Woody's recurrent moodiness. He does not deal well with rejection, with obstacles, with disappointments, and sometimes his depression feels to him global and requiring much attention from both of us, even while I know that in a week, he will not remember he was in despair. As I grow older, companionship is precious to me and so is solitude. We are always working to balance them. Many friends have dropped away as time has gone by. There are periods in my life that have blown down friendships like the wake of tornadoes leaves a swath of broken and upended trees. My intense involvement in the antiwar movement was one such period; my early militance in feminism was another; my blind period was another. Friendships of many years vanished with my disability, but I have retained several deep friendships and made new ones. Some friends live on the Cape, but many of our best friends live elsewhere, and we must make appointments to get together or rely on e-mail. I have more friends who are poets than those who write fiction, although Ruthann Robson does both: Diana der Hovanessian, Martin Espada, Elizabeth McKim, Celia Gilbert. With all those women, I exchange poems regularly. That feedback is vital to me. Etheridge Knight was a friend too, still sorely missed, as is May Sarton, whom we used to visit every August at York, Maine, bringing her a bottle of the champagne she loved and a jar of my jam. But other friends are naturalists, scientists, fishermen, carpenters, women judges, Web-masters, theater and radio people, academics, lawyers, shellfish farmers, a lobbyist, a cook, a chief of police, other publishers of small presses, journalists, painters.

Leapfrog Press has forced Woody to learn new skills, and he relishes the knowledge and ability he has gained. I would never have started a press, knowing how much time reading manuscripts takes from other reading I would rather be doing, but I believe in the importance of small independent presses and I am delighted with his success. After we had begun the press, we learned gradually that almost all the small presses we most admired had inherited or otherwise earned money behind them. We go hand-to-mouth and have no idea how long we can afford to carry on, but it still feels good.

We teach workshops together when we can, separately if I am doing poetry; we give readings, usually separately but sometimes together. I spent a lot of effort learning to perform well, but I do not really want to come across as a performer. I don't want the audience to focus on me but on the poem. My voice is my instrument. Woody and I wrote a novel together in 1996–1997, *Storm Tide,* the first time we had collaborated since 1977, when we wrote our play. This was a smoother collaboration. It's easier to write with someone than alone, if you respect each other and communicate well. But editors don't like it. Serious novelists, like poets, are supposed to work alone—as opposed to the theater, film, opera, where you are expected to work as part of a team. Now we are collaborating on *So You Want to Write,* a craft book that comes directly out of the forty or so workshops in fiction and personal narrative we taught together.

Writing about my life has been strange. I have always considered myself a good friend, but I see how many people have fallen out of my life or been pushed. I also recognize that frequently I have not inspired loyalty or deep affection. I think of friends who have dismissed me, used me, treated me as a resource. Then I think of others who have stood by me in emotional and physical trouble, who have given of their own precious time and scarce resources to succor me, and I am grateful and delighted to have such friends. I think of those willing to read manuscripts and give feedback in busy lives when nobody really wants to read a manuscript, no matter how eagerly they may read the book it becomes.

Memory is such a tricky baggage. Sometimes it comes unbidden and shakes me. I will hear my mother's slightly husky alto voice. I will see my grandmother letting the braid of her hair down like Rapunzel as she sat on the bed's edge, the rickety sagging double bed with the maple headboard that we shared. I remember the pattern in the curtains that hung over us—cacti in blue and gray, what I now know to be the saguaro cacti I have seen in the Sonora Desert. The taste of sheep's cheese or mango or pâté brings into focus an adventure in Crete or Cuba or the Dordogne. I put on a pair of silver snake earrings and remember a party and the giver. But my mind is a rough sieve and much escapes. It dissolves in time as in running water and rushes away, lost. The bad times blur and fade. I remember the pain but few particulars.

I am always wanting to learn things. I would like to refurbish my Greek, unused for thirty years. I have enjoyed the Internet since it existed, long before the ease of the Web. I had to learn klunky protocols, Kermit, X, Z, to get into sites that fascinated me, then all text. I look forward to faster and more powerful computers that enable me to do more and more research and explore more connections. I could not tell you how many friends I communicate with by e-mail—far more than I ever did by regular mail. I love e-mail, the quickness of it, the back-and-forth, the lack of compulsion to fill a page. You have one sentence to say? Fine. You have a whole page? Okay. It's 6 A.M. and none of your friends are up? Great. You can send them a message they can open at noon or midnight.

Writing is a task ever fresh. Things that once were laborious now are second nature, but there is always another mountain higher and more beautiful, visible only when I have climbed this one. I am always discovering new poets and sometimes new fiction writers to delight in. Discoveries come weekly. There is so much I will never come to learn before I die that I would love to investigate and saturate myself in. I read more poetry than fiction, and a great deal of nonfiction, usually what I am researching for the next or the current novel.

I imagined that writing a memoir would be easy; I was mistaken. It has proved as hard as eating bricks for breakfast. I have been aware of huge segments of my life brushed past or detoured around. Every day I am aware I can see but might not be able to in the future. No day goes by that I am not thankful I live in a beautiful place and have so far been able to make a living without leaving here for longer than a week or two at a time, with rare exceptions when I go broke. This is not easy—living where I want and surviving economically. The Cape is not your best place to earn money.

I have to say honestly I have never regretted staying childless. My privacy, my time for work and our time for intimacy are precious. I feel my life is full enough. There is a lot I regret—opportunities I missed or stomped on, friends I have lost or mislaid or offended, money wasted here and there. There are things I wish I had: more time, a pied-à-terre in Boston or Cambridge, more money. People read me and cherish my work—it is deeply meaningful to many of them, both the fiction and the poetry—but I do not have the kind of reputation that squeezes prizes out of the network that grants them. I would like very much not to have to work so hard, but I see no sign I will be recognized in that way until I am dead. Lots of academics use my work and produce interesting criticism, but they are not the ones who control free money. Therefore I give a great many readings, lectures and speeches, workshops, and hit the road as often as any other traveling salesman. I dream of a slower life, but I don't see it coming.

Recognizing that more than half my life is over, I try to gain some perspective and wrest some wisdom from my journey. I know I am an intense, rather angular passionate woman, not easy to like, not easy to live with, even for myself. Convictions, causes jostle in me. My appetites are large. I have learned to protect my work time and my privacy fiercely. I have been a better writer than a person, and again and again I made that choice. Writing is my core. I do not regret the security I have sacrificed to serve it.

No day passes that I am not grateful I live with a man who finds me attractive, who loves me, who looks out for me, whom I can trust, whom I can care about passionately and deeply. That means a great deal to me, peace in the center of my domestic life. I did not have it before I lived with Ira. It isn't that we do not disagree or fight or become irritable with each other. We're volatile and strong-willed people. But we are each other's best friend and each other's proper mate. We continue to interest each other. We make a good unit here on our land with our visitors and fellow residents—deer and birds and raccoons and possums—and our family of cats.

ON GUARD

I want you for my bodyguard,
to curl round each other like two socks
matched and balled in a drawer.

I want you to warm my backside,
two S's snaked curve to curve
in the down burrow of the bed.

I want you to tuck in my illness,
coddle me with tea and chicken
soup whose steam sweetens the house.

I want you to watch my back
as the knives wink in the thin light
and the whips crack out from shelter.

Guard my body against dust and disuse,
warm me from the inside out,
lie over me, under me, beside me

in the bed as the night's creek
rushes over our shining bones
and we wake to the morning fresh

and wet, a birch leaf just uncurling.
Guard my body from disdain as age
widens me like a river delta.

Let us guard each other until death,
with teeth, brain and galloping heart,
each other's rose red warrior.

TWENTY-FOUR

OBOE

Oboe is dying. He has deteriorated so quickly it was upon us before I realized what was happening. Even a week ago, he was responsive, affectionate, interested in everything. He enjoyed the holidays and greeted every person who came into the house. He was eating and drinking normally—for an aged and unwell cat—until last Thursday.

We took him to the vet's the first week in January—two weeks ago—for his quarterly shot, and while he had lost half a pound, he was in decent shape. But in the last ten days, he shriveled. He is so thin it is hard to touch him, and he seems to find being caressed almost unpleasant. I force a little food into him and vitamins, but he does not want to eat. It takes him five minutes to urinate. He has lost strength in his back legs and cannot jump onto the couch or the sink, where he usually asks for fresh cold water. Most of the time he cannot seem to lift his head. To look at him, to touch him, makes me weep. The other cats are good to him. Each of them has lain with him, washing him, keeping him warm. They seem almost to take turns.

I wish I had the strength to call the vet, but I don't yet. I cherish a ridiculous hope that he will rally. He has seemed to fail before. But I know from all the time I have spent with cats that he is too far gone to recover. He has no reservoir of energy. He is running on empty, and he knows it. He is withdrawing into death. I want him to fight, but he has been fighting for all this time and so far winning. Now I think he has lost the war. We all will. I see in his end the vision of my own.

The hard part to know is when to take him to the vet. I wanted him to live as long as he was enjoying his life, and until just a week ago, he was. He loved his mother and his harem and Max. Most of all he loved us, especially me. To be with me was his bliss and his right: to be with me when I write, to be with us when we make love, to sleep with us at night, pressed to my side. He never stayed out overnight, never caught a bird, never ran away from me, never scratched me. He has a strong and definite personality, but it is of a courtly and passionate gentleman.

He was born in my bed, and I helped feed him as a kitten when Dinah lacked enough milk. He was mine from the time he opened his eyes, when he was a shapeless blob of kitten. He has slept with me all his life, always in the bed that was his too. There is a special empathic link between us, as there was with Arofa, as there was with Colette. He is the only male cat with whom I have ever had that close and tight a connection, since Fluffy. He accepted the other cats who came into the house, protected and taught them. He was the best top cat I can imagine.

You always wonder when you contemplate taking a cat to be euthanized, if you are being selfish. Is it because I have not had a night's sleep in a week? Am I being callous? Ira is no help in making the decision, as he wants to deny Oboe's condition. He is not the one who gets up every hour in the night when Oboe cries and carries him into the bathroom so he can try to drink water and try to urinate. We are both overwound emotionally and on short fuses. This is an impossibly rough decision.

It is snowing hard, big flakes but little wind. We had a dry warm fall, right up to New Year's. Then the second week of January, the jet stream moved and Arctic air blew in with high winds, intense cold, and snow. The snow is deep on our land and the air feels serrated, tearing at the nose, at the lungs.

This morning we took Oboe to the vet to die. He was still conscious, but he could no longer stand. He got up six times last night, went to the water bowl, sat over it with his head drooping, drank some water, tried to urinate, tried for ten minutes at a time. He began to cry last night. He had been stoical, but now the pain was too much. I held him all evening and all night. I told him it would be over today, I promised him there would be no more pain. I told him what a wonderful cat he had been and how much we all loved him, and how I knew he had enjoyed his life. I don't think there has ever been a cat more doted on, more adored, better pleased with his life and his position in the world.

On the way there, I did not put him in a carrier but held him on my lap. It was still snowing and the roads were difficult, so we used the truck with its four-wheel drive. He crawled into my coat. He was incredibly light, all sharp jutting bones, and he found it hard to rest in a comfortable position.

On the vet's table he lay down as if exhausted on the towel I had brought so the metal table would not chill him. The vet did the injection quickly and smoothly and he was dead within a minute—no noise, no jerking, just silence. His eyes stayed open. I have been crying for a week and my sinuses are inflamed. How ridiculous that grief can be measured in used tissues. I have gone through a whole box.

The temperature has dropped to five degrees several times, so the ground is frozen a foot down. It happens that when the vet first told us Oboe could die any moment two years and four months ago, I had Ira dig a grave. Many times since, he has suggested filling it in, but I was unwilling. I felt, with all the weight of superstition, that if we filled it in he would die. Now that he is dead, we did our best to bury him in the frozen earth eight inches deep in snow with more falling on us. We put in potting soil from the shed, what dirt we could break loose. It is a very makeshift grave, so we put a plank and cinder blocks on top to keep coyotes from digging him up. We will finish the job when there is a thaw. I believe he is deep enough to be safe from scavengers.

I decided we should bring his body in while we were working on the grave, so that the other cats would not think he had simply disappeared. I put him on a towel on the bed and uncovered his still beautiful head. Even in death, his face kept its sweet soulful quality. His mother sniffed him and understood. Dinah cried and cried all over the house and now is in a sleep of exhaustion. When I came back in to get his body for burial, Malkah was standing over him, keening. She will not get up on my bed now. Max didn't see and Efi didn't understand.

There is an emptiness in the house. It is going to be a hard transition for all of us. It is the dead of winter when I always feel my mortality. This is a time when nature feels alien and dangerous. Whenever I think of him in the cold dirt, I weep. And feel myself losing body heat. In the death of every creature we have loved, we taste our own.

It is the first morning without him. Every morning of his life that we were home, even these last mornings when he was almost too weak to lift his head, he would crawl onto my lap while I drank my morning cappuccino. I would pet him and he would purr extravagantly. It was our morning routine, Dinah on Woody and Oboe on me. This morning there was Dinah, but no Oboe.

The cats settle into a new pattern. We wait to see if Max will assume the top cat position he never wanted. He is like someone elevated to the presidency who never had the ambition. He liked being ruled by Oboe. He always accepted that occasional slap humbly. Oboe, one-third his size, was his peerless leader. We watch the cats to see the new configuration as they adjust to the loss of the one who was everybody's favorite—except Efi, who loved him but loves Malkah more.

Now it is two months after Oboe's death. Max is definitely top cat. He has endured his first serious fight. He marks his territory and defends it. He is even more affectionate than before, but also frets more. He is a worrier as well as a warrior. He cannot remain the sole male cat in the house, so we will get a kitten sometime late this spring. No one fills Oboe's place in the morning or in my days and nights. No one can. Malkah is bolder and comes to bed confidently every night, sleeping plastered to my side. We all go on, and in a few months, a new kitten will come and distract us all and a new configuration will form. I am going to plant a burning bush over Oboe this week. It is a bush that is beautiful in all seasons, as was he.

Cats continue to teach me a lot of what is important in my life, and also, how short it is, how we need to express our love to those for whom we feel it, daily, nightly, in every way we can. With everyone we love, we have only a limited time, so we must learn to celebrate it body and soul. They have taught me how precious every moment we can enjoy can be with whatever we love, because it all passes and so do we. Writing is a futile attempt to preserve what disappears moment by moment. All that remains of my mother is what I remember and what I have written for and about her. Eventually that is all that will remain of Ira and of me. Writing sometimes feels frivolous and sometimes sacred, but memory is one of my strongest muses. I serve her with my words. So long as people read, those we loved survive however evanescently. As do we writers, saying with our life's work, *Remember*. Remember us. Remember me.